Antique American
Switchblades

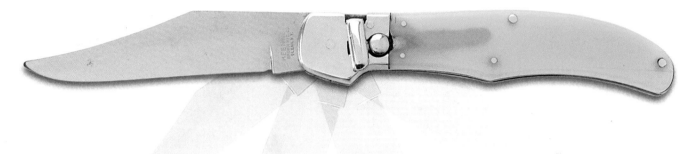

Mark Erickson

Identification & Value Guide

©2004 Mark Erickson

Published by

kp krause publications
An F+W Publications Company

700 East State Street • Iola, WI 54990-0001
715-445-2214 • 888-457-2873
www.krause.com

Our toll-free number to place an order or obtain
a free catalog is (800) 258-0929.

Library of Congress Catalog Number: 2004100738

ISBN: 0-87349-753-8

Designed by Tom Nelsen
Edited by Kevin Michalowski

Printed in the United States

Dedication

For my father, Bernard Erickson, who taught me compassion.
For my mother, Ruth, who kept me on the straight and narrow path.
For Breee who helped me find the time that I needed.
For my children who inspire me to be the best I can be.

Acknowledgments

I would like to thank everyone who helped me with this project. Special thanks to Fred "Fritz" Jaeger who went above and beyond the call to help me find the answers that I was searching for. I would also like to thank Tom Williams, historian for Camillus; David A. Swinden, Imperial Schrade Corp. Executive V.P., retired; Debbie Chase; Betty Kelley; Olie Olsen; Gertrude Endthoff, historian for South Milwaukee, Wis.; and all of the helpful librarians across the country without whom I would have some large gaps in my information. Thank you all for helping me to achieve my dream.

Foreword

The goal of this book is to provide you with as much accurate information about antique American switchblade knives as I possibly can. I have tried to include as many pictures of actual knives as possible, but some are just nearly impossible to find. I have included information about some knives that I could not find pictures for, including values, in an effort to be thorough. You will find an appendix in the back of this book that contains a list of manufacturers of switchblade knives. Another one contains a list of miscellaneous tang stamps and yet another with a "mostly complete" list of knife model names by manufacturer, which includes other information about the knives. I hope that these appendices prove useful to the collectors. There is also another appendix that I think you will find interesting which has tracings of the blades of most pre-1958 American made switchblades in actual size! You can simply lay your knife on top of the corresponding tracing and you'll be able to tell how much your blade has been sharpened! I think that this will prove very useful for the novice and expert alike in determining the actual condition of the blades!

No matter how much we know about any particular subject, there is always more to be learned. The study of these knives has been a constant learning experience for me these past 15 years. Each new day has brought some interesting fact, tidbit or lesson about these great old knives. I am striving to provide the most accurate and informative guide possible. I intend to keep studying these knives and accumulating information about them. I would be very grateful for any help that you may be able to provide. If you have a knife not pictured in this book or information that you notice is lacking, I hope that you are willing to take the time to contact me through my website at http://www.AntiqueAmericanSwitchblades.com, or email me at Shursnap@mwt.net. The more information I am able to compile, the better job I can do in recording and preserving it. I would also appreciate feedback and suggestions about the book through these venues.

I hope that this book will help everyone to better understand a knife that has been very misunderstood in this country for the past 50 years, or so. My main goals are: to educate those who want to learn more about these knives, and to preserve this information as a Historical reference for future generations. I have provided information which I feel collectors will find very useful and will help them to better understand and evaluate these knives. It is also my hope that non-collectors will find it very informative and enjoyable reading and maybe even gain a new appreciation for these fabulous pieces of our past. I have combined a personal affection for these wonderful antique knives with an impressive database of information that has been compiled over the past 15 years. I threw in a little detective work to help solve some mysteries and to answer a few "often asked" questions about antique American switchblades. This book is the fruition of all my efforts. I can assure you that it is a labor of love.

Contents

Introduction

What do you think of when you hear the word switchblade? Do images of gangs from the 1950s come to mind? Maybe you think of large, intimidating Italian stilettos in the hands of dangerous criminals? Those are the images that were thrust in front of the American public by sensationalistic and narrow-minded media and politicians during the 1950s. Certain members of Congress took it upon themselves to convince everyone that these knives were to blame for much of the crime in this country. They were trying to find a way to outlaw switchblade knives in the United States. They painted images of switchblade knives as the "weapon of choice" for gang members and dangerous criminals. They wanted the public to believe that these "evil knives" were relatively new to this country and that their only possible use was as a dangerous weapon. They never mentioned the fact that switchblade knives were a useful tool appreciated by hunters, fishermen, trappers, store clerks, farmers, mechanics, firemen and many others in this country. Switchblades were very popular with women, especially in the early 1900s. Not only did having a switchblade in the purse save many broken fingernails, switchblades were also very handy tools to have in the sewing kit. They often still turn up in old sewing machine drawers. Switchblade knives were extremely handy for the fisherman and there was a time when most tackle boxes were not complete without a switchblade knife inside. They were also very popular watch fobs and many gentlemen put them on the end of their watch chains.

Somehow the Congressmen who were feverishly trying to outlaw these knives, and gain attention for themselves, overlooked all of these facts. They didn't bother to mention that the majority of the switchblades manufactured in the United States prior to 1958 measured from 2 ¼ inches to 4 inches closed and could be comfortably carried in the pocket or coin purse. It also escaped their attention that many were designed to put on a chain with your keys. Does this sound like a group of dangerous weapons, with no other purpose than to maim or kill? It saddens me to realize that we had a Congress that could be manipulated into outlawing interstate commerce of one of the most useful and beloved tools in the history of our country. Maybe they should have outlawed hammers while they were at it. They are certainly dangerous weapons in the hands of a criminal.

History

Would it surprise you to know that switchblade knives had actually been in this country for over 75 years when these public figures were busy telling congress how switchblades were new to this country? The manufacture of switchblades in the United States began in the 1880s, shortly after the first switchblade patents were granted in this country. They were in mass production by the mid 1890s and fast becoming the most useful cutting tool one could carry and gaining in popularity and public acceptance. Over a 50-year period from the mid 1890s to the mid 1940s there had been approximately 20 different companies who had manufactured switchblade knives in this country. There were switchblades specifically designed for hunters, fishermen, soldiers, farmers, veterinarians, mechanics, office workers, seamstresses, high school girls, Boy Scouts and also for Girl Scouts. How's that for a list of dangerous criminals? They were also a very popular advertising giveaway and can be found with advertising from around the country, both on the handles and etched on the side of the blades.

The origins of the switchblade knife go back much farther than one might imagine. I know that they were being manufactured in England in the mid 1800s and France and Italy were making them well before that. I am very confident that they were brought to this country from Europe by the mid 1800s, and quite possibly before that.

As a Collectible

Fortunately knives are appreciated and sought after by collectors from around the world, so the value of knives, especially antique collectible knives, seems to be on a steady rise. Collectors the world over are constantly hunting for knives to add to their collections and the demand for antique knives is very high. Collector fever is very catchy and can make people do strange things. The hunt for a particular knife can be extremely challenging and exciting. The price that a collector is willing to pay for a knife can depend upon many things and the harder it is to find, usually the higher the price a collector is willing to pay. This behavior quite often leads to exorbitant prices being paid for very rare knives and surprisingly you don't often hear of buyer's remorse when it comes to rare antique knives. You do, on the other hand, hear a lot of "oohs" and "ahhs" whenever these knives are brought out for other collectors to appreciate.

If you ask most collectors why they collect knives you'll most likely hear something like "for the joy of collecting", or "I've loved knives since I was a boy", or possibly "I love the hunt." I have yet to have someone tell me "as an investment", and yet there is obviously much potential for knives to be an excellent investment. It's not only a good investment of your time, but if you buy using your head and not your heart, it can also be a good investment of your money. That doesn't mean you have to get cheap knives, but more that you need to make wise and informed purchases. Some of the best deals to be had are on more expensive knives, especially if you know something that others don't.

I love to find and collect antique knives and I am extremely interested in the history behind them. These are the main reasons that I collect knives and that I wanted to write this book, but I've noticed something in recent years. The increases in antique knife values in the past 15 years have surpassed inflation and most available interest rates. To my way of thinking, this makes knives a pretty good investment if you are knowledgeable and careful of what you buy. There are no guarantees that the values will continue to rise at the rate that they have been, but there's also no reason to assume that they will not. I'd never suggest that you cash in your IRAs and put the money in knives, or anything else that foolish. I do, however, feel that it is fine for you to think of your hobby as a good investment.

Knife collecting has brought me much enjoyment and even excitement at times. I have always been a collector. When I was very young I collected pennies, then I moved on to stamps and by the time I was in sixth grade my passion had shifted to antique padlocks and keys. To this day I still have a great appreciation for locks and keys and I know part of the attraction is the history behind them, just as it was for the stamps and pennies. It is much the same with antique knives. I am fascinated by the differences and the history behind them. The only regrets that I have are the ones that I let get away. Since I started collecting I've always felt that my time and money have been well spent.

The values listed in this book may seem high to some of you, but you must keep in mind that prices are for knives in MINT condition. Antique knives in MINT condition are very rare and will command much higher prices than even the "near mint" examples. These values have been determined from data compiled from years of research and careful study. I have tried to take all factors into consideration in determining these values and I believe them to be very realistic and accurate in the current collecting climate. These knives were the constant companions of our fathers, grandfathers and great grandfathers, etc. and they are fascinating reminders of our history. The interest in collecting them has been steadily increasing as people become aware that they are available and as easy to find as turning on your computer.

Which knives should I collect?

There are so many different knives to collect that most of us simply cannot afford to collect them all, though some of us would like to. Most collectors end up focusing their collecting attention on a particular type of knife. Some collectors are interested in a specific manufacturer and that is the only brand of knife they will collect. Many collectors are interested in a particular pattern or type of knife that may have been used by many manufacturers over the years and that is all that they search for. Other things that may become a collector's focus are: handle material, function, number of blades, country of origin, type of blade, advertising knives, size and more. I know of several collectors who like only very small knives and I have seen some wonderful displays of these collections.

Even after you determine what you like the best you may still have a few choices to make. Many collectors fancy the Italian stilettos that were imported into this country in vast quantities in the 1950s. If you chose to focus your attention on these knives there is a wide enough variety of tang markings and size variations to keep a collector busy for many years. Each country offers a good selection of antique switchblades to collect. France, England, Germany, Mexico, India and even Japan have contributed many different vintage switchblades and there is a large following of these knives as well.

In my opinion, the most interesting and challenging switchblades to be collected were made in the United States between 1884 and 1958. You can find anything from the ultra-rare bolster-release switchblade patented by George Korn in 1884 to the Imperial minis that were made in the late 1950s. Even making the choice to collect only American made switchblades would be an overwhelming task if you try to collect them all. The best advice I can give you is to go with what you like. Whatever catches your attention or tickles your fancy would be a good place to start. You can always change your mind and go another direction later.

Probably the best suggestion I would have for the "adventurous" collector would be to attempt to acquire one of each pattern that was produced by each manufacturer over the years. This would give you the most exposure to the various knives available and might help you to figure out what you like the most. In each section I have listed the different patterns that each company produced. This should prove very helpful in keeping track of what you have and what you're still looking for as you go. There were approximately 20 companies that manufactured switchblades in this country between 1884 and 1958 and over the years there were many short production runs and one-of-a-kind knives made.

I hope that the information contained in this book will help collectors, new and seasoned alike, to figure out which knives they are most interested in and give them the information needed to assist them in their collecting endeavors. Whichever direction you choose to go you will need to know what things to look for before you start buying the knives that you choose to collect.

Take a Good Look

Like anything else you're thinking of purchasing, you want to closely inspect a knife before buying it. There are many factors to consider when evaluating a knife. A switchblade knife is a bit more complicated to inspect than a horse's teeth, but with a little knowledge and practice you should become quite proficient at it. Here is an outline that should prove helpful in this situation:

1) Evaluating the Blade

a) **Blade markings legible?** If the tang stamp is not legible or has been obliterated from blade cleaning it will have an affect on the value. Many had blade etchings originally and the condition of these will also affect the value.

b) **How full is the blade?** By using the Blade Tracings appendix in the back of this book you should be able to determine how full the blade is on most antique American switchblades.

c) **Overall condition of the blade?** Does the blade have heavy patina, spotting, scratches, pitting or rust? Is the blade straight and unbroken?

d) **Visually check base of the blade for breakage.** The design of the lock on many of the antique switchblades can cause the base of the blade to chip or break if too much pressure is applied to the blade when it's locked open. Unfortunately

this condition exists on many of the antique knives in varying degrees of severity. This is one of the things that can cause the blade to have movement when locked open and if severe enough, the blade will not lock open at all. In most cases it allows the blade to droop when open.

2) Closely inspect the handles

a) **Do the handles look original?** It is very important that a knife have handles that were original to the knife. If they have been replaced, even if it was nicely done, it has an affect on the value. If they have been replaced with handles that were never used on that particular knife it detracts from the value even more. The possible exception to this would be a common knife that does not have a high value to begin with. In this circumstance you can actually increase the value by adding attractive, professionally installed handles. Although it will hurt the authenticity of the piece, eye appeal can have a large affect on what a collector is willing to pay and if it makes the knife more interesting, the value will go up. The downside is that eventually the value of the piece in original condition may surpass its "eye appeal value" so I would not recommend changing the handles.

b) **Damage assessment.** The next thing to determine is the condition of the handles. You should be looking for scratches, cracks, dings, dents,

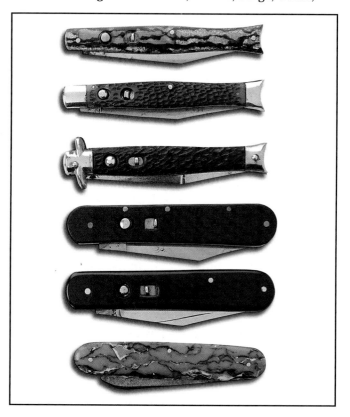

shrinkage, deterioration and breakage. If you need a magnifying glass to find these flaws they are not very significant and the knife could still grade Near Mint. If the flaws are obvious to the naked eye then they must be further evaluated and considered when determining the value.

c) **Accessories and Misc.** If the knife is equipped with bolsters or other accessories you must also determine the condition of those and the affect that they may have on the value.

3) Function

a) **Does it work properly?** Make sure that the blade opens fully and locks as it should when the button is pressed. If it is slow to open or won't open on its own it has an affect on the value. Even if it opens properly, if the spring has been replaced and you can tell by looking at it, it has an affect on the value.

b) **Evaluate blade position and lockup.** When the knife is closed the blade tip should be inside the handles. If the tip protrudes slightly it is referred to as "peeking" and will affect the value. If it protrudes quite a bit it is referred to as "proud" and has an even larger affect. When the blade is full open it will automatically lock on most antique switchblades. It is important to evaluate the amount of play or movement that it has when in this position. Ideally it will not move at all. Often there will be some up and down movement that is often referred to as wiggle. If this movement is more extreme it is often called droop. If the blade has movement side to side it is referred to as wobble and is usually a sign that the knife could use some repair. Each of these factors has an affect on the value, with proud or drooping blades having the greatest impact.

c) **The safety.** Whether or not the safety works does have an affect on the value, but it is not dramatic. Some safeties were so poorly designed that they never worked properly from the factory or functioned marginally, at best. On these knives it would have no affect on the value if it does not work. As for the rest, if the safety does not function properly there should be a minor deduction in the value.

d) **Miscellaneous.** There are a few other minor things to be considered. As with any crevice, the area between the handles where the blade rests, or *channel* as I call it, tend to collect things. Most of these antique knives were carried in a pocket at one time or another and so it is common to find dirt and pocket lint hiding

under the spring and packed into the bottom of the channel. Normally this will clean out easily, but if it has been exposed to any moisture this *sediment* will often cause rust to form on the spring and backspring that definitely affects the value. Another area that is susceptible to collecting foreign materials is the safety. Quite often things will settle into the pocket made by the safety hole and discolor the safety itself and may even cause a bit of mold to grow in there. Usually this will clean out fairly well, but sometimes when it is very dirty, the sediment gets underneath the handles and can cause the button spring to rust. The third area is between the liners and the blade. If any moisture and dirt collects in this area it can cause the base of the blade to rust which can obliterate the tang stamp and cause functional problems with the knife over time. There are ways to clean this out without taking the knife apart so if it's caught in time you can avoid costly damage down the road. Using a wax lubricant in this area is one way of reducing the risk.

All of these things are considerations when evaluating a knife for purchase and have an affect on the value, but how much affect should they have? There are obviously varying degrees of severity for each one and some things are more important than others in determining the actual condition of the knife. You need some guidelines to follow and a system that will help you to determine how each factor contributes to the overall picture. That's where knife grading comes into play.

Parts Terminology

The knife-collecting community commonly accepts a variety of different terms to describe knife parts. Many of these names seem well thought out and apply well. Some of them are a bit vague and can be used to mean more than one thing. This can be very frustrating when trying to describe something over the phone or via email. And with several different terms for the same part, it is sometimes even difficult discussing knives in person, if you don't have the knife handy as a reference. For the most part I use the commonly accepted terms, but I have made a few minor alterations and additions to my terminology to try to reduce some of the confusion. I hope that some of my substitutions will be embraced by other collectors, but if not I guess they'll just have to survive in this book to help you better understand which things I am talking about.

Basically I prefer to evaluate the knife from the front with the blade pointing upwards and this is the reference position for my terms. The more commonly accepted method is to reference the knife as though the tip is pointing toward you. Bolsters are commonly referred to as front and back. Suppose you have a knife with four bolsters. How can you tell someone over the phone which one of the four is missing? Would you say the front back bolster, or maybe the back, back or the back, front? Using my terminology you have top and bottom bolsters on the front and back of the knife. Would you know which bolster I'm referring to if I said the top front? It is much easier to understand in my opinion. The main addition that I have made is to come up with a term for the recess between the handles where the blade rests. I have yet to hear a commonly accepted term for this. The most common reference seems to be "inside the frame", but I feel it deserves a name and the best one that I could come up with is *channel*.

The only major parts that do not show up in the diagram are the main spring that throws out the blade and the base of the blade and the grooves cut into it for locking the blade open and closed.

These parts are all internal and difficult to show in the diagram. The spring is fastened in place with a pin that goes through the liners. On many switchblades this pin goes all the way through the handles making it much easier to replace the spring when it breaks. The Shur Snap Jumbo Jack was used as the model for the parts diagram, and on this knife the spring pin does not come through the handles. In order to replace the spring properly you would have to remove the handles first.

Most antique switchblades used either holes or, more commonly, grooves cut into the base of the blade combined with a spring tensioned lever which locked into those grooves to hold the blade in both the closed and open positions. A button on the other end of the lever protrudes out of the handle and when pressed it pivots the lever lifting the end out of the groove to release the blade so it will open, or so it can be closed.

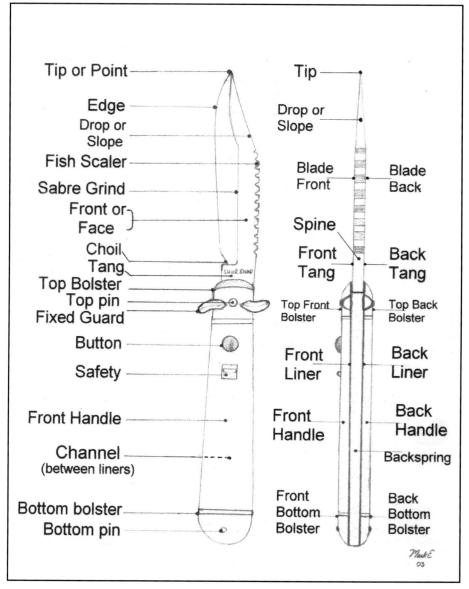

Styles, Shapes & Trade Names of Blades

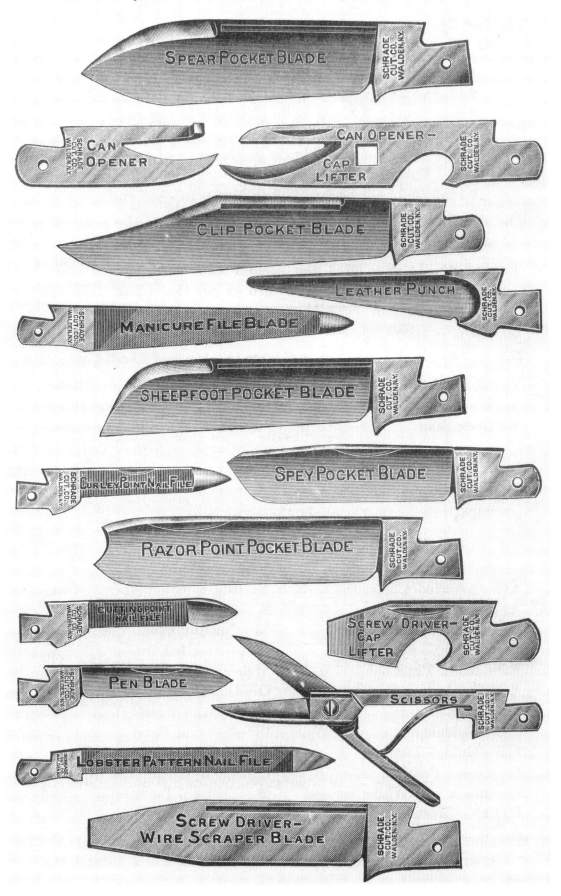

Spear Pocket Blade

Can Opener

Can Opener — Cap Lifter

Clip Pocket Blade

Leather Punch

Manicure File Blade

Sheepfoot Pocket Blade

Curley Point Nail File

Spey Pocket Blade

Razor Point Pocket Blade

Cutting Point Nail File

Screw Driver — Cap Lifter

Pen Blade

Scissors

Lobster Pattern Nail File

Screw Driver — Wire Scraper Blade

Grading Switchblade Knives

It never ceases to amaze me when I find another knife book and look in the front to see what they recommend for grading a knife. What could be more important for the collector of knives than being able to accurately grade a knife and determine the value? One might expect a whole chapter to help collectors determine and apply values to their knives. Yet in book after book I see less than a page with some vague ideas and a few different grading levels. Even with good pictures, how is the average collector supposed to fill in all the blanks and properly grade a knife? It is, at best educated guessing in most cases, and uneducated guessing in far too many. I'm sure that there are many collectors out there who would like to stop guessing and be able to accurately grade a knife. I'm going to do my best to help bring some unity and sanity to the grading of knives. My system is designed for switchblade knives, but it could be adapted for other knives as well.

What is it worth?

As with anything, a knife is only worth what someone else is willing to pay for it. This fact of life applies to any item. It doesn't matter what someone says it is worth. If nobody is willing to pay the asking price then it's not worth that much, at least not at that particular moment. Often the price that seemed way too high before seems like a much better deal after the object is gone. The mistake I feel is more common than paying too much for a knife is not buying a knife because you were advised that the seller wanted too much for it. I can't tell you how many times I've heard that and later find out what a good deal it really was. If your luck is like mine, you can rest assured it will not be there when you go back. I can think of several times that I fell for that bad advice and I ended up wishing I had bought it. There were a few that I've never been able to find again. Unfortunately, there are a lot of "well meaning" advisors out there who don't have enough information to give good advice on antique switchblades. The key here is information. You need as much information as you can get your hands on to make educated decisions and keep yourself from making costly mistakes. This book is designed to provide you with the information that you need.

How to determine value

First let me say that there is no way to place a value on a knife that everyone will agree is fair. Obviously the buyer and seller will have different views on what a particular knife is worth and there's no way to come up with a value that will make everyone happy. Knowing this fact, I have spent the past 15 years compiling information about these knives and the prices they sell for. My scope was not limited to any single market and I have observed the sale and trade of knives at knife shows, flea markets, gun shows, auctions, antique stores, classified ads, and one of the newest and biggest markets, the Internet. I have kept track of thousands of knives and built up a very impressive database of information. I have taken into consideration the condition and selling price of each knife as well as other factors to compile this database for determining values. Those who know me, or may have seen my user name on many occasions online, should know that I have been very active in the knife-collecting world in the past years. I have been both trying to fulfill my thirst as a collector and at the same time, amass as much information about knives as possible. This is the foundation for the values that I place on the models of knives featured in this book. Although I have many favorite knives and personal opinions about many things, I have not let these, or any other factors that should not be involved in putting a value on a knife, affect my efforts to accurately determine the values in this book. Just the facts.

I have tried to take everything into consideration when valuing the different models of knives in this book. There are so many factors that determine the value of a knife. Manufacturer, age, rarity, blade types, handle materials, collector interest, current market values, and more all play a part. Because I have tried to take all factors into account, many of the values that I have placed on knives may seem extravagant or out of line compared to what seem to be similar knives. Many knives that appear to be nearly the same, or at least very comparable, in reality are not. One example might be a 4 7/8-inch Schrade Cutlery Co. knife with celluloid handles priced at $1,000. If you look at a Presto 5-inch with plastic handles the price is $600, which seems like a big difference for two similar knives. Considering that the Presto knives were only made for about 25 years, where the Schrade knives were made for 50 years it might be even harder to understand. Once you realize that most of these Schrade knives were handled in bone, and celluloid is a rarity and the majority of the Presto knives were handled in plastic, this begins to make more sense. Combine these facts with the fact that Presto made a higher percentage of the large knives than Schrade did in comparison with the rest of their switchblade line, and it makes even more sense. There are even more factors involved, but you get the idea. Another good example can be found in the 3 3/8-inch knives. With Schrade Cutlery Co., the majority of their 3 3/8-inch knives were doubles and the singles are quite scarce and will command higher prices than the doubles. With Presto it is the opposite. The 3 3/8-inch singles far outnumber the 3 3/8-inch doubles combined with the fact that some of the celluloid used by the George Schrade Knife Co. tends to crack and deteriorate worse than Schrade Cutlery Co. celluloid. So nice examples of 3 3/8-inch double Presto knives are much harder to find. Therefore the Presto doubles will command higher prices than the singles.

Another major consideration is collector interest. I also try to pay attention to which manufacturers and knife patterns, handles, etc. seem to be the most popular with collectors. This is a factor that can constantly shift, but usually doesn't change dramatically. Sometimes certain things can spark interest in knives and get collectors excited. More information or better information will often accomplish this. It's hard to be interested in something that you don't know much about and even harder to buy something without a good working knowledge of its value.

Knowing facts about which knives were made with what blades and handle materials and which combinations are more common and which are very rare are vital to placing accurate values on these knives. I have made thousands of observations about antique American switchblades and I have scoured the country and internet in search of these knives and information about them. I constantly monitor online auctions and make frequent visits to gun shows, knife shows and flea markets. I have learned what is common and what is rare when it comes to most of these knives and I know when they were made and for how long. I have kept track of these things in an effort to put it all together to try to create an accurate and informative reference. The basis for a system of value must start with some real, current market prices that have actually been paid for certain knives. You can then calculate value for other knives that may not be currently on the market by comparing the rarity and other factors to determine the difference between the two. If you consider all the factors you should be able to place fairly accurate values on even the most obscure knife by using relative values of other knives. The values of these knives are all related and based largely upon supply and demand, but they're also partly based on appreciation and respect for the knife and what it represents.

Obviously I could not take every single factor into consideration on every single knife, no matter how hard I tried. Location is a factor that can have an affect on the value that is hard to account for. I have noticed that some areas of the country seem to be willing to pay more for collectible knives. This might be explained by a lack of exposure to the knives or a lack of availability. There may be areas where they are not considered very valuable, but I haven't encountered that, personally. The only reason I could think of for that situation would be a lack of collector interest in an area. In the past geography could have been a great obstacle, but with the introduction of the Internet one can bypass the local market. In some cases I may have missed a factor or two, but I have tried to take everything into account and believe these values to be a true representation of the current climate of the collecting world. Even so, as with most things in life, there are no guarantees, implied or otherwise.

Why do we grade knives?

Now that you know more about the factors that influence the value placed on a particular knife, it is important to understand how to apply this value when knives are found in so many various states of condition. Obviously a knife that is as nice as the day it was made is worth much more than one with broken rusty blades. What if you have a knife that looks like the day it was made except for one little scratch on the back handle? This is where grading comes in. You just went from Mint to Near Mint condition and believe it or not there is a BIG difference between the values of these two grades. Even though the two knives would look almost identical, the Near Mint knife would be worth 25 percent to 50 percent less than the Mint one. Fortunately the difference in value becomes more subtle as the knives become less perfect. In order to place an accurate value on a particular knife you must know two things: A realistic value for that particular knife if it were in Mint condition and how to grade a knife to determine its true condition. You can then determine any knife's value as a percentage of its Mint value.

Which grading system is best?

Unfortunately there is no universally accepted system for grading knives and even if there were, it would have to be adapted for switchblades since there are extra factors that must be considered when grading a switchblade knife. It is very difficult to depend upon someone else's evaluation of a knife, especially if you're thinking of buying it without first examining the knife yourself. Often things like pride, emotion and greed play a role when others grade their own knives. These things have no business being involved in grading a knife. The only things that should be considered are the actual condition and function of the knife — period. The major downfalls of most of the grading systems that I have evaluated is that they do not have enough grading levels to allow for accurate assessment and they don't have enough instruction to help the average collector do a good job of properly grading a knife. That is why I have developed my own grading system. It is similar to other systems, but makes it possible to grade with a higher degree of accuracy. It is also specifically designed for switchblade knives. With the help of the accompanying instructions, charts (and photographs), I think that anyone will be able to accurately evaluate switchblade knives and determine their value. Anyone can learn to grade knives like an expert with this information and a little practice.

My system is based on the theory that to grade a knife properly you must start with the idea of a perfect knife. You must then determine what flaws the knife being graded has, as well as how severe they are. By using the charts I have provided you can determine these things and add up the points to achieve a "score" for the knife. This score will hopefully correspond with one of the 17 grading levels and yield a grade for the knife from Mint to Junk, with 15 grades in between. The system actually uses four main grades between Near Mint and Poor combined with + and – for each grade. Those grades are Excellent, Very Good, Good and Fair. Mint is at the top of the scale and Parts and Junk are at the bottom, for a total of 17 possible grades. It sounds much more complicated than it actually is. The accompanying charts (and pictures) will help you to use and understand this system.

What is Mint?

Mint is a term, borrowed from coin collectors, which basically means that the knife is in the same condition as when it left the factory. The knives pictured in this book are, for the most part, NOT in mint condition. Their sole purpose is for the collector to actually see what the knives look like. The knives pictured in this book are in various conditions from Mint all the way down to Poor and are a good representation of what a real collection might look like. Often it is hard to find a Mint example, so the collector will often buy one of lesser condition in hopes of someday upgrading to a better one. Some knives are so rare that even an example in Poor condition is a prized possession and proudly displayed in a collection. I have not graded the knives pictured in this book and do not intend to imply that they are worth the values posted by them, though many may very well be.

It is important to understand that a MINT antique knife is very special and collectors will pay a premium for perfection, but anything less than perfection and that premium disappears. In other words, they might pay up to 50 percent more for a knife that is perfect, than one that may only have one or two tiny flaws. Such has been the mindset in much of the knife-collecting world for many years. Personally I think this way of thinking is fast becoming outdated as interest in knife collecting is on the rise and demand for knives to collect is increasing, thus creating a much tougher market than in past years. MINT knives should always command much higher prices, but as collectors are willing to settle for "less than perfect" knives to put into their collections, the competition for those knives is increased and therefore the prices increase also.

I feel that 25 percent is a more realistic premium for perfection in today's market. Therefore, if you have a knife with only one tiny imperfection, it is not mint and the value of that knife is approximately 25 percent less than the Mint value. Another way to express the same figure would be that it is worth 75 percent as much as a MINT knife. An example would be a MINT knife is valued at $1,000 and you have an example with one tiny flaw, such as a small scratch on the back of the blade,

it would grade as Near Mint and your knife is worth 75 percent of $1,000, which is $750. I know even that figure seems extreme for a tiny flaw, but such is the case when it comes to MINT examples. The difference in value is much less dramatic in any other situation where the knives are close in condition. To further that example, if you have another knife that is the same model with only two tiny flaws, that knife would grade Excellent+ and would be worth 70 percent of $1,000 which is $700. In other words, any flaws once you've gotten away from the 25 percent drop from mint, equates to approximately 5 percent detract in value according to my system. Please see accompanying Grading List.

Tools of the trade

Fortunately there are no expensive tools to buy if you want to grade knives. A good magnifying glass or jeweler's loupe should be a close companion for the avid knife collector. Many situations will present themselves where this tool will prove most useful. Good lighting is important so you can better see any flaws that might exist. It's always nice to have a clean soft surface upon which to lay the knife so a clean soft towel or piece of felt might be a good idea. Paper and pencil are the only other things that you are likely to need to complete the task of grading. It's also a good idea to have a clean soft cloth about your person to gently wipe the knife when you're finished with it. If you're grading a knife that belongs to someone else it's always a good idea to ask the owner of the knife before doing anything with his knife. This includes asking before picking it up and before wiping it off. You always want to clean fingerprints and foreign materials from your own knives before storing them so a soft cloth; good quality metal polish and some wax lubricant will all come in handy at the end of the grade.

The Blade

The blade is everything. A knife without a blade is simply knife parts. A knife with a badly broken blade is simply knife parts. A knife with a heavily sharpened blade might be an example to have in your collection until a better one comes along, but most likely would end up being knife parts. If it happens to be an extremely rare knife it may be an exception. An example of this would be a KORN'S PATENT knife, which is so rare that to have one in any condition you would be very lucky. I think I have made my point. A knife is not a knife without a decent blade. Therefore the condition of the blades on a knife is the most important factor when grading and is the factor that has the most affect on the final grade.

There are many factors to consider when evaluating the condition of a blade. A mint blade is 100 percent full and has never even been sharpened. It has no blemishes whatsoever. The least serious deduction on a blade would be to have been carefully sharpened at one time, leaving some light scratches or marks on the blade. Even this is tiny infraction is enough to reduce a knife to Near Mint, at best. There are several other flaws to look for including: heavy patina, spotting, deep scratches, nicks, rust, pitting, bent or broken. Each of these flaws has different levels of severity, which must be evaluated and scored as accurately as possible. I have included a chart as well as a few pictures, to help you understand and identify these flaws and to determine the proper score for each blade.

Handles

Handles are much more than something with which to hold onto a knife. Handles give a knife character. They basically take an inanimate object and bring it to life, in our imaginations, at least. Handles are what catch a collector's eye and make him stop to get a better look. Handles have the power to captivate our minds and hearts and cause us to spend money on knives that our spouses had other plans for. Sure, there are lots of other features that catch our eye, but handles rate right at the top. Because of these factors, handles are the second most important things to consider when grading a knife. Many collectors use the term scales, but that term is also sometimes used to describe liners, so I much prefer to say handles.

There are many different materials that have been used to make knife handles throughout history, but I'm only going to focus on the ones that have been used in the manufacture of switchblade knives in the United Stated prior to 1959. The most common handle materials on this list would be: Jigged bone, Stag, Celluloid, Plastic, Bakelite, Aluminum, Tin, Brass, Nickel Silver, Sterling Silver, Gold-plated metal, Genuine Pearl, and Dark Wood (Ebony). There are different flaws relating to the different materials, due simply to the fact that their characteristics and vulnerability to the ravages of time, as well as susceptibility to damage are different. In other words, some flaws only occur on certain materials and not others and one must be aware of this when grading. Also included in this section are the bolsters, if the knife has them, as well as the condition of the liners and backspring. All of the miscellaneous details, other than those relating to the blade or function, will fall under this category. Examples would be: dirt or tarnish on the safety, dirt inside the liners, tarnished button, etc.

I have provided charts and photographs to help you evaluate these flaws and to accurately score the handles for grading purposes. The flaws will range from the tiniest scratch or nick to the extreme of handles missing entirely, and many steps in between. There may still be some "gray areas" when using the charts since it would be nearly impossible to cover every possible combination of flaws. Though I may not cover every possible scenario with the charts, they should be able to guide you to a very accurate assessment of the handles in almost every situation. If it comes down to a hard choice between two conditions that are only 1 point apart, it most likely will not affect the overall score if you make an educated choice between the two.

Function

The function or action of a knife is a very important factor when considering its value. This is especially true with switchblade knives. With regular knives you'll hear collectors mention "Walk" and "Talk" when referring to function. These terms simply refer to the affect of the backspring on the blade when opening and closing the knife. Most pocketknives have a "halfway open" spot where the blade should stay in position when stopped there. They should also have a little snap when going into the full open and closed positions. The basic function of a switchblade is similar, but we have terminology all our own.

When it comes to switchblades, we want to know how the blade "Sits" when closed. We want to know how well it "Fires" when that button is pressed. We want to know how well it "Locks" when the blade is open. Other terms related to switchblade functions that we don't like to use are: Peeks, Proud, Wobble and Droop. Some things that we like to hear are: Sits deep, Fires strong, Good snap and Tight lockup.

All of these aspects related to the function of a switchblade must be considered when trying to score the function of your knife. Other things that must be considered as part of the function are the spring and the safety. If the spring is weak, broken or has been "poorly replaced" it has an affect on the score. If the safety does not function properly in both the open and closed positions, it has an affect on the score. The exception to this would be a situation where a particular knife is notorious for a certain condition, like a poor safety design, and some of the safeties might not have worked properly when the knife was made. One example that comes to mind is the Edgemaster My-T-Mite, which has an inferior design for lockup, and many of the knives did not lock open properly when they were new. The blade appears to lock when it flies open, but on many of them slight pressure will dislodge the blade from the open position. This would not be considered a flaw unless the blade is wobbly or looser than normal.

All of these factors determine the overall function of a switchblade knife and must all be considered to achieve an accurate score for grading. The charts are designed to take all things into consideration and to give you the information you need to determine an accurate score. Unfortunately, with this many factors and various levels of severity, it is hard to allow for every possible scenario and still keep the point level low and the grading process fairly simple. As with the blade and handle evaluation, you may find yourself with a choice between two possibilities and you will just have to use good judgment.

Non-Factors

Often in life we are taught to look at certain things in a certain way. We are even taught that it's OK to overlook certain flaws in others and their behavior in order to get along better. Our perception of life and our surroundings are strongly affected by our environment and the lessons learned from our parents. We learn about relationships, love, loss, respect and more and all of these lessons have an affect on us and our perception of things. Simply stated we become products of our environment. We are emotional, sentimental and often "slightly unbalanced" creatures with our own unique perception and outlook. This is all part of who we are and it is very important to us and those we love. It is NOT important to grading a knife. Things like emotional attachment, sentimental value, pride, greed and dishonesty have no place when it comes to grading knives, though they often find their way into it. My system, though very straightforward and fairly simple, can still be misused or abused when these "Non Factors" come into play.

Honesty, accuracy and the "plain and simple facts" are all that are needed to properly grade a knife. If you use my charts (and pictures) as a guide, combined with a little common sense and some very basic math, you'll be an expert grader in no time.

Charts and Scoring the Knife

There are three main charts to help you determine actual condition and come up with associated point value used for the final scoring. There is one chart for each category; Blade, Handles and Function. On each chart the various flaws are listed in order of severity with the least severe at the top working down to the more serious ones. There are several factors involved and various levels of severity for each point level. Therefore there are multiple possibilities listed in each point range. You must make the choice that best describes the condition of that aspect of the knife that you are grading. If it is a close choice between two possibilities and a definite decision cannot be made, you must choose the one with the higher point value. There will be only one choice from each chart which will have a corresponding point value. Carefully read all of the choices under each point value starting at the top and working down until you find the choices that best describe that as part of the knife you are grading. You must use the highest point value that contains a choice that fits your knife. As you become more familiar with the charts the process should become much easier and faster. Once you have made your determination on each chart you should write down the point value and

proceed to the next chart. When you have done this for all three charts you simply add up the three point values and that total is the score of your knife.

The charts provided for grading in this chapter are not perfect. It would be nearly impossible to account for every possible circumstance. I have tried to account for every likely circumstance and to give collectors the information necessary to determine the actual condition of their knives. There may be many possible situations where the grader will have to use common sense to fill in a blank or make a determination. These charts are simply tools to help you more accurately grade your knives and I hope that you find them useful.

The Final Tally

Once you have the score it is easy to determine both the grade of the knife and the value. Simply look on the Grading List and find the corresponding number which will give you the actual grade, as well as a multiplier. To find the value of the knife you are evaluating you simply multiply the mint value listed in the book by the multiplier that corresponds to your score. It's that easy.

There are a few "gray areas" that may require you to make a decision based upon your individual needs or opinion. One of these situations can occur if your knife happens to have a certain combination of flaws which could cause it to score slightly higher than it should. Although it is unlikely for this to occur, it is possible. It should only make a difference of one or two steps and if the buyer and seller agree that the rating should be higher you could adjust it slightly.

If your score were 17 or higher your knife would fall into the Junk category. Even though the score places it into the Junk category it still may be useful for parts or display. If you determine that there are useful parts then it should be graded as a Parts knife. Even if there aren't any useful parts, I have learned that junk knives still have some value. The main reason for this is simply that we, as collectors, have a respect for these knives and it would be disrespectful to simply throw them away. I myself have paid $20 for a knife that was absolutely worthless in most people's eyes. Some knives are even rare enough that a Junk example is good enough to display in your collection, which makes it worth more than the Junk value. One thing you should remember though is that the grade remains the same, even if the knife is determined to be worth more because of special circumstances. The grade is simply the actual condition of the knife.

Blade Chart

✻ *You can use blade tracings in the back of the book to determine blade loss.*

In order to use this chart effectively you must understand the adjectives that are used:

1. **Faint:** Hard to see with the naked eye, but obvious with a magnifying glass
2. **Light:** Obvious to the naked eye, but not deep at all
3. **Medium:** Very obvious to the naked eye, but still not deep
4. **Deep:** Heavy scratches, but not too deep or wide
5. **Gouged:** Scratches that are deep and, or wide
6. **Tiny:** Means just that, so small that you almost need a magnifying glass to see it.

Here are the other terms that you must understand to effectively use this chart:

1. **Patina:** Effects of age which cause darkening of the blade
2. **Scratch:** Lines which actually leave impressions in the steel, usually from sharpening
3. **Rust:** Corrosion caused by moisture, salt, etc, which destroys the integrity of the steel
4. **Surface Rust:** Very fine and light rust which gives the area a brownish hue, not heavy
5. **Light Rust:** More serious than surface rust and will leave pitting if cleaned off.
6. **Pit or Pitting:** Effects of rust on metal. Invades the metal leaving dark craters or holes
7. **Peppering:** Several tiny pit marks which resemble pepper sprinkled on the surface
8. **Age spots:** Spots on the blade which are not rust or pitting and would buff off with effort
9. **Nicks:** Chip/break usually along sharpened edge
10. **Bent:** Self-explanatory, often at the tip
11. **Broken:** Self-explanatory, but there are various degrees of damage
12. **Sharpening:** Sharpening reduces the blade and over time becomes very noticeable. The amount of sharpening can be determined using the Blade Tracings Appendix in the back of this book.
13. **Etching:** Words or designs applied to the face of the blade using acid or other methods.

Scoring

1 Point

- Medium to heavy patina making the blade light to medium grey
- Sharpened leaving the blades 100 percent full with faint, or no marks.
- 1-5 faint scratches which are barely visible.
- 1 or 2 tiny, almost unnoticeable rust spots
- Few tiny age spots which are barely noticeable (not pitting or rust)
- 1 tiny nick in sharpened edge of blade (must be

barely noticeable)
- Tang stamp altered slightly from blade cleaning, but clear and legible
- If blade originally etched and etch is faded slightly

2 Points

- Heavy patina which makes the blade dark grey
- Blades sharpened leaving 98 to 100 percent intact✻
- Many faint scratches which are barely visible
- 3 to 6 tiny, almost unnoticeable rust spots or pepper spots
- Several tiny age spots (not pitting or rust)
- 2 or 3 tiny nicks in sharpened edge of blade (must be hardly noticeable)
- Tang stamp faint, but legible due to blade cleaning
- Blade etching barely readable, if etched originally

3 Points

- Blades sharpened leaving 96 to 98 percent intact✻
- A few noticeable scratches, but must be very light
- 7 to 12 tiny, almost unnoticeable rust or pepper spots -or- small spot light rust
- A few medium size age spots which don't look too bad (or light rust)
- 1 small nick in sharpened edge of blade that's pretty noticeable, but not bad
- Tip of the blade bent slightly, but not broken
- Tang stamp hard to read due to blade cleaning
- Blade etching no longer visible, if etched originally

4 Points

- Blades sharpened leaving 94 to 96 percent intact✻
- Many light scratches, which are noticeable, but not deep
- Light peppering in one or two areas -or- light surface rust in small area -or- small pit
- Very tiny tip break where just 1/16" or so is broken off and hardly noticeable
- Tang stamp hard to read due to light rust or pitting

5 Points

- Blades sharpened leaving 92 to 94 percent intact✿
- A few medium scratches which are very noticeable, but still not deep
- Heavy peppering in one area -or- medium area of very light surface rust -or- medium pit
- Medium tip break where less than ¼" is broken off and doesn't look too bad
- Badly bent tip, would be likely to break off if straightened
- Tang stamp no longer visible due to cleaning

6 Points

- Blades sharpened leaving 90 to 92 percent intact✿
- Many medium scratches which are very noticeable, but still not deep -or- 1 or 2 deep ones
- Heavy peppering over a large area -or- large area of surface rust -or- small area of pitting
- Medium tip break combined with nicks in blade edge
- Tang stamp no longer visible due to heavy rust or pitting

7 Points

- Blades sharpened leaving 85 to 90 percent intact✿
- Few deep scratches -or- a lot of medium scratches -or- one small gouge that's not too obvious
- Heavy peppering on both sides of blade, or on both blades -or- surface rust covering whole side
- Large tip break of more than ¼" -or- large chip or two in edge -or- medium are of pitting
- Medium bend in blade which does not prevent normal operation

8 Points

- Blades sharpened leaving 80 to 85 percent intact✿
- Many deep scratches -or- one medium gouge, preferably in the back side of the blade
- Light rust in a few spots with some light peppering and, or surface rust
- Break with blade loss to 20 percent -or- smaller break combined with small chips

9 Points

- Blades sharpened leaving 75 to 80 percent intact✿
- Deep scratches covering whole side or some on each blade -or- 2 to 3 small gouges
- Heavy rust in one or two small spots -or- light rust in large area -or- few large pits
- Blade bent badly enough to cause scraping when closing or opening

10 points

- Blades sharpened leaving 70 to 75 percent intact✿

- Deep scratches on both blades -or- one large deep gouge and misc. scratches
- Heavy rust in several spots or a few spots on both blades -or- light rust over large area -or- a large area of deep pitting
- Break with loss of 20 to 30 percent -or- 1 of two blades broken in half -or- both have small breaks

11 Points

- Blades sharpened leaving 60 to 70 percent intact✿
- Deep scratches covering both blades -or- two deep gouges and misc. scratches
- Heavy rust over a large area or small areas on two blades -or- light rust over entire blade side -or- two to four large areas of deep pitting
- Break with loss of 30 to 40 percent -or- smaller break combined with chips
- Blade bent badly enough that knife will not close or open properly

12 Points

- Blades sharpened leaving 50 to 60 percent intact✿
- Combination of light scratches, deep scratches and deep gouges covering most of one blade
- Heavy rust covering whole side or large areas on two blades -or- light rust covering both sides of blade -or- several areas of deep pitting
- Break with loss of 40 to 50 percent -or- 1 of 2 blades broken off at tang

13 Points

- Blades sharpened leaving 40 to 50 percent intact✿
- Combination of deep scratches and deep gouges covering both sides of one blade of 2 blades
- Light to heavy rust covering entire blade surface -or- deep pitting covering most of blade surface
- Break with loss of 50 to 60 percent -or- both blades broken approx 25 percent loss to each

14 Points

- Blades sharpened leaving 30 to 40 percent intact✿
- Combination of deep scratches and deep gouges covering entire blade surface
- Heavy rust covering entire blade surface -or- deep pitting covering entire surface
- Break with loss of 60 to 70 percent -or- both blades broken approx 30 percent loss to each

15 Points

- Blades sharpened leaving 15 to 30 percent intact✿
- Blades scratched, gouged and rusted to the point of being totally useless
- Break with loss of over 70 percent -or- both blades broken with approx 40 percent loss to each

✿ You can use blade tracings in the back of the book to determine blade loss.

Handle Chart

In order to use this chart effectively you must understand the adjectives that are used:

1. **Faint:** Hard to see with the naked eye, but obvious with a magnifying glass
2. **Light:** Obvious to the naked eye, but not deep at all
3. **Medium:** Very obvious to the naked eye, but still not deep
4. **Deep:** Heavy scratches, but not too deep or wide
5. **Gouged:** Scratches that are deep and, or wide
6. **Tiny:** Means just that, so small that you almost need a magnifying glass to see it.

Here are the other terms that you must understand to effectively use this chart:

1. **Crack:** A break in the handle material of varying degree
2. **Hairline:** A tiny crack no wider than a human hair and usually through a pin
3. **Scratch:** Lines which leave impressions in the steel, usually from sharpening
4. **Dent:** Impression in a surface from a blow or pressure
5. **Ding:** A tiny dent or nick in a surface that is hardly noticeable
6. **Chip:** Missing a piece of material as from a blow or cut
7. **Bursting:** The visual appearance of internal cracking caused by deterioration of celluloid
8. **Broken:** Self explanatory, but there are various degrees of damage
9. **Rust:** Corrosion caused by moisture, salt, etc, which destroys the integrity of the steel
10. **Surface Rust:** Very fine and light rust which gives the area a brownish hue, not heavy
11. **Light Rust:** More serious than surface rust and will leave pitting if cleaned off.
12. **Pit or Pitting:** Affect of rust on metal. Invades the metal leaving dark craters or holes
13. **Peppering:** Several tiny pit marks which resemble pepper sprinkled on the surface
14. **Age spots:** Spots on the blade which are not rust or pitting and would buff off with effort

Scoring

1 Point

- All Handles: 1-5 faint scratches on one handle / 1 tiny ding that is barely visible
- Shrinkage of handles with no more than 1 /32-inch gap by bolster or from edge of liner
- Backspring or liners: 1-5 faint scratches / Heavy patina / or Light spotting
- Bolster: Few faint scratches, barely visible

2 Points

- All Handles: 5-10 faint scratches on the handles / 2-5 tiny dings / 1-3 light scratches on both handles / metal handles: noticeable loss of finish
- Shrinkage of handles with no more than 1 /16-inch gap by bolster or from edge of liner
- Backspring or liners: 5 or more faint scratches / Medium spotting / 1-3 light scratches
- Bolster: Several faint scratches / Few light scratches

3 Points

- All Handles: 3-5 light scratches / 6 or more tiny dings or 1-3 regular dings / 1-3 deep scratches / metal handles: 10-15% loss of finish
- Shrinkage of handles with no more than 1 /8-inch gap by bolster or from edge of liner
- Backspring or liners: Many faint and light scratches / 1-3 deep scratches / Light peppering
- Bolster: Several light scratches / 1-3 deep scratches / Light peppering

4 Points

- Handles: Many light scratches / Many tiny dings / 4-6 deep scratches / 1 hairline pin crack / 1 small chip / Metal handles: 1-3 tiny dents / metal handles: 20-30% loss of finish
- Shrinkage of handles with no more than 3 /16-inch gap by bolster or from edge of liner
- Backspring or liners: 4 or more deep scratches / Medium peppering / Light pitting / Light rust
- Bolster: 4 or more deep scratches / Medium peppering / Light rust

5 Points

- Handles: 4 or more deep scratches / 4 or more dings plus scratches / 2 short hairline cracks / 1 tiny crack / 1 medium chip / Metal handles: 3-6 tiny dents or 1 medium dent / some surface rust / metal handles: 30-40% loss of finish
- Shrinkage of handles with no more than ¼-inch gap by bolster or from edge of liner
- Backspring or liners: Multiple deep scratches / Heavy peppering / Medium pitting / Medium rust
- Bolster: Multiple deep scratches / Heavy peppering / Medium rust / Few deep pits / 1 loose

6 Points

- Handles: Multiple deep scratches / Multiple dings and scratches in both / 3 or more hairline cracks / 2-3 tiny cracks / Large chip / Metal handles: Multiple tiny dents in both or 1 medium dent in front handle or large dent in back handle / some surface light rust / metal handles: 40-50% loss of finish

- Shrinkage of handles with more than ¼-inch gap by bolster or from edge of liner
- Backspring or liners: Heavy pitting / Gouged / hairline break / Heavy rust
- Bolster: Gouged / Heavy Rust / 2 or more loose

7 Points

- Handles: Multiple hairline cracks / 4 or more tiny cracks / 1-3 medium cracks / 1 large crack / 2 or more large chips / Broken handle missing ¼-inch chunk or smaller / Metal handles: 1 large dent in front handle / Multiple large dents in back handle or multiple medium dents in both / fairly serious rust / metal handles: 50-70% loss of finish
- Repairs: 2 small handle patches nicely done / 1 handle replaced and doesn't match well
- Backspring or liners: Solid rust / Broken with small piece missing
- Bolster: 1 missing

8 Points

- Handles: Multiple large cracks / multiple large

chips / Broken handle missing chunks from one handle / Celluloid showing signs of bursting / metal handles badly dented / bad rust / metal handles: 70-90% loss of finish

- Repairs: 1 large or 3 or more small patches nicely done / both handles replaced poorly or wrong handles done nicely.
- Backspring or liners: Missing
- Bolster: Missing all

9 Points

- Handles: Both broken and missing pieces / Obvious celluloid bursting / Metal handles gouged through and dented / rust holes / metal handles: 100% loss of finish

- Repairs: 2 or more large patches nicely done / 1-4 small patches poorly done
- Backspring missing entirely

10 Points

- Handles: Both damaged beyond repair / or missing entirely / Celluloid bursting on both handles with obvious breakdown causing knife corrosion
- Repairs: 5 or more poorly done repairs (obvious), in other words they are worthless or gone!

Function Chart

Here are the terms that you must understand to effectively use this chart:

1. **Peek:** Blade tip barely protrudes from handle when closed
2. **Proud:** Blade tip protrudes quite a bit from the handle when closed
3. **Lockup:** When blade is locked into position by the *catch*
4. **Wiggle:** Slight movement up and down when locked open (direction of the blade travel)
5. **Droop:** Excessive movement up and down when locked open *See diagram*
6. **Wobble:** Side to side movement when locked open (opposite direction of blade travel)
7. **Lazy:** When a blade opens much slower than normal or barely opens by itself
8. **Weak:** Spring that lacks the strength to throw the blade open properly
9. **Strong:** Spring that forcefully throws the blade into full open position
10. **Kickback:** Spring too strong and blade bounces back from full open without locking*
11. **Safety:** The sliding knob near the button that prevents accidental opening of the blade

* This is common with the smaller blade in many of the double bladed switchblades. Especially

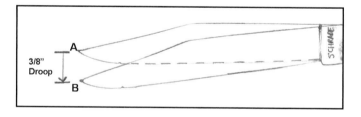

if the spring has been replaced, or the knife has been over-lubricated, or the blade is loose.

Scoring

1 Point

- Very slight wiggle when blade is open, not measurable
- Spring is just a bit weak and knife seems a bit slow, but works just fine
- Minor kickback of small blade only on a two bladed knife
- Safeties work, but marginal. Blade opens slightly when engaged, etc.

2 Points

- Measurable wiggle of not more than 1/8"

- Spring is noticeably weak and knife appears a little lazy, but still works fine
- Severe kickback of small blade only on a two bladed knife
- One safety of two doesn't work (unless known to have defective safeties when new)

3 Points
- Wiggle of not more than ¼"
- Spring weak and knife lazy, but still opens all the way
- Kickback of both blades on a two bladed knife
- Both safeties not functional on a two bladed knife
- Slight wobble, not measurable
- Blade barely peeks when closed. Less than 1/16" from tip to liner

4 Points
- Droop of 3/8" or less
- Very lazy and will not throw blade all the way open when button pressed
- Noticeable wobble with 1/8" or less side to side movement
- Blade peek of 1/8" or less from tip to liner
- Opens fine, but noticeable that spring is not original

5 Points
- Droop of ½" or less
- Broken spring
- Wobble of ¼" or less
- Blade proud ¼" or less from tip to liner

6 Points
- Droop of 5/8" or less/ barely stays locked
- Poorly replaced spring that is obviously not correct or damage to handles from the repair
- Extreme wobble of 3/8" or more
- Very proud blade of 3/8" or less from tip to liner

7 Points
- Won't lock open at all/ or droop of more than 5/8"
- Won't stay closed/ or hair trigger and blade releases prematurely
- Extremely proud blade over 3/8" from tip to liner

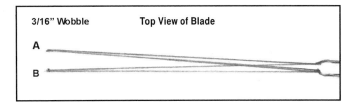

Measuring *wiggle, droop and wobble.*

The two diagrams shown in this section help to demonstrate the difference between wiggle, droop and wobble and show how to measure them. Wiggle and droop both refer to the movement inline with blade travel with droop being the more severe condition. Wobble refers to the movement from side to side or opposite of blade travel. Each can be measured by placing the knife blade on a piece of paper and use a pencil to chart the movement and a ruler to measure it. If the movement is so slight that it is barely measurable it is referred to as slight, otherwise there should be a measurement to gauge the severity of each. To accomplish this you must hold the knife firmly while tracing the blade in one position and then while still holding the knife firmly, move the blade until it stops and trace again. Then you simply measure the distance between points A & B which are the positions of the tips in each tracing. You can also simply hold the knife and push the tip with the pencil against the paper until it stops and measure the line that the pencil makes on the paper, but this doesn't seem to be quite as accurate as the tracings.

Grading List

Points	Grade	Mint Value multiplier
0	Mint	100%
1	Near Mint	75%
2	Excellent +	70%
3	Excellent	65%
4	Excellent –	60%
5	Very Good +	55%
6	Very Good	50%
7	Very Good –	45%
8	Good +	40%

Points	Grade	Mint Value multiplier
9	Good	35%
10	Good –	30%
11	Fair +	25%
12	Fair	20%
13	Fair –	15%
14	Poor	10%
15	Parts	5%
16	Junk	2.5%

George Schrade
1860–1940

George Schrade Knife Co.

46 SEYMOUR STREET – BRIDGEPORT 8, CONN

Manufacturers of Automatic Knives for over a Half Century

Many people refer to George Schrade as the father of the switchblade knife in America. There are certainly some arguments against this. He did not patent the first switchblade in America. William T. Whitehouse did that, with nothing less than a coil spring-fired knife patented on October 25, 1877. Schrade did not start a knife company and remain with it his entire life to make his mark on the industry. He did not even manufacture the most switchblades made in this country. Why then, would anyone refer to him as the father of the switchblade in America? I can sum it up in three words: Creativity, Influence and Ambition. He was responsible for inventing many things, including several different knives, and in one way or another he can be connected to most of the switchblades made in this country prior to 1958.

George Schrade was born on February 13, 1860 in Williamsport, Penn. to Jacob L. and Henrietta Schrade. George had three brothers; William, Jacob Louis and Joseph. When the boys were old enough they learned the machinist trade at the business owned by their father and another man. That business was called Gottlieb Schrade of New York. George was very mechanically inclined and quickly became an excellent machinist. They were known for fabricating models of inventions for people to use in the patent application process. It is said that someone brought an idea into the shop one day for a knife that would open automatically and wanted them to make a prototype so he could apply for a patent. They were not able to make his idea work, but George didn't forget about it. It was on his mind until he finally designed a model that would work and on December 4, 1891 he applied for a patent on his design. On March 8, 1892 he was granted U.S. Patent # 470,605 for his switchblade knife.

George attempted to manufacture the knife on his own with the help of a few good cutlers, but he had trouble finding good help and keeping up with demand. Edward Whitehead of Walden Knife Company was intrigued with George's knife and convinced George to move the production of his knife to Walden, N.Y. Part of the Walden Knife Co. factory was designated for the manufacture of George's switchblade with George himself overseeing the production. This is where the Press Button Knife Company was born. George stayed there until 1903 when he sold his rights to his first patent to the Walden Knife Co. and, along with two of his brothers, J.Louis and William, started the Schrade Cutlery Company there in Walden. George applied for, and was granted, two more switchblade patents in 1906 and 1907. The significance of these patents is that they introduced a safety to prevent the knife from opening accidentally in one's pocket. There were some other improvements as well and you can learn more about these patents in the Schrade Cutlery Company chapter of this book.

Schrade was an avid inventor and he received patents for other things besides knives. He can be credited with a drill gauge, dime bank, weaver scissors, player piano and knife machinery including a shielding machine that automatically cut the recess into handles to install a shield. This last invention was the one that prompted Schrade to sell his interest in the company to his brothers and head for Europe to market this and other machinery. His son, George M. Schrade, accompanied him and they left shortly after 1910. After some combined success, followed by failure in England, they moved on to Germany where they spent a lot of time. It is said that Schrade actually started a cutlery company while in Germany and actually manufactured a switchblade knife that he designed while he was there. I have not been able to confirm this, but it seems possible. It is also said that with the onset of WWI the German government confiscated his factory and inventory and sent him and his son packing back to America. Regardless of the details, Schrade invented another

switchblade knife in 1918 that is commonly referred to as the Flylock. U.S. Patent #1,258,150 was granted on March 5, 1918. The fact that Schrade was unable to manufacture this knife on his own might suggest some truth to the German story. Schrade made a deal with Challenge Cutlery Corporation of Bridgeport, Conn. to manufacture this newest design. Schrade and his son oversaw the production and stayed with the company until they went out of business by 1929.

Since Schrade was still owed money by the company when they went under, he was paid in the form of knife machinery and materials. This was all that Schrade needed to finally start his own knife company — the George Schrade Knife Company. He even started this company in the same building that had just been vacated by Challenge Cutlery Corp. It would seem likely that the building might have been included in the deal he made with Challenge, but I have not confirmed this. He was in full production by 1930 and even the Great Depression couldn't dampen George's spirit. The company prospered and both he and his son received more patents pertaining to switchblade knives. They produced a line of switchblades that were sold under the marketing name of "PRESTO". They also produced a line of small switchblades called Pullballs, which were stamped with the company name. They didn't stop there. Since Remington had a factory right there

in Bridgeport it only seems natural that they would contact George when they were interested in selling a line of switchblade knives. George manufactured the entire line of Remington knives, as well as most of W.R. Case & Sons switchblade line.

Schrade remained active in the business and received his last switchblade patent in 1940. It probably would not have been his last if not for the fact that he died September 9th of that year. That date most definitely marks the end of an era and a great loss to the knife industry in this country. George M. Schrade remained in control of the company until it was sold in 1956 to Boker of Germany. George's grandson, Theodore, was retained as manager of the company from then until 1958 when the company closed its doors for good.

Schrade may not have invented the first switchblade and he may not have made the most switchblades either, but he sure had a huge influence on the industry in this country. George Schrade was somehow connected to most of the switchblades that were ever produced in the USA prior to 1958. He's definitely the best known maker of switchblade knives in this country and I feel that his contributions and achievements over the years have, without a doubt, earned him the name "Father of the switchblade knife in America".

Antique American Switchblade
Manufacture Timeline

1890	1900	1910	1920	1930	1940	1950	1960

{ --George Korn--}   { --Crandall--}   { -----Union Cut Co-----KaBar-----}   {--Queen--}
(Korn's Patent)   (Union Cut Co)   (Keenwell)   (KaBar)   (Queen)

{ AutoKnifeCo }   {--Case XX--Levers & Zippers--} {Bowie Knife}
(Aut Knife Co)   (CASE)   (CASE TESTED)   (CASE Bradford)   (Bowie Knife)   (Edgemaster)
(Hatch Cutlery)
(Wilzin's)

{-----------Press Button Knife Co------------ } { ----Aerial Cutlery---- } { ----Colonial---- }
(Press Button Knife Co) (Walden Knife Co)   (AC Mfg. Co.)   (Shur Snap)
*(Graef & Schmidt) *(Elliot W Langley)   (Pronto) (Jiffy)
*(Torrey) *(Torrey) *(Simmons Hdwre)   (Snappy)

{ Russell Knife }   { ----Flylock----- }{ -----George Schrade Knife Co-------}
(Russell)   (FlyLock)   (G Schrade Knife Co)
                         (Challenge)   (PRESTO)
{ Kruschke }   *(Cattaraugus)   *(CASE)
                                               *(Remington)

{ -------------------Schrade Cutlery Co----------------------- }{-----Schrade Walden-----}
(Schrade Cut Co, Walden, NY)   Imperial
*(Wade & Butcher)   *(Keen Kutter) *(LL Bean)   (Schrade Walden)
*(Norvell Shapleigh) *(Shapleigh)   (Hammer Brand)
*(E. Weck)   *(Buffalo Cut Co)   (Edgemaster)
                                                                (Imperial)

{ - Utica - }   { -----------Camillus--------- }
                             (Camco)

1890	1900	1910	1920	1930	1940	1950	1960

Please Note: All of the above switchblade timelines are Approximations and although they are accurate, to the best of my knowledge, they may vary slightly.

Tang stamps in parenthesis underneath the Manufacturer's stamp, are either knives made under contract for other companies, or other tang stamps used by that manufacturer.

* The asterisk indicates knives made under contract.

Aerial Cutlery Manufacturing Co.

Marinette, Wis.   1909–Present

J.D. Phillips started the Aerial Cutlery Supply Company at 319 West 1st Street, Duluth, Minn. in 1909. It was strictly a jobber business where he bought cutlery that was manufactured by other companies and resold it through his company. One of his main suppliers was the Morris Cutlery Company of Morris, Ill. Phillips was joined in his business by Thomas Madden and they were lucky enough to acquire a couple of ambitious young salesmen; brothers Christian Frederick Jaeger and Frederick Henry Jaeger.

store and went on to learn the barber trade. Fred apparently hooked up with J.D. Phillips and Aerial Cutlery Supply, though I'm not sure how this came about, and began selling cutlery for him. Eventually, both brothers ended up selling cutlery for the company and sell, they did! The Jaeger boys proved to be fantastic salesmen and their experience with the logging industry proved helpful during their travels. In their visits to the logging camps and mines, they were able to gain access to places

In 1903, Frederick Richard Jaeger, the father of Chris and Fred, was killed in an accident at the Sawyer-Goodman Mill, leaving behind a widow and six children with no visible means of support. Fred and his older brother, Chris, ages 14 and 16 respectively at the time, had to grow up fast and became the breadwinners for the family. The only job they could find that would pay a "man's wage" was packing shingles with a traveling shingle mill. The boys were hard workers and they traveled with the mill, all the while sending money home to their mother. After a few years the brothers went separate ways. Chris got a job at a drug

that other salesmen could not. Loggers and miners accounted for a large percentage of their early sales. The ambitious brothers managed to sell cutlery faster than the Morris Cutlery Company could supply it!

J.D. Phillips was a good businessman and he recognized the ambition and ability of the brothers, as well as the need to expand his business to keep up with demand. In 1912 Phillips promoted the Jaeger brothers into management positions. Aerial Cutlery Supply Company became a manufacturing company when they purchased the Morris Cutlery Company on March 5, 1912. The story is still told in the Jaeger family about the brothers traveling to Illinois to close the deal. Some details about the appearance of the factory, a sign in a second story window, hiring a lawyer to come and close the deal on a Sunday and his $5 fee, add character and feel to the story. The selling price for the Morris Cutlery Company was $3,500, lock, stock and barrel and it included a 90-day lease on the building. On March 16, 1912 the company name was changed and was registered as the Aerial Cutlery Manufacturing Company and all of the equipment and supplies from the old Morris Cutlery Company were transported by train to Duluth. Fred Fauble, who had been the treasurer for Morris Cutlery, came to work for Aerial as their Master Cutler and he remained with the company for 30 years. In later years he handcrafted the first fighting knife for jungle warfare in WWII that was accepted by the U.S. military. Richard Jaeger, the younger brother to Chris and Fred, also joined the company. I don't know how much cutlery was actually manufactured by Aerial in Duluth, but I would guess not very much since they were only in operation there for less than a year.

It was decided to move the entire company to Marinette, Wisconsin in 1913 and by June of that year they were manufacturing cutlery in their new location.

Marinette was the Jaeger brothers' hometown. The town had promised to give them a building to use for their factory as incentive to come to Marinette, if they could guarantee $10,000 would be paid in labor costs in the first two years. They easily accomplished this and were handed the deed in 1915. The building they were given had previously been the old Menominee River Company Store and was located at 108 Hosmer Street in Marinette. The building proved to be "less than ideal" and several renovations were done to the building over the years. These changes are reflected in the slightly changing address of the company over the years. The earliest address is 108 Hosmer and by 1922 it was 108-114 Hosmer. Another change is reflected in the 1950s when it's listed as 112-116 Hosmer as well as a couple of other variations. J.D. Phillips remained president of the company until 1915 when personal health problems forced him to sell his interest in the company to the Jaeger brothers. Christian Jaeger, who had been treasurer, became president

when Phillips left. The company officers as of 1916 also included Frederick Jaeger as secretary and treasurer and Richard Jaeger and Thomas Madden as directors.

Aerial Cutlery Manufacturing Company is probably best known for their "picture knives." In 1879 Reuben and Henry Landis applied for a patent for the idea of putting pictures and advertising on knife frames and covering them with clear celluloid handles. The first two companies to produce the knives were the Canton Cutlery Company and the Novelty Cutlery Company. Both companies were located in Canton, Ohio. Novelty Cutlery Company catered to individuals and made mostly custom knives using the customer's own photos and art. These two companies didn't have much competition until the patent ran out around the turn of the 20th century. While several companies made these knives in the early 1900s, the Aerial Cutlery Manufacturing Company was the only serious competition for the original firms. Picture knives became a large part of the Jaeger brothers business and at one time they probably controlled the market. The interest in this type of knife dropped off dramatically by the 1930s and Aerial, as well as the other companies making them, had to turn their attention elsewhere. Aerial was still manufacturing other cutlery, but barber supplies were becoming their focus. They not only sold their cutlery under the name Aerial Cutlery Manufacturing Company, but were also known to use "Jaeger Brothers" to market their products. In fact, a catalog from 1930 bears the "Jaeger Brothers" name. I was fortunate enough to gain access to this catalog and have the opportunity to bring you some images from it, including the information on a particular knife that they sold.

Aerial Cutlery Manufacturing Company sold a very interesting switchblade knife. The model K112 Sportsman knife was a switchblade with an unusual backspring release that was activated by pivoting with your thumb, a lever mounted over the bolster. This model was handled in pyralin (celluloid), a very popular handle material for knife makers throughout the first half of the 20th century. The model K112S had stag handles and the model K112GS had genuine imported stag handles. These three models were featured in the aforementioned Aerial product catalog from 1930. Some of the K112 knives were handled in tortoise celluloid and some were also done in clear cel-

The "Sportsman" No. K112.

The "Sportsman"

No. K112. This hunting knife is slightly shorter than the K111, but has a patented safety lock arrangement, which is also a self-opener, by pushing the attachment on bolster with thumb. Fits the pocket and stays locked open or closed. Has large high finish saber clip blade, and pyralin handle. Per dozen $18.75

No. K112S. Same as K112, but has stag handle instead of pyralin. Per dozen $18.75

No. K112GS. Same as K112, but has genuine imported stag handles. Per dozen $21.00

ALL ILLUSTRATIONS SHOW THE ACTUAL SIZE OF EACH K[

Photograph of the original Aerial factory on Hosmer Street in Marinette. This picture was taken in September of 1913.

luloid over pictures. I did not find evidence of any other colors or handle materials, though others could have been used at a different time. As I had suspected for some time, these knives were manufactured, without handles, under contract by Union Cutlery Company of Olean, NY. The knife is nearly identical to a knife sold by the Union Cutlery Co. with their tang stamp. That knife had jigged bone handles. It was a model # 61126L and some of them had the famous KaBar "Dog's Head" emblem embedded in the handle. The most obvious clue is the same tang stamp of Oct. 23, 1916, on the back tang on all of these knives. Fred "Fritz" Jaeger still remembers meeting the family that owned Union Cutlery Company when he was younger. I don't know for how many years Aerial sold these models or how many were made, but apparently it was not a large number since these original knives are very hard to find.

Aerial continued to produce cutlery for many years. During WWII they manufactured bayonets for the U.S. Government. Shortly after WWII they began a steady transition from cutlery manufacturing to barber and beauty supplies and by the late 1950s had phased out the manufacture of knives almost completely. In May of 1961 an M-6 bayonet, which was made for NATO, marked the end of Aerial's cutlery production. The fact that Aerial stopped manufacturing cutlery created a mystery which has had knife collectors debating for years! Thanks to much patience, persistence, and a little inves-

tigative work I was able to solve most of this mystery.

Lee Einer Olsen was a stockbroker in the 1920s. When the market crashed in 1929 he found himself out of work. He soon got work as a salesman for the Hudson Cutlery Company of Howard City, Mich. Olsen bought the company in the 1940s and changed the name to the Olsen Knife Company. His wife was Elda Jaeger, younger sister of Fred and Chris Jaeger. The company began having financial problems in the 1960s and since Aerial wasn't making knives anymore, Chris and Fred decided to give all of their stored knife machinery, dies and knife parts to their sister and brother-in-law in an effort to help them through difficult times. Around 1967 the Olsen family hauled all of Aerial's remaining cutlery equipment to Michigan. In with that equipment was a group of K112 Sportsman switchblade knives as well as many other patterns that had been made by Aerial. The stock included some complete knives, but much of it was loose parts. Olsen's son, Lee Jr., became active in the company and he ended up being in control of the company in the late 1970s and into the 1980s. In the final years that Lee Jr. was in charge he tried to breathe some life into the company by selling off the remainder of the Aerial knives that his father and mother had gotten years earlier. He put together as many of the switchblade knives as he could from original parts and then he manufactured approximately 600 reproductions of the knife using "AC Mfg Co, Marinette, Wisc." and "Jaeger Bros, Marinette, WIS." tang stampings right there at the Olsen Knife Company. All of these knives were handled in stag. He made all of the parts for the reproductions from scratch and with noticeable differences. As a result they can be identified and not confused with the original knives. The telltale differences are the release lever and overall measurements.

To sum it up, there are less than 200 switchblade knives that Lee Jr. put together from original K112 parts and approximately 600 of the copies that were manufactured at the Olsen Knife Company for a total of approximately 800 of these switchblade knives that originated in Howard City, Mich. in the late 1970s. Unfortunately, despite all of Lee Jr.'s efforts the financial problems could not be overcome and he was forced to sell the company in 1982 to a group of four investors. The investors continued to use the Olsen Knife Company name and sold knives for nearly three more years before the company closed its doors for good in 1985. Currently the switchblade knives that came from the Olsen Knife Company are considered to be less collectible than the original knives and bring less money, but part of the reason for that is the lack of information on where they came from and how many are around. Now that we have the information, and fairly accurate production numbers, it should have an effect on how collectable they are and should increase the value of the knives. The originals will still command higher prices, but the difference in price should be less than it has been.

Aerial Cutlery Manufacturing Company became Aerial Beauty & Barber Supply just prior to 1960, which reflects the change that took place in their product line. The name was again changed in later years to Aerial Company Inc. and a new 36,000-square-foot facility was built around 1990 and another 40,000 square feet added in 1994. The new address is 2300 Aerial Dr., Marinette, WI and, contrary to what some other knife books would have you believe, the company is still in business and they are a strong force in the Barber and Beauty Supply Industry.

Aerial & Olsen Knife Co. Knives

How to tell the Difference

It would seem logical that while fabricating parts for the K112 switchblades that Lee Jr. got the idea to manufacture his own version of the knife with some slight variations to generate even more income. He paid tribute to the Jaeger Brothers, who owned Aerial Cutlery Mfg. Co. by using their name on most of the tang stamps of these reproduction knives. He also stamped some with Aerial Cutlery Mfg. Co. and all had the patent date of Oct 23rd, 1916 stamped on the back of the blades. He manufactured approximately 600 of the reproduction knives and it's actually quite easy to tell the reproductions from the originals even though they are very similar in appearance.

The switchblades stamped "Jaeger Bros" are all reproductions. Interestingly the catalog put out by Aerial in 1930 was entitled "Jaeger Brothers" and though they did use that marking on much of their cutlery, I do not believe it was ever used on the original K112 knives.

The quickest way to tell an original K112 from a reproduction is by looking at the release knob. The original knives have a pattern of small circles on the knob and the reproductions have a checkered pattern and are slightly larger than the originals. The difference can be seen in the Aerial section by comparing the original tortoise celluloid-handled knife with the other two in the section. There is also a cut from the original Aerial catalog in the Aerial section text with a drawing of the K112. Another way to tell is by looking at the tang of the blade. The tangs on the original knives runs straight into the bolster and the reproductions and some of the "parts knives" have a curved tang. The original knives also have a longer tang measuring slightly over $5/8$ inch compared to the copies which measure approx. $3/8$ inch to the curve. This can be easily measured with the blade open from the underside of the blade. It is a quite noticeable difference. The reproductions were shorter overall than the originals. The original knives measure approximately 8 inches open and the reproductions are at 8 $1/8$ inches approximately.

The blade grind varies also, with the sabre-grind line being pretty much centered on the blades of the original knives and being higher on the reproductions, usually _ inch or less from the top of the blade, or spine. The bolsters are also slightly different with the original bolsters being a bit wider at $^{13}/_{16}$ inch compared to $^{11}/_{16}$ inch for the reproductions which were also a bit thicker than the originals. The fact that they have stag handles does not mean that they are reproductions! The original knives were handled in two types of stag, although the stag used on the reproductions was often burned to give it character and an appearance of age and it definitely has a different look than naturally aged stag. There are a couple of other slight differences, but this should be plenty of information to help any collector tell the difference between the knives.

Here is a chart with various measurements from an original compared to a reproduction.

Item Measured	Original Aerial	Reproduction
Tang Length	$^5/_8$ inches	$^3/_8$ inch to curve
Across Bolster	$^{13}/_{16}$ inches	$^{11}/_{16}$ inch
Length Closed	4-$^1/_2$ inches	4-$^5/_8$ inch
Length Open	8-$^1/_4$ inches	8 $^1/_8$ inch
Sabre-grind line	near middle of blade	$^1/_4$ inch from spine

Model # K112. Tortoise celluloid handles with nickel silver bolsters and brass liners. Sabre-ground clip blade is stamped "A.C. MFG. Co." over "Marinette, WIS." back "PAT Oct 23rd, 1916". This is an original Aerial Cutlery Mfg Co. knife from the 1920s. Measures 4 ½" closed and 8 ¼" open. **Mint value: $1,600**

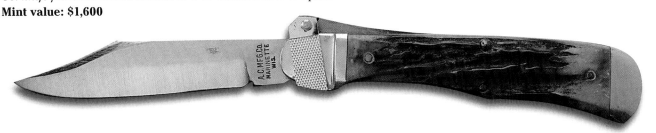

This is an Olsen Knife Co. made knife which was assembled using some authentic parts, including the blade, from Aerial Cutlery Mfg Co. Model # K112. Stag handles with nickel silver bolsters and brass liners. Sabre-ground blade is stamped "A.C. MFG. Co." over "Marinette, WIS." back reads "PAT Oct 23rd, 1916" Measures 4 ⅝" closed and 8 ⅛" open. **Mint value: $500**

This is an Olsen Knife Co. copy of the Model #K112. Stag handles with nickel silver bolsters and brass liners. Sabre-ground clip blade is stamped "JAEGER BROS." over "Marinette, WIS." back reads "PAT Oct 23rd, 1916" Measures 4 ⅝" closed and 8 ⅛" open. **Mint value: $500**

Automatic Knife Company

Middletown, Conn.   1891–1893

Started in 1891 in Middletown, Conn., the Automatic Knife Company produced a knife based on Arthur Wilzen's patent of April 9, 1889. The knife, while not a full-fledged switchblade, was spring-assisted in opening. Instead of opening all the way, when the tabs that protrude from the end of the knife are pressed, the blade is released and a spring throws it open part way so you can easily grab the blade and open the rest of the way with your fingers. No more broken fingernails.

The original factory was located at the foot of Green Street, opposite Union Depot in Middletown, Conn. Two brothers, Doras A. and Norman Stiles, managed the company. In 1893 the company was sold to Walter

the same time that production of the knife stopped.

Apparently, all of the knives manufactured were two-blade knives and were made with different handle materials and blade combinations. They were offered with handles of German Sterling Silver, Pearl, Ivory, Bone, Imitation Stag, Silverine and Aluminum. These knives are hard to find and the few that I've seen have had sterling or aluminum handles with embossed designs or pictures. I have seen one with pearl handles. Some tang stampings that you may encounter are: "Aut Knife Co, Middletown, CT", "Hatch Cutlery, So Milwaukee, Wis" and "Wilzin's. Also see the Hatch Cutlery Company section for related information.

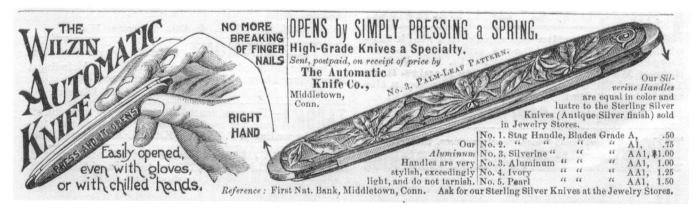

Hatch from South Milwaukee, Wis. and Doras A. Stiles stayed with the company as manager. After Hatch took over the company the stamping was changed to "Hatch Cutlery" in an arch over "CO" over "So Milwaukee" over "WIS". These knives were displayed at the Chicago World's Fair in 1893. Earlier that same year Walter Hatch lost his house to a fire, his factory also suffered damage from a fire. As near as I can tell they continued to manufacture knives in Middletown for a couple of years before that factory was shut down around 1895, which makes this stamping very collectible.

Interestingly, Doras A. Stiles patented an improvement on the Wilzin design involving a change to the liner and release mechanism. U.S. patent # 526,167 was granted to Doras on Sept. 18, 1894, about

	Observations 3" double spring assist knife
1.	Many had spear blade/file blade combination.
2.	Most have metal handles.
3.	Knives bearing the "So Milwaukee" stamp seem to be rarer than the "Middletown" marked knives.
4.	This knife is a 7 out of 10 on the Rarity Scale.

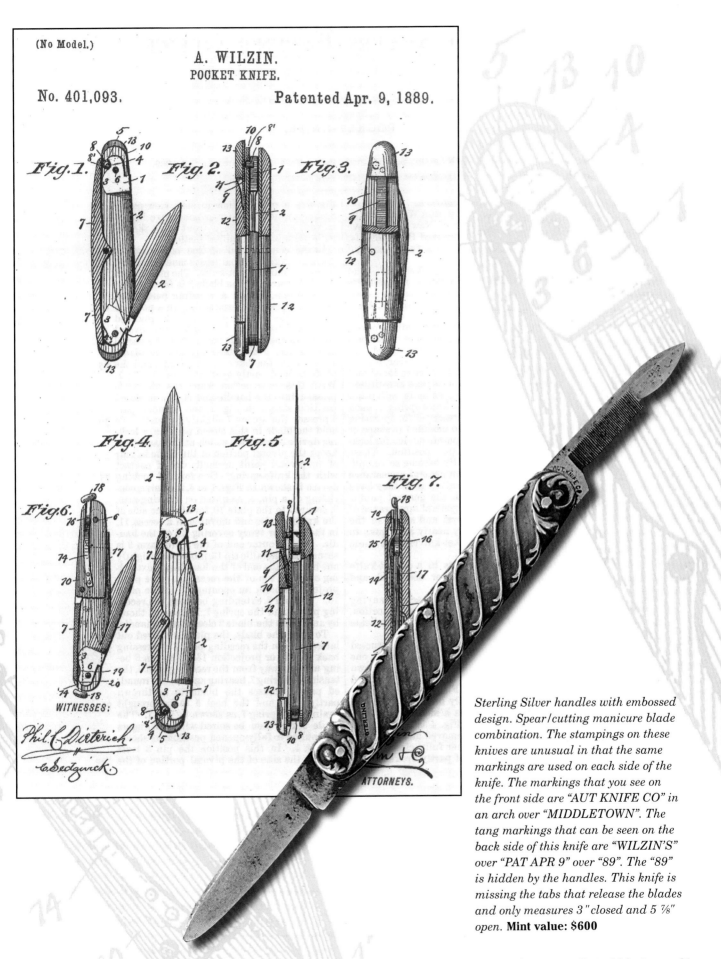

(No Model.)

A. WILZIN.
POCKET KNIFE.

No. 401,093. Patented Apr. 9, 1889.

Fig.1. Fig.2. Fig.3.

Fig.4. Fig.5. Fig.7.

Fig.6.

WITNESSES:

Phil. C. Dieterich.
C. Sedgwick.

ATTORNEYS.

Sterling Silver handles with embossed design. Spear/cutting manicure blade combination. The stampings on these knives are unusual in that the same markings are used on each side of the knife. The markings that you see on the front side are "AUT KNIFE CO" in an arch over "MIDDLETOWN". The tang markings that can be seen on the back side of this knife are "WILZIN'S" over "PAT APR 9" over "89". The "89" is hidden by the handles. This knife is missing the tabs that release the blades and only measures 3" closed and 5 ⅞" open. **Mint value: $600**

Bowie Knife Co.

Newark, N.J. 1945–1950

The 1947 Newark City Directory lists the Bowie Knife Company as a manufacturer located at 327 Academy in Newark. It also lists the owner as Bernard Mogel. This would seem to rule out the speculation that the Bowie Knife Co fishtail switchblades were contracted knives. The significance of this company to switchblade collectors is that they manufactured a distinctive fishtail switchblade knife. This was apparently the only switchblade pattern with their stamp on it. I've seen no evidence of any other models. This fishtail switchblade measures 4 inches closed and 7 ³⁄₁₆ inches open. It has distinctive handles with a factory checkering pattern cut or molded into them. The handles appear to be Bakelite and I've only seen them in three colors: white, black and tan. What sketchy information I've been able to find would indicate that they were in business from about

1945 to 1950. Whatever the case, the knives must not have been made in very large numbers because they are very scarce and collectable old switchblades.

	Observations
1.	These knives all have a checkering pattern on the handles.
2.	The three most common handle colors are black, tan or white.
3.	Brass liners
4.	Some tang stamped upside down

Tan bakelite checkered handles and brass liners. Clip blade is stamped "BOWIE KNIFE" over "NEWARK, NJ" and back tang is blank. Fishtail measures 4" closed and 7 ³⁄₁₆" open. **Mint value: $750**

Buffalo Cutlery Company

Buffalo, N.Y.   1939–1944

There doesn't seem to be much information available on the Buffalo Cutlery Company. I know that it was located at 14 Stock Exchange Bldg, Buffalo, N.Y. The president of the company was Abe Halbreich and they were in business from approximately 1939 to 1944. They were also apparently a cutlery jobber, contracting cutlery to be made with their tang stamp and selling it. Buffalo Cutlery's claim to switchblade fame comes from them contracting Schrade Cutlery Company to make some switchblades for them with the Buffalo Cutlery Co. tang stamp. As far as I know they only contracted for the 3 ⅜-inch double blade and I haven't seen any other models with this tang stamp. Since it was a small company and not in business for long, they did not have the opportunity to sell many of these knives, making them very rare and quite collectable. I would appraise a double in mint condition at $800 at the time of this printing. I was not able to find an example to include in the book, but I'm going to keep looking .

Camillus Cutlery Co.

Camillus, N.Y. 1902–Present

Camillus Cutlery Company got its start in Camillus, NY in the 1890s when Charles Sherwood built a small knife factory on the banks of Nine Mile Creek. The business, originally called Camillus Knife Company, struggled until 1902 when Sherwood sold the company to Adolf Kastor who was a large importer of German cutlery. Kastor changed the name to Camillus Cutlery Company and breathed new life into the company. Adolf and his brother Nathan still operated A. Kastor & Bros., their import company in New York City as a separate entity until 1947, when they put the entire business under the already popular Camillus Cutlery Company name.

Camillus, although not particularly known for their switchblade knives, did indeed manufacture two different models. The most widely known is the MC1 an orange-handled paratrooper knife with shroud cutter, which they manufacture under contract for the U.S. Government. They took over this contract from Schrade Walden around 1960 and they still manufacture them today. The contract was given to Logan Smyth of Florida around 1990, but their knives were of low quality and were rejected by the government and the contract was restored to Camillus. These knives were designed for military use, primarily for paratroopers. It is designed to leave the manually

opened shroud cutter blade open and attach the knife to the jumpsuit with a lanyard tied to the lanyard ring on the knife so it is ready for use. The automatic clip blade is just a back up and for general use. These knives were manufactured strictly for military use, but many have found their way into the open market and they are a "double interest" collectible because they are sought after by knife collectors and military collectors alike. In December of 1965 one of these knives was onboard the Gemini space mission so among other claims, this knife has been in outer space.

Although not many people are aware of it, Camillus did make another switchblade model for civilian use and more specifically, for advertising. This knife was based on U.S. Patent 2,197,136, granted to Maurice Share and William D. Wallace on April 16, 1940. They were assignors to Camillus Cutlery and I have confirmed that they were employees of Camillus. The knife is called the #80 Flylock model by Camillus and was primarily designed to be an advertising knife. Measuring 3-1/8 inches closed, this knife usually had celluloid handles and nickel-silver bolsters. Instead of a button release, it had an unusual backspring release and was stamped CAMCO, which was a trademark of Camillus Cutlery Company. Apparently this model was not very popular because there don't seem to be many of them around. I would guess that the release mechanism might have had something to do with that since it is in an inconvenient spot for easy opening. I have included an original factory drawing of the knife that was supplied to me by Camillus. These knives were manufactured during the 1940s and must not have been pro-

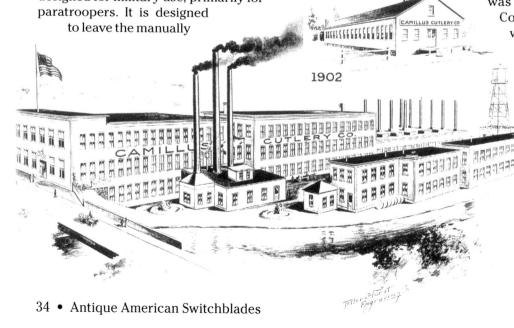

1902

duced in very large numbers. Camillus is still making knives today at the same location.

Observations	
3-⅛-inch #80 Flylock	
1.	Backspring release.
2.	Should have brass liners and bolsters.
3.	Most likely will have advertising on handle.
4.	Tang stamp CAMCO

MC1 Paratrooper	
1.	Most have bright orange jigged handles, with some shade variations.
2.	Should have an automatic clip blade and a manual shroud cutter blade. (hooked)
3.	Should have a lanyard ring on the automatic blade end.

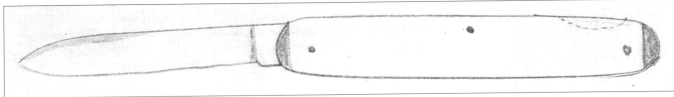

Tang stamped "CAMCO", this switchblade measures 3 ¼" closed approx. Normally had celluloid handles and nickel silver tip bolsters and used as advertising knives mostly. A small button near the bottom, or back of the knife triggers unusual backspring release. This picture is from an actual fabrication sheet from the Camillus factory. Rare knife. **Mint value: $450**

Orange jigged plastic handles, brass button and safety, steel liners and lanyard ring. Clip/shroud cutter combination. Clip blade is stamped "CAMILLUS" over a line, over "NEW YORK" over "USA" with no other markings. You may find "Stainless Steel" stamp on some of these. Camillus reference number MIL-K-25594C, US Gov # MC1. **Mint value: $200**

CASE
W.R. Case & Sons

Bradford, Penn.   1902–Present

When it comes to knife collecting there's one company name that stands out in the crowd and is recognized the world over. That name is Case. The story of the Case family and their ties to the knife industry in America is a long and complicated one. I'm not going to try to tell the whole story of how the Case family married into many of the major knife companies of the late 19th and early 20th centuries. I will briefly mention that they are connected to a number of knife manufacturers including, Cattaraugus, Union Cut Co. (which later became KaBar), Standard Knife Co., Kinfolks, C. Platts & Sons Cutlery Co., Robeson, and Crandall Cutlery, to name a few.

Although there was more than one Case Company and many different Case stampings, the Case Company that is most interesting to switchblade collectors is W.R. Case & Sons.

J. Russell Case, son of W.R. Case, who was the main investor in the company, started the firm in Little Valley, N.Y. in 1902. J.Russell was the grandson of Job Russell Case, for whom he was named. J. Russell had worked for Case Brothers Cutlery Co., which was

owned by his uncles John, Jean and Andrew Case. He left there in 1902 and started W.R. Case & Son as a jobber and sold knives that were manufactured by other companies. He started his first manufacturing plant in Bradford, Penn. in 1905 with some financing from his father and the help of his brother-in-law H.N. Platts. At this time the company name was changed to W.R. Case and Sons, even though H.N. was only a son-in-law. J. Russell used the image of his grandfather, Job, and the year that his grandfather was born in his advertising to give the impression of an established company. He eventually acquired the "Tested XX" trademark from his uncles' failed business in 1914.

W.R. Case & Sons got involved in switchblades around 1920, but I suspect that the seed was planted by J. Russell's other brother-in-law, Herbert Crandall. W.R. Case & Sons acquired Crandall Cutlery Co. November 15, 1911. Crandall had marketed a "scale release" switchblade prior to the merger. During WWI Case contributed to the war effort by making more than 80,000 pocketknives under contract to the U.S. government. W.R. Case & Sons outgrew their original factory in the late 1920s and in 1929 they moved into a new facility on Russell Blvd. in Bradford. Most, if not all, of W.R. Case & Sons' switchblade lineup was contracted knives from other manufacturers, the majority of which came from none other than George Schrade and his George Schrade Knife Company of Bridgeport, Conn. Ten basic models of switchblades can be found with a Case tang stamp on them and they are as follows:

1.   2-7/8" pullball
2.   3-3/8" single-blade
3.   3-3/8" double-blade
4.   4-1/8" single-blade
5.   5" single-blade
6.   4" fishtail
7.   4 3/8" lever-release
8.   5-3/8" lever-release
9.   5-1/8" Coke bottle Zipper
10.   5-3/8" Clasp Zipper.

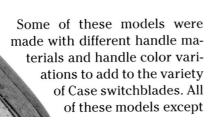

Some of these models were made with different handle materials and handle color variations to add to the variety of Case switchblades. All of these models except for the lever release and Zipper switchblades were made under contract by the George Schrade Knife Co. for W.R. Case & Sons.

There is speculation that the Zippers never actually went into production and were just prototype knives made at Case, but I have no proof either way at this point and although they are extremely rare, it would seem that there are too many in existence to support this theory. The release for which they are named is very unique. It consists of a large squarish button on the handle that is pushed sideways instead of downward. Most collectors believe that the lever-release switchblades were indeed manufactured by W.R. Case & Sons, but again I am aware of no proof. This author has suspected a possible connection with J.A. Henckels Cutlery of Germany. Henckels produced some lever-release switchblades in the early 1900s that strongly resemble the lever knives mar-keted by W.R. Case & Sons. Case did contract knives, scissors, leather cases, razors and manicure items to be made for them in Germany between 1923 and 1940, which is approximately the same time for Case selling the lever-release knives. There is also a possible George Schrade link here because Schrade traveled to Germany before WWI and while he was in Germany it is likely that he established connections and may have assisted Case with the lever knives in one way or another. I don't know if there is a connection, but it would seem possible, especially since George manufactured most of Case's switchblade line. The Case lever-release knives were introduced around 1920 which was shortly after the end of the war with Germany.

The George Schrade Knife Co. produced the rest of the Case switchblade line between 1929 and 1956, when the George Schrade Knife Co. went out of business. The switchblade production most likely stopped prior to 1956 because Connecticut banned switchblades in 1955, prior to the passing of Public Law 85-623 in 1958 by Congress. I suspect that they actually stopped producing them in the late 1940s. Case also produced edged weapons for the U.S. Government during WWII including the V-42 stiletto, the V-44 navy machete and others. W.R. Case & Sons remained a family business until 1972 when it was sold to American Brands Inc. The firm has since changed hands a few times and is still in business to this day.

Model # 5161L. Stag handles, nickel silver bolsters and release lever with brass liners. Sabre-ground clip blade is stamped "CASE" over "Tested XX" back is blank. Bottom bolster also stamped "CASE" over "Tested XX". Lever release knife measures 4 ⅜" closed and 7 ¹³⁄₁₆" open.
Mint Value: $3,100

Model # 5171L. Stag handles, nickel silver bolsters and release lever with brass liners. Sabre-ground clip blade is stamped "CASE" over "Tested XX" back stamped "5171L". Bottom bolster also stamped "CASE" over "Tested XX". Lever release measures 5 ⅜" closed and 9 ¼" open.
Mint value: $3,500

Model # 5172. Stag handles with nickel silver bolsters and unique Zipper release. Clip blade stamped "CASE" over "TESTED XX". This knife is referred to as the Clasp Zipper and is even more rare than the Coke bottle model. Knife measures 5 ⅜" closed and approx. 9 ¼" open.
Mint value: $8,500

Model # C61050L. Bone stag handles with nickel silver bolsters and unique zipper release. Swedge ground clip blade is stamped "CASE" over "TESTED XX". This knife is referred to as the Coke bottle Zipper and is quite rare. Knife measures 5 1/8" closed and approx. 9" open.
Mint value: $5,500

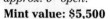

Model # 31211 ½. Black celluloid handles, nickel silver bolsters and brass liners. Clip blade stamped "CASE" back tang stamped "31211 ½". Measures 4" closed and 7 ¼" open.
Mint value: $1,500

Model # 31211 ½. Yellow celluloid handles, nickel silver bolsters and brass liners. Clip blade stamped "CASE" back stamped "31211 ½". Measures 4" closed and 7 ¼" open. **Mint Value: $1,500**

Model # 61213 ½. Jigged bone handles, no bolsters, brass liners. Clip blade stamped "CASE, Tested XX" back is hard to read, but should be "61213 ½". Measures 4" closed and 7 ¼" open.
Mint value: $1,750

Model # 91210 ½. Onyx celluloid handles with brass liners. Clip blade stamped "CASE" back stamped "91210 ½". Measures 3 ⅜" closed and 6" open. **Mint value: $750**

Cattaraugus Cutlery Company

Little Valley, NY   1886–1963

Cattaraugus Cutlery Company had its origins with J.B.F. Champlin & Son, a knife jobber business started by John Brown Francis Champlin around 1882. John's son, Tint, was involved in the business also. The name was changed to Cattaraugus Cutlery Company in 1886 when J.B.F. and Tint were joined in the business by some of John's brothers-in-law, the Case brothers, Jean, John, William Russell and Andrew Case. The Case brothers left Cattaraugus within a few years and went on to form their own company, Case Brothers Cutlery Company, around 1896 in Little Valley, N.Y. They invented the famous "Tested XX" trademark. (There is disagreement about some of these events and I was unable to come up with much evidence, so I'm going with the version endorsed by Case.) Cattaraugus got into manufacturing around 1890 when they bought out the Beaver Falls Cutlery Company, which had gone out of business. Cattaraugus continued to make quality knives in Little Valley, N.Y. for nearly 75 years.

Although Cattaraugus never manufactured switchblade knives, they did contract for some switchblades. This was done mostly between 1918 and 1929, when George Schrade was producing his Flylock knives at Challenge Cutlery Corp. in Bridgeport, Conn. Cattaraugus contracted at least three different models of the Flylock switchblades to be produced by Challenge Cutlery and they were as follows:

1.   3 ⅜-inch double
2.   4 ⅛-inch clip blade single
3.   5-inch clip blade single

The large clip blades had the standard black grooved Bakelite handles that were used on the Flylock stamped knives. The 3 ⅜-inch knives were made with different handle materials, though I suspect only a few options were available. The only ones I've seen were in sterling silver or mottled celluloid. One interesting note on the tang stamps: because of limited tang space and the long company name, the name is shortened by removing one "u" to Cattaragus. Might also have been a mistake at the factory?

There was a fourth switchblade sold under the Cattaraugus name. It measures approximately 3 inches closed and the one that I've encountered had genuine pearl handles. It is unique in that there are no buttons. The blades are released by pressing down on the blades themselves. You press the small blade to release the large and visa versa. The release is similar to switchblades made in England in the middle of the 19th century, but this is the first small double that I've seen like this so I really don't have any others to compare it to. I hope to solve this mystery and would appreciate any information.

To sum up, there are four basic models of Cattaragus switchblade knives, including the unusual 3-inch double. All of the Cattaraugus switchblades are very rare and highly collectible. Even in poor condition, they will command much higher prices than their Flylock counterparts. To find one in any condition is and I'd suggest you not miss your chance if you have one come your way!

Mottled celluloid handles with green, black, dark orange and more. Nickel silver tip bolsters and brass liners. Spear blade stamped "Cattaragus" arched over "CUTLERY Co" over "LITTLE VALLEY" over "NY" and the back reads "Flylock" over "REG US PAT OFF". The pen blade is stamped "Flylock" over "REG US PAT OFF" and the back is marked "US PAT" over "3-5-18". This knife was made under contract at the Challenge Cutlery Corp. by the FLY-LOCK division and is extremely rare. Measures 3 ⅜" closed and 7 1/16" open. **Mint value: $1,000**

Challenge Cutlery Corporation

Bridgeport, Conn

The Challenge Cutlery Corporation was incorporated in 1905 in Bridgeport, Conn. The company had roots in England with the B.J. Eyre Company of Sheffield, which was started in 1867 and purchased in 1877 by the Frederick Wiebusch Company of New York, along with the "Challenge" trademark. Challenge Razor Works was started in Bridgeport in 1889 as a subsidiary of F.Weibusch & Co. The Challenge Cutlery Company of Bridgeport, Conn came into being in 1899 with the purchase of the Hatch & Holmes Manufacturing Company on the corner of Kossuth & Seymour Streets in Bridgeport. This is NOT the same company that made the Hatch spring-assisted knives discussed in other chapters in this book. (See Automatic Knife Co. and Hatch Cutlery sections for more information on those)

Challenge Cutlery Corp's claim to switchblade fame is their association with George Schrade and his patented Fly-Lock knife. George invented and patented his Fly-Lock switchblade design soon after he returned to the United Stated from Germany after the start of WWI. He contacted Challenge Cutlery Co. and convinced them to manufacture his newest switchblade design. He actually went to work for Challenge as manager of the switchblade division and eventually sold the patent rights for his Fly-Lock to Weibusch and Hilger. They later sold the rights to P.L. Van Alstyne in 1923 and the Flylock Knife Company was formed. George Schrade's son George M. Schrade also went to work for Challenge in their Fly-Lock division. A portion of the plant was used to produce the Fly-Lock knives that were eventually made in several variations of six basic patterns listed in the Flylock Knife Company section. There are two major variations on the tang stamps used on the Fly-Lock knives over the 10-year span that they were made. The two main markings that are found are "Flylock" and "Challenge Cut Co", which is stamped on the front of the tang. The ones that are stamped Challenge Cut Co are also marked Fly-Lock on the back of the tang. This was an early marking

that was used from 1918 until Van Alstyne formed the Flylock Knife Company in 1923. Total production of the Fly-Lock knives ran from 1918 to 1929, when Challenge Cutlery Corp went out of business. I have only come across four switchblade patterns with the Challenge Cut Co tang stamp and they are:

1. 3 ⅜-inch double
2. 4 ⅛-inch single blade
3. 5-inch single blade
4. 5-inch single blade with folding guard

One interesting knife that I came across is featured in this section. It is a 5-inch pattern with normal markings. What makes it unusual is that it's a large-frame knife with a tiny release button. It also has handles with an unusual jig pattern. The handles appear to be Bakelite, as was used on other large Challenge knives though it has a glossier look. At first I had thought it could possibly be a prototype where they tried out the smaller button at the factory. Often they did not bother to properly fit or finish prototypes since they were just experimenting. It is more likely that this knife has been taken apart and altered. Outwardly the knife does not appear to have been taken apart and from what I have been told it has not been tampered with for the last 40 years, at least. One might be able to tell more by taking the knife apart, but that would seriously hurt the value if it were indeed a factory prototype. I'll just price it both ways and leave it at that.

Although these four patterns are the only ones I've encountered thus far, there's a good chance that there are others patterns with the Challenge stamping as well. I hope that you will let me know if you happen across any others. Please see the chapter on the Flylock Knife Co for more information. There definitely seem to be less of the Challenge marked knives around than the Flylock marked knives, so the Challenge knives should bring slightly higher prices.

3 ⅜" doubles

The first 5 knives pictured have the following things in common: They are all 3 ⅜" double blade knives with spear/pen blade combination. Front of spear blade stamped "Challenge Cut Co." over "Bridgeport, Conn." and the back is stamped "FLY-LOCK" in an arch. The front of the pen blade is stamped "Challenge Cut Co" over "Bridgeport, Conn." and the back is stamped "US PAT" over "March 5, 1918". These knives all should measure 7" open.

Black jigged imitation stag handles with nickel silver tip bolsters and brass liners. **Mint value: $625**

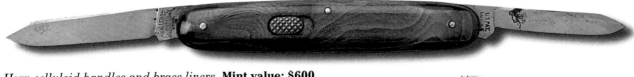

Horn celluloid handles and brass liners. **Mint value: $600**

Gold plated metal handles with fancy embossed pattern and shackle and nickel silver liners. **Mint value: $700**

Silver colored metal handles with delicate embossed pattern and shackle and nickel silver liners. **Mint value: $650**

Silver colored metal with beaded border and nickel silver liners. **Mint value: $600**

5" Singles

The knives pictured below have the following in common: They both measure 5" closed and 8 ¾" open. The front tang is stamped "CHALLENGE" in an arch over "Cut Co" over "B'PORT, CONN" and the back tang is stamped "FLY-LOCK" in an arch over "US PAT" over "MARCH 5" over "1918".

Left: Black Bakelite handles with steel liners and bolsters. This knife is very unusual because of the smaller than normal button and odd jig pattern on the handle. It may have been altered or it could possibly have been a rough prototype. One would need some sort of proof to authenticate as a prototype. **The value for an authenticated prototype: $2,000**
Value if simply an altered knife: $300. *Right: Black Bakelite handles. Steel liners, nickel silver bolsters and folding guards.*
Mint value: $1,000

Colonial Knife Company

Providence, R.I.   1926–2002

The Paolantonio brothers came to the United States from Italy prior to 1912. They already had experience at making knives when they came to this country from one of the most famous knife producing cities in the world, Frosolone, Italy. The brothers, Frederick, Dominick and Anthony worked for the Empire Knife Company of Winsted, Conn. for a few years. The brothers all left Empire and separately formed four separate knife companies between 1914 and 1926. Finally, in 1926 the brothers united to form Colonial Knife Company, located at 9 Calendar St. in Providence. The business thrived and they moved to 287 Oak St. and have been manufacturing knives there ever since.

Colonial Knife Company manufactured five basic models of switchblades in the 1940s and 1950s. They were one of only two U.S. companies who were still manufacturing them on a large scale in 1958 when Congress banned interstate commerce and manufacturing for the purpose of interstate commerce, of the knives. How's that for irony? The two companies in the nation who still manufactured switchblades on a large scale, could still legally make them, but could only sell them in the state where they were manufactured and both companies were locate in Rhode Island!

Many of the antique American switchblades have acquired colorful nicknames over the years. Some of my favorites are the ones associated with the Colonial switchblades. In the following list of knives I have included the length closed, tang stamp and nicknames in parenthesis. The eight basic patterns of switchblade knives Colonial produced were as follows:

1. 2 ¼-inch Snappy (fishtail)
2. 2 ¼-inch Snappy (bowtie)
3. 3 ⅜-inch Shur Snap (cigar)
4. 4-inch Shur Snap (fishtail)
5. 4-inch Shur Snap (bowtie)
6. 4 ⅛-inch Shur Snap (fatjack)
7. 4 ⅛-inch Shur Snap (stubby)
8. 5-inch Shur Snap (jumbo jack)

The names Shur Snap and Snappy were introduced in 1948. The 4 ⅛-inch fatjack was made with two more tang stampings besides the Shur Snap mentioned above. Those stamps are "Pronto" and "Jiffy" and these knives must have been made in smaller numbers because they are harder to find than the Shur Snaps. With the addition of these two important variations there are a total of 10 knives that you'd have to collect to have a good representation of Colonial's switchblade lineup.

The Jumbo Jack and Stubby knives all have large round buttons. The Fatjack knives, including the Pronto and Jiffy, all have a smaller button with some being flat and some slightly rounded. The buttons on the rest of the Colonial Shur-Snap knives help to tell us at what stage of production they were made; early, middle or late. I like to refer to these time differences as generations, and there are four total. Those knives with large brass buttons are the oldest. I call them first generation and they were made in the late 1940s and early 1950s. A large button other than brass would be second generation from the early 1950s. Small rounded buttons are third generation from the mid 1950s, and small flat buttons are fourth generation and were made in the late 1950s. For the record, the handles on these knives were NOT made of celluloid as many collectors think. I wanted to be sure so I did the fire test on several handles. Celluloid is extremely flammable and will ignite immediately upon contact with flame, while plastic will smoke Also, the odors are very different. The Colonial handles are some sort of plastic, not celluloid. Interestingly, all of the Colonial switchblades have the brand name over "Colonial" over "PROV USA" stamped on the front tang, but on most of the fishtails, jacks and Snappys all that can be seen of the bottom stamp is "USA". During the manufacturing process grooves must be cut into the tang of the blade for locking purposes and most of the time these grooves were cut right through "PROV", usually obliterating it, though sometimes part of it is still visible.

Not all models were affected because of size and other differences.

Sadly, the Colonial Knife Company went out of business in February 2002. A new company, Colonial Cutlery International, is rising from the ashes. One of its officers is a grandson of one of the original Paolantonio brothers. The new business also produces pocket knives.

2 ½" Snappy

The knives pictured here have the following in common: They all measure 2 ½" closed and 4 ½" open. Tang stamp is "Snappy" over "Colonial" over "PROV USA". They all have brass liners.

Left: Bowtie with yellow plastic handles, metal bolsters with finger guards, ring and keychain. Large button means it is an early production model. **Mint value: $250**

Right: Bowtie with brown swirl plastic, metal bolsters with finger guards, ring and keychain. Large brass button means it is a very early production model. **Mint value: $250**

Left: Bowtie with white plastic handles, metal bolsters with finger guards, ring and keychain. Small button means late 1950s production. **Mint value: $250**

Right: Bowtie with tan swirl plastic handles, metal bolsters with finger guards, ring and keychain. Small button means lat 1950s production. **Mint value: $250**

Left: Fishtail with yellow plastic handles, no bolsters has ring and keychain. Small button means late 1950s production. **Mint value: $275**

Right: Fishtail with white plastic handles, no bolsters. This is an unusual one in that it does not have a keychain or ring as most do. I do believe that it is original and therefore a bit of an oddity. **Mint value: $300**

3 ⁷⁄₁₆" Jacks

The knives pictured here have the following in common: They all measure 3 ⁷⁄₁₆" closed and 6" open. The tang stamp is "SHUR-SNAP" over "COLONIAL" over "PROV USA" and the back is blank.

Left: Brown swirl plastic with tin bolsters. This knife has a large brass button and a clip blade with sabre grind. **Mint value: $260**

Right: Maroon swirl plastic handles with tin bolsters. This knife has a large button and a clip blade with sabre grind. **Mint value: $260**

White plastic handles with no bolsters. This knife has a small round button and a clip blade with sabre grind. **Mint value: $250**

Black plastic handles with no bolsters. This knife has a small flat button and a clip blade with sabre grind. **Mint value: $250**

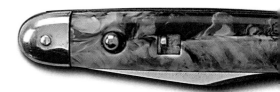

White plastic handles with tin bolsters. This knife has a small round button and a clip blade with sabre grind. **Mint value: $250**

Red and white striped (barber pole) plastic handles with tin bolsters. This knife has a small round button and a clip blade with sabre grind. **Mint value: $275**

Three Shur-Snap jacks to show other variations.

4" Fishtails & Bowties

The knives pictured here have the following in common: They are all 4" closed and 7 ¼" open. Clip blade is stamped "SHUR-SNAP" over "Colonial" over "PROV USA" and back tang is blank.

Bowtie with red and white striped plastic handles with a "New York City" emblem attached. These handles fondly referred to as "Barber pole". Metal bolsters with finger guards and brass liners. This knife has a sabre-ground blade and a small rounded button. Obviously a souvenir sold in New York in the 1950s and has added interest and value because of this. **Mint value: $275**

Bowtie with white plastic handles and tin bolsters with finger guards. Large brass button, sabre ground blade and brass liners. **Mint value: $250**

Bowtie with white plastic handles and tin bolsters with finger guards. Large button, sabre ground blade and brass liners.
Mint value: $250

Bowtie with tan swirl plastic handles and tin bolsters with finger guards. Small rounded button, sabre ground blade and brass liners. **Mint value: $250**

Bowtie with black imitation stag plastic handles and tin bolsters with finger guards. Large button, sabre ground blade and brass liners. **Mint Value: $265**

Fishtail with black imitation stag plastic handles and tin bolsters. Large button, sabre ground blade and brass liners.
Mint value: $265

Fishtail with white plastic handles and tin bolsters. Large button, sabre ground blade and brass liners.
Mint value: $250

Fishtail with red swirl plastic handles and tin bolsters. It has a small round button and brass liners. **Mint value: $265**

Fishtail with white plastic handles tin bolsters. Unusual in that it has a small round button with large hole. I have seen others and believe this to be a transitional knife from 2nd to 3rd generations. Colonial was not one to waste parts and it would seem that they must have used up all of the large-hole handles in stock, though I haven't run into many of these transition knives. This adds interest to the knife and I feel that it adds somewhat to the value as well. It also has brass liners.
Mint value: $285

Fishtail with green swirl plastic handles and no bolsters. Knife has the small flat button, clip blade and brass liners. **Mint value: $265**

Fishtail with blue swirl plastic handles and no bolsters. Knife has the small flat button, unusual flat clip blade (similar to Edgemaster) and brass liners. It is very late production and harder to find. **Mint value: $275**

Bowtie with black imitation stag plastic handles and tin bolsters with finger guards. Large button, sabre ground blade and brass liners. **Mint Value: $240**

Fishtail with black imitation stag plastic handles and tin bolsters. Large button, sabre ground blade and brass liners. **Mint value: $240**

4 ⅛" Stubby & Fat Jacks

The knives pictured here have the following in common: These Jumbo Jacks measure 5" closed and 8 ⅞" open. Blade is stamped "SHUR-SNAP" over "COLONIAL" over "PROV USA" back of tang is blank.

Stubby, tang stamp "SHUR-SNAP" over "COLONIAL" over "PROV USA" and back tang blank. Tan swirl plastic with tin bolsters and finger guards. Sabre ground blade and brass liners. These are hard to find. **Mint value: $325**

Fatjack, tang stamp "PRONTO" over "COLONIAL" over "PROV USA" and back tang blank. Green/black swirl plastic. Sabre ground blade and brass liners. These are hard to find. **Mint value: $325**

Fatjack, tang stamp "JIFFY" over "COLONIAL" over "PROV USA" and back tang blank. Red/blue swirl plastic handles. Sabre ground blade and brass liners. These are very hard to find. **Mint value: $350**

Fatjack, tang stamp "SHUR-SNAP" over "COLONIAL" over "PROV USA" and back tang blank. Tan swirl plastic handles. Sabre ground blade and brass liners. **Mint value: $275**

Fatjack, tang stamp Fatjack, tang stamp "SHUR-SNAP" over "COLONIAL" over "PROV USA" and back tang blank. Red swirl plastic handles. Sabre ground blade and brass liners. **Mint value: $275**

5" Jumbo Jacks

The knives pictured here have the following in common: These Jumbo Jacks measure 5" closed and 8 ⅞" open. Blade is stamped "SHUR-SNAP" over "COLONIAL" over "PROV USA" back of tang is blank.

Black imitation stag plastic handles and tin bolsters with finger guards. This knife has a fish-scaler sabre clip blade and brass liners. **Mint value: $360**

Black imitation stag plastic handles and tin bolsters with finger guards. Sabre clip blade and brass liners.
Mint value: $350

White plastic handles and tin bolsters with finger guards. Sabre clip blade and brass liners. **Mint value: $350**

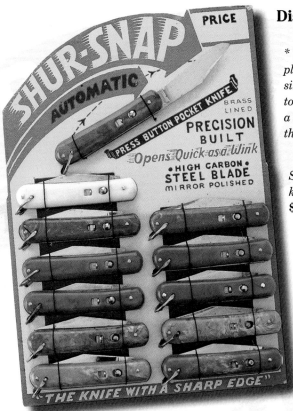

Display Cards

* These cards are so rare and especially with original knives on them, plus the fact that it would be nearly impossible to find a truly Mint set since you're dealing with several knives plus the card, prompted me to make an exception and list their values as Near Mint. If you had a truly Mint set there are many collectors who would pay much more than the values that I have listed here.

SHUR-SNAP display card from the 1950s has 12 original Fatjack knives held in place by an elastic cord. **Near Mint value with knives: $4,000* Mint card empty: $400**

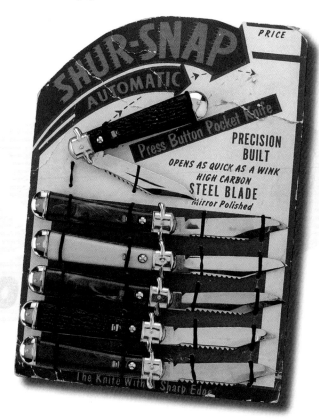

SHUR-SNAP display card from the 1950s has six original Jumbo Jack knives held in place by an elastic cord. Although this is not the display card that came with the Jumbo Jack knives, it is an original SHUR-SNAP fishtail card and retailers in the 1950s often reused the display cards so it is quite possible that this card is just as it was when taken off the shelf in 1958. **Near Mint value with knives: $2,560* Mint card empty: $400**

SHUR-SNAP display card from the 1950s has 12 original fishtail and bowtie knives held in place by an elastic cord. These knives, though all near mint and authentic, weren't likely together in the 1950s since they are all different and represent three different time periods in production. I thought it would be interesting to show the subtle variations by putting them together on the display card. **Near Mint value with knives: $3,200* Mint card empty: $400**

Crandall Cutlery Company

Bradford, Penn. 1905–1912

Herbert Crandall started Little Valley Knife Association Incorporated in 1900. He was a jobber selling knives produced by other manufacturers, many made to his specifications. In 1905 Crandall incorporated as a knife manufacturing company in Bradford, Penn. The town was also the home to W.R. Case & Sons. Sometime between 1900 and 1912 Crandall Cutlery Co. marketed a small "scale-release" switchblade with jigged bone, or pearl handles. It measured approximately 3 inches closed and was opened by applying side pressure to the handle which pivoted slightly releasing the blade. I do not know if Crandall manufactured the knife or if it was contracted, but if they did make it, it was probably based on U.S. Patent # 736,525 which was granted to E. Kaufmann of Germany on Aug.18, 1903. It is very similar to the Simmons "scale-release" which was marketed by E.C. Simmons Hardware Co. prior to 1923. It is possible that Crandall made the Simmons knives as well.

W.R. Case & Sons absorbed Crandall Cutlery Co. in 1912. This was about the same time that H.N. Platts, the second son (in-law) in W.R. Case & Sons, was leaving. Ironically, Herbert Crandall was also a son-in-law of W.R. Case, so when he joined the company, after the merger, it was technically still W.R. Case & Sons — for awhile anyhow. Herbert's grandson, J. Russell Osborne, would eventually become president of W.R. Case & Sons.

Observations 3" Scale-release knife	
1.	Two blades with one at each end of the knife.
2.	Jigged bone, or pearl handles which act as the release for the blades.
3.	On the rarity scale this is a nine out of 10. Extremely Rare!

Cutino Cutlery Company

Kansas City, Mo.   1922–1935

The Cutino Cutlery Company was founded in 1922 in Kansas City, Mo. Edmund Cutino had been operating a drug and sundry company when in 1922 he purchased the entire cutlery stock of Pape-Thiebes Cutlery Company of St. Louis and was instantly in the cutlery business. The only reason that Cutino is interesting to switchblade collectors is because they marketed a 3 ⅜-inch double switchblade with metal handles that strongly resembles a Schrade double. The knives were actually very decent quality. Some had delicate, but elaborate engraving on the handles. They also had safeties of the type for which George Schrade held the patent. Though they were made in Germany, they were marketed in the U.S. in the 1920s and 1930s. They are basically a German copy of George Schrade's double-safety knife, only slightly different. I do not know how many were sold, or for how long, but they seem to be very scarce. The tang is actually stamped with "Cutino Co." over "Germany", so it would appear that Cutino Cutlery Company actually contracted the knives to be made with their name stamped on them. I don't believe they were marketed in this country after 1935. Even though these switchblades were not manufactured in the United States, they were sold here and I thought it might be useful information for the collectors who are lucky enough to find one and be interested.

3 ⅜" doubles

Metal handles have delicate engraving of a peacock and brass liners. Spear/pen blade combination with spear blade stamped "Cutino Co." over "Germany" with back tang blank. The pen blade has the same markings. Measures 3 ⅜" closed and 7 ⅛" open. **Mint value: $450**

Metal handles with Masonic emblem and brass liners. Spear/pen blade combination with spear blade stamped "Cutino Co." over "Germany" and the back is blank. The pen blade has the same markings. Measures 3 ⅜" closed and 7 ⅛" open. **Mint value: $400**

Edgemaster

Unknown

Edgemaster was the marketing name used to sell a line of the most colorful of the antique American switchblades. The synthetic handles can be found in practically any color. The Edgemaster line was designed to compete directly with the switchblade line of Colonial Knife Company of Rhode Island and could possibly have been another line for that company. Unfortunately I have been unable to confirm who actually made them. At first I had suspected that the Edgemaster line was created by one of the Imperial Knife Associated Companies in an effort to compete with Colonial in a tough market. Colonial switchblades were very inexpensive to manufacture and they were able to sell them very cheaply. I've heard stories of 69-cent switchblades and some knives that sold for even less. Imperial, though they also sold inexpensive switchblades, did not have anything to compete directly with Colonial's knives. Schrade Walden made higher quality switchblades that were much more expensive. They didn't even have any switchblade knives in that low price range and I had wondered if they might not have developed the Edgemaster line to get themselves into the "low-end" market. After doing much research, neither appears to be the case. I have made contact with many people who have intimate knowledge of the Schrade and Imperial product line during that period and none have confirmed these theories. I believe that the next most likely theory is that Edgemaster was indeed an independent company. Any information that readers might have and be willing to share about Edgemaster would be greatly appreciated! I hope to solve this mystery. Edgemasters were made in five basic models with several variations in handles and bolsters. They were all single-blade knives as follows:

1. 2 ½-inch key chain knife
2. 3 ½-inch jack
3. 4-inch fishtail
4. 4 ⅛-inch fatjack
5. 4 ⅛-inch paratrooper

The 2 ½-inch key chain knives came with colorful synthetic handles and had a key chain attached to a tiny lanyard ring. This model was marketed under the name "My-T-Mite" and most often sold on cardboard display cards like the one pictured in this section. While most of the Edgemaster knives are simply stamped "Edgemaster" over "USA", these little knives also have "PAT. PEND." stamped underneath the "USA". It seems odd, but I have only observed this stamping on this model. The next model measures 3 ½ inches closed and is a basic single blade jack pattern. These were not made with tin bolsters like the Colonial Shur Snap equivalents sometimes were. They are distinguishable from a Shur Snap from a distance because of an extra pin near the middle of the knife that holds the spring in place. This pin is not visible on the Shur Snap jacks. The next model measures 4 ⅛ inches closed and was also handled in colorful synthetic materials with a lanyard ring. The model is commonly referred to as the "fatjack". Interest in WWII created a market for military-style knives for many years after the war. One of the most interesting of these WWII knives was the MKII paratrooper switchblade. Edgemaster came up with a similar model with metal shell handles with fake bolsters and fake jigging pattern to resemble the switchblades used by paratroopers in the war. Both tin and brass handles were used on these knives with the brass models being scarcer than the tin ones. Both are scarcer than the synthetic handled fatjacks. Probably the most common knife made under the Edgemaster name is the 4-inch closed fishtail model without bolsters.

Edgemasters really were the most colorful switchblades made in America, with a large variety of color combinations, swirl patterns and even sparkles used to make the knives stand out. The fishtail knives seem to be the most colorful of the Edgemaster models. Although this is the most common model, there were four variations made of it in much lower numbers and they are harder to find:

1. The first variation has brass bolsters at both ends of the knife. The bowtie version is very rare.

2. Another variation was the bowtie model, which had tin bolsters with the ones nearest the blade having built in finger guards. This particular style was marketed under the name "Push-O-Matic" and often sold on cardboard display cards such as the one pictured in this section.

3. The third variation has clip-on solid brass handles and this knife is sometimes referred to as the "brassy".

4. The fourth variation has clip-on tin shell handles that were painted in a variety of colors and patterns. This model is often referred to as the "tinny" and is hard to find in mint condition because they were not made for very long and the paint chips off quite easily. I believe this knife wasn't in production for very long.

Observations	
1.	Early production fishtails had sabre clip blades and later production had flat clip blades.
2.	Fishtails seem to be the most common pattern.
3.	The 4 ⅛-inch metal-handled knives seem to be the least common in this size.
4.	Definitely the most colorful antique American switchblades!
5.	Bowties with metal handles are harder to find and more valuable.

2 ½" My-T-Mites

The knives pictured here all have the following in common: These My-T-Mites measure 2 ½" closed and 4 ⅛" open. The clip blade is stamped "Edgemaster" in script over "USA" over "PAT. PEND." and back of tang is blank.

Grey marbled plastic handles, small bail with keychain attached and brass liners.
Mint value: $225

Black plastic handles, small bail with keychain attached and brass liners. **Mint value: $225**

Green swirl plastic handles, small bail with keychain attached and brass liners.
Mint value: $225

Red sparkle plastic handles, small bail with keychain attached and brass liners.
Mint value: $225

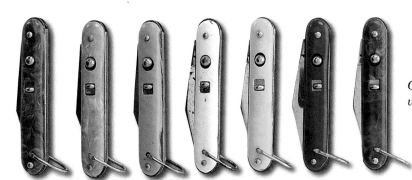

Group of seven My-T-Mites to show various handle colors.

3 ½" Jacks

The knives pictured here all have the following in common. The knives actually measure slightly under 3 ½" at 3 ⁷⁄₁₆" closed and 5 ⁷⁄₈" open. The clip blades are stamped "Edgemaster" in script over "USA". All have brass liners. These can be distinguished from the similar Shur Snap jacks by the blade grind and also the extra pin in the middle of the handles which holds the spring. This pin is not visible on the Shur Snap knives.

Cigar jack with green swirl synthetic handles.
Mint value: $250

Cigar jack with red/orange swirl synthetic handles. Value enhanced slightly by less common attractive color. **Mint value: $260**

Cigar jack with purple swirl synthetic handles. Value enhanced slightly by less common attractive color.
Mint value: $260

4" Fishtails

The knives pictured here all have the following in common. The knives measure 4" closed and 7 ⅛" open. The clip blades are stamped "Edgemaster" in script over "USA".

Fishtail with flat clip blade and candystripe plastic handles with brass liners. Knife has a flat clip blade. The candystripe handles are very popular with collectors, which enhances the value. This knife may have been rehandled, but even so it is a beautiful knife and has much collector appeal
Mint value: $400 If rehandled- $275

Fishtail with sabre-ground clip blade and blue sparkle plastic handles with brass liners. The sparkle handles are attractive and harder to find. **Mint value: $275**

Fishtail with flat clip blade and reddish orange plastic handles with brass liners. **Mint value: $225**

Fishtail with sabre-ground clip blade and light-green swirl plastic handles with brass liners. **Mint value: $225**

Fishtail with sabre-ground clip blade and maroon/black swirl plastic handles have tin bolsters and brass liners.
Mint value: $250

Fishtail with sabre-ground clip blade and aqua green plastic handles that have brass bolsters and brass liners. These knives with brass bolsters are pretty scarce. **Mint value: $325**

Bowtie with sabre-ground clip blade and blue & white striped handles with brass liners. The handles are painted tin hollow shells that are clipped onto the liners by a bendable tab. This model is sometimes referred to as the "tinny". These are actually quite rare and I believe that they were never produced in large numbers combined with the fact that the paint easily peels off the tin, makes it very hard to find a mint example. **Mint value: $350**

Bowtie with sabre-ground clip blade and yellow plastic handles that have tin bolsters with finger guards and brass liners. Edgemaster bowties are harder to find than the fishtail pattern and command higher prices. **Mint value: $300**

Bowtie with sabre-ground clip blade and solid brass handles with finger guards and brass liners. I fondly refer to this knife as the "brassy" and it is hard to find a mint example of this knife. **Mint value: $350**

Group of 10 Edgemaster 4" fishtails to show various handle colors.

Bowtie with flat clip blade and blue plastic handles that have tin bolsters with finger guards and brass liners. The flat blade would indicate a knife made near the end of production in the late 1950s. **Mint value: $300**

4 ⅛" Singles

The knives pictured here have the following in common: They measure 4 ⅛" close and 7 1/16" open. Clip blade is stamped "Edgemaster" over "USA". All have bails so they can be attached to cords.

Fatjack with wild purple swirl plastic handles, clip blade and brass liners. **Mint value: $275**

Paratrooper style with brass handles that are formed to resemble jigged bone, clip blade and brass liners.
Mint value: $300

Paratrooper style with tin handles, clip blade and steel liners. The tin handles are coated with a finish similar in appearance to brass. **Mint value: $275**

Paratrooper style with black painted tin handles that are formed to resemble jigged bone, clip blade and steel liners.
Mint value: $ 275

Display Cards

* These cards are so rare and especially with original knives on them, plus the fact that it would be nearly impossible to find a truly Mint set since you're dealing with several knives plus the card, prompted me to make an exception and list their values as Near Mint. If you had a truly Mint set there are many collectors who would pay much more than the values that I have listed here.

Edgemaster cardboard display card from the 1950s with 12 original jacks which are held in place by an elastic cord. Retailers often restocked the cards and sometimes put different models on them.
Near Mint value with knives: $3,400*
Mint value empty card: $500

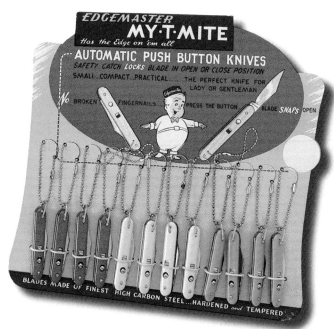

Edgemaster cardboard display card from the 1950s with 12 original My-T-Mite key chain knives held in place by the key chains and elastic cord. I believe that this card is exactly the way it was and with the exact same knives when it was shipped from the factory. It is extremely rare to find one of these cards, let alone to have the original knives on it. **Near Mint value with knives: $3,500***
Mint value empty card: $500

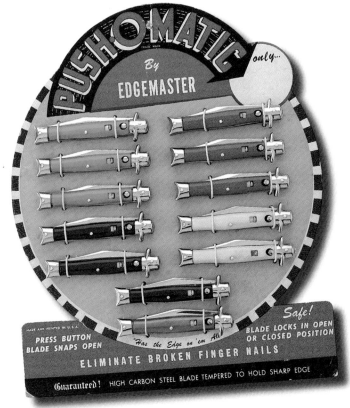

Edgemaster cardboard display card from the 1950s with 12 original Push-O-Matic bowtie knives which are held in place by an elastic cord. I believe that this card is exactly as it was and with the same knives it had when it left the factory. It is extremely rare to find one of these cards, let alone with the original knives on it. **Near Mint value with knives: $4,100***
Mint value empty card: $500

E. Weck & Son

New York, NY   1893–Present

Edward Weck was born in Solingen, Germany. He immigrated to the United States when he was 15 years old. Edward worked for Paul's Brothers, a cutlery import company in New York. I'm not exactly sure when he started his own cutlery business at 148 Fulton Street in New York City, but I believe it was early in the 1890s. I don't believe that Weck ever manufactured any knives. His business was primarily as a jobber/wholesaler of cutlery manufactured by other companies. He did however have a razor manufacturing plant in Brooklyn at one time. He incorporated as E. Weck and Son and contracted to have many different knives made with the E. Weck & Son tang stamp. Schrade Cutlery Co. of Walden, N.Y. did most of their contract work. Two of the basic knife patterns that Schrade produced with the E. Weck & Son stamping were switchblades.

1. **4 ⅞-inch hunting knife with folding guards**. Schrade's model G1543 ¾ is commonly referred to as a Hunter's Pride and this name is etched on the front of the blade.
2. **3 ⅜-inch double-** Schrade's two-bladed safety knife.

I am aware of three handle variations of the double that were made for E. Weck, but there may be more. I've seen them in:

a) Tortoise celluloid Schrade's model # 7404S
b) Ivory celluloid Schrade's model # 7404W
c) Jigged bone w/ tip bolsters Schrade's model # 7403T

I believe these switchblades were contracted between 1910 and 1925. This particular tang stamp is pretty hard to find, making them worth much more than their Schrade Cutlery Co. counterparts.

Observations 4 ⅞" Hunter's Pride	
1.	These knives usually had jigged bone handles.
2.	Most had "Hunter's Pride" etched on the blade.
3.	Folding guards should be made of nickel silver.

Observations 3 ⅜" Double	
1.	Handles usually tortoise celluloid, ivory celluloid or jigged bone.
2.	Some were made with nickel-silver tip bolsters.
3.	Blade combination usually spear/pen.

Tortoise celluloid handles and brass liners. Pen blade is stamped "US PATS" over "Feb 13, 06" over "Feb 26, 07" over "Sept 13, 10". This knife is worth a bit more because of the early patent dates. **Mint value: $750**

Ivory celluloid handles and brass liners. This knife is even more collectable because it has the original leather snap purse that came with the knife. Pen blade is stamped "US PATS" over "Dec 21, 09" over "Sept 13, 10" over "June 6, 16".
Mint value: $700 w/original leather purse add $75

Jigged bone handles with nickel silver tip bolsters and brass liners. The bone handles and tip bolsters add to the value of this piece. Pen blade is stamped "US PATS" over "Dec 21, 09" over "Sept 13, 10" over "June 6, 16". **Mint value: $750**

Flylock Knife Company

Bridgeport, Conn. 1918–1929

At the outbreak of WWI George Schrade found himself in Germany. He had traveled to Europe to market some of the knife machinery he had invented. While in Germany it is believed that he invented another switchblade and bought a factory and was actually producing knives there. When the war broke out the German government confiscated George's factory, tools and materials for the war effort. I have not been able to substantiate this with any concrete evidence, so I guess it is just hearsay for now, but considering George's ambition, it seems very likely. George definitely did return home to the United States soon after the war broke out. The resourceful George wasted no time. Shortly after he returned he quickly patented another switchblade knife, which he referred to as the Fly Lock. United States patent # 1,258,150 was granted to George on March 5, 1918, which many of you will recognize since it is stamped on the back tang of most Flylock knives. Unfortunately, George lacked the resources to manufacture the knife himself so he took his patent to Challenge Cutlery Corporation in Bridgeport, Conn. They agreed to manufacture the knives if George would oversee the Flylock division, which he did. His son George M. Schrade joined him. From 1918 until 1923 the knives were stamped "Challenge Cut Co." on the front and

"Fly-Lock" on the back. At some point George sold the rights to his patent to Weibusch and Hilger, who owned Challenge, and they later sold the rights to P.L. Van Alstyne in 1923 and the Flylock Knife Company was formed. The address used for marketing the Flylock knives was N. 106-110 Lafayette St, New York, N.Y. and they were incorporated in 1925.

Flylock was the marketing name used by the Challenge Cutlery Corporation for all of their switchblade knife line. The word is somewhat descriptive of the release mechanism and function of the knives. You push down on the oblong button and then slide it toward the center of the knife with your thumb, releasing the blade which flies open into a locked position. The knife was produced in 6 basic models:

1. 2 ⅞-inch double
2. 3 ⅜-inch double
3. 3 ⅜-inch single-blade attached to letter opener
4. 4 ⅛-inch single-blade
5. 5-inch single blade
6. 5-inch single blade with folding guards.

Although there were only these basic models, variations in handle materials, bolsters, tang stamps

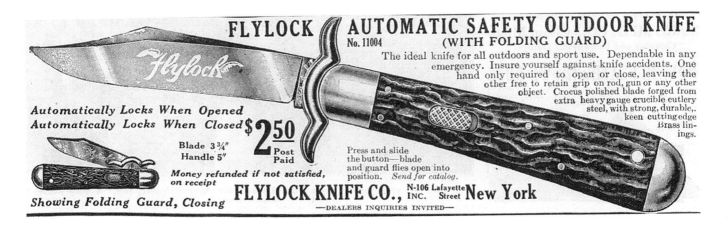

and different blades make for a large variety of Fly-locks to collect. They were only made under the Fly-lock Knife Co. name between 1923 and 1929, which is when Challenge Cutlery Corp went out of business. Interestingly, many manufacturers had their own special names for celluloid. This was most likely because of poor public reaction to a fairly volatile substance. Flylock Knife Company called their celluloid Amerith, so you may see a few references to this in the knife descriptions. Though the black stagged handles on the larger knives all look the same I believe at least two different materials were used over time. Some appear to have rubberized handles and the others appear to be bakelite.

Challenge still owed George money when they went out of business, so he took payment in the form of knife machinery and materials from the defunct company. It's likely that something was negotiated for the building also since it was the same building in which George Schrade started up his new company, The George Schrade Knife Company of Bridgeport, Conn. He started his own line of switchblades and no longer produced the Flylock knife. I would assume that this is because he had sold the patent rights and wasn't able to regain them. (See section on Challenge Cutlery Corporation for more information relating to the Flylock).

With One Hand
Blade opens and locks automatically. Locks automatically closed. Blades forged from best obtainable
STAINLESS CUTLERY BLADE STEEL

Flylock Automatic Safety Fishermen's and Outdoor Knife With scaling back.
Length of blade 3¾ inches.
Length of handle 5 ins.
At your dealers or sent postpaid for
$3.00

THE FLYLOCK KNIFE COMPANY, Inc.
106 Lafayette St.   New York

Observations

1.	3 ⅜-inch doubles seem to be the most common.
2.	Some letter openers have been ground down to look like a 3 ⅜-inch single. Don't be fooled.
3.	4 ⅛-inch clip-blade is harder to find than the hawkbill and is more valuable because of it.
4.	Some worn 4 ⅛-inch hawkbills have had blades ground flat and look like sheepfoot blades.

2 ⅞" Doubles

The knives pictured here have the following in common: They measure 2 ⅞" closed and 5 ⅞" open. Spear/pen blade combination and spear blade stamped "Flylock" over "REG. US PAT OFF" back stamped "FLYLOCK" over "KNIFE CO" over "B'PORT, CONN". The pen blade has the same tang stamp as the spear, but the back is stamped "US PAT" over "MARCH 5" over "1918". All have a small shackle to attach to watch chain or keychain.

Model # 3130R. Green mottled Amerith (celluloid) handles and brass liners. **Mint value: $500**

Model # 6505WR. White Gold handles with decorative edge and nickel silver liners. **Mint value: $525**

Model # 6505GR. 14K Gold plated metal with light lines with decorative edge and brass liners. This knife also has an original watch chain attached which I would date from the 1930s. It's always an enhancement when a knife has something extra like this chain which has probably been with the knife since it was new, even though it was not sold with the knife. **Mint value: $550**
Vintage watch chain add $35

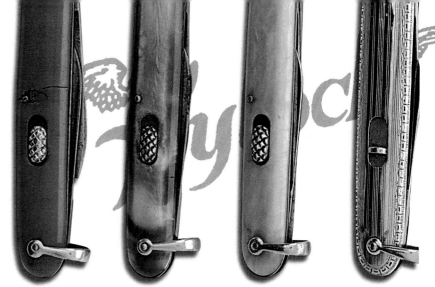

Group of four knives to show other variations. I am still researching the silver knife with the unusual buttons. At first I thought the knife had been altered, but upon close inspection it does not appear as though it was ever taken apart. The buttons are the same on both sides and are actually much easier to activate than the regular buttons. I hope to discover that it is a prototype, or limited production run, but I can't say anything for sure right now. I would be grateful for any information that my readers could supply. The handles pictured here are, from right to left: silver colored metal, marine pearl amerith (celluloid), Honeyswirl amerith and red amerith.

3 ⅜" Doubles

The knives pictured here have the following in common: They measure 3 ⅜" closed and 7 1/16" open. Spear/pen blade combination and all but two have the same markings. Spear blade stamped "Flylock" over "REG. US PAT OFF" and back reads "FLYLOCK" over "KNIFE CO" over "B'PORT, CONN". Pen blade tang stamp is the same as the spear blade and the back reads "U.S.PAT" over "MARCH 5" over "1918".

Black imitation stag handles and brass liners.
Mint value: $525

Model # 1125. Blue pearl amerith (celluloid) handles with advertising and brass liners. Front handle says "Golden Loaf" Flour and the back says Tennant & Hoyt Co.
Mint Value: $550

Model # 1127. Black celluloid handles with advertising and brass liners. Front handle says: Compliments of Frank J Petru and the back says: John Sebek, which makes me wonder if this might not be a salesman's sample? An authenticated salesman's sample will be more collectable and have a higher price tag than regular switchblades because of added interest as well as rarity. Since I have not authenticated this one yet, the price is for a standard advertising knife. **Mint value: $525**

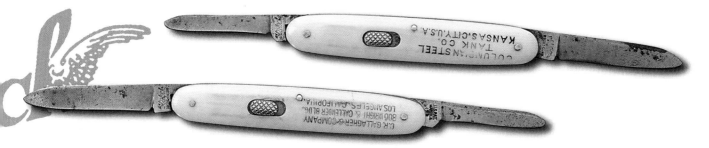

Model # 1120. Ivory celluloid handles with advertising and brass liners. This knife has different markings on the blades. Front stamp is the same as the others, but the back tang of the spear blade reads "THE FLYLOCK" in an arch over "KNIFE CO" over "B'PORT, CONN". This is an earlier stamping, most likely from mid 1920s. Front handle says: C.R. Gallagher & Company over 806 Wright & Callender Bldg over Los Angeles, California. The back handle reads: Columbian Steel Tank Co, Kansas City USA. It seems even more likely that this knife is a salesman's sample since the advertising on each side does not seem related, but again I have not confirmed it so the price is for a standard advertising knife. If it were a salesman's sample it would add from 5 percent to 25 percent to the price and even more in certain situations. **Mint value: $525**

Silver metal handles with beaded border and steel liners. Please note that this is not sterling silver, simply silver colored metal. If it were sterling it would be valued higher. **Mint value: $525**

Model # 1121. Tortoise celluloid handles with nickel silver tip bolsters and brass liners. This knife also has different markings than most of the knives in this group. The markings are the same except for the back tang of the spear blade which reads "THE FLYLOCK" in an arch over "KNIFE CO" over "B'PORT, CONN". Tortoise celluloid handles are popular among collectors because of their beauty, combined with the tip bolsters on this knife, adds a premium to the value. **Mint value: $575**

Model # 1125. Blue pearl celluloid handles with nickel silver tip bolsters and brass liners. These handles are very attractive and are one of my personal favorites. Combined with the tip bolsters they add a small premium to the value. **Mint value: $550**

Model 1112 ½ R. Gold metal handles with a beaded border and a shackle to attach to watch chain, etc. Knife has nickel silver liners and 14K gold plated handles. **Mint value: $650**

Model # 1125. Blue pearl celluloid handles and brass liners. **Mint value: $525**

Group of five doubles to show more variations.

4 ⅛" Singles

The knives pictured here have the following in common: They all measure 4 ⅛" closed and approximately 7" open. Black grooved bakelite handles and steel liners. All single blade knives with front tang stamped "Flylock" over "REG US PAT OFF" over "US PAT 3-5-18" and back tang reads "FLYLOCK" over "KNIFE CO" over "B'PORT, CONN" with minor variations.

Painted tin handles formed to look like stag with steel liners. There are no markings on the back tang of this knife. These knives are too early to call them paratroopers since they were all made prior to 1930, but that's what they resemble. This knife apparently even had a bail originally. I've only seen two of these knives in this size in all of my travels, so they are quite rare. **Mint value: $850**

Black grooved bakelite handles with nickel silver bolsters and steel liners. This knife has a hawkbill blade with same markings as others except for the addition of "THE" in front of "FLYLOCK" on the back tang. The blade is etched "Flylock", though faint, it's there. All of the larger knives had an etching on the front of the blade, with the possible exception of the metal handled ones. If the etch is intact, even faint, it adds to the value. **Mint value: $700**

Black grooved bakelite handles with nickel silver bolsters and steel liners. I'm pretty sure that this blade is actually a hawkbill blade, but after some sharpening and possibly a broken tip, it was ground to resemble a sheepfoot blade. I have not been able to confirm that they were ever made with a sheepfoot blade, but I don't believe that they were. The etching is still visible on the blade and other than missing the tip, it's in excellent condition, but would have to be graded down a bit because of the blade.

5" Singles

The knives pictured here have the following in common: They measure 5" closed and 8 ¾" open. Clip blade stamped "Flylock" over "REG. US PAT OFF" over "US PAT 3-5-18" and the back reads "THE FLYLOCK" over "KNIFE CO" over "B'PORT, CONN".

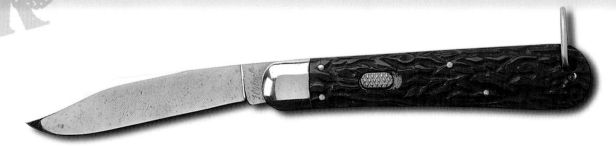

Model # 11000. Black grooved bakelite handles with a bail. Steel bolsters and steel liners with a nickel silver release button. The etching is still visible on the blade. **Mint value: $750**

Model #11005. *Black grooved bakelite handles with nickel silver bolsters and steel liners. This knife has a stainless steel fish-scaler blade, which is unique since the knife was made prior to 1930 and stainless steel was a pretty new concept. The fish-scaler blade is harder to find also and this one has a crisp clean blade etch of "Flylock" and also "Stainless Steel" as well as having an "S" stamped on the back tang to signify Stainless.* **Mint Value: $900**

Black painted tin handles formed to look like stag with steel liners. This knife with metal handles is very rare. It predates the paratroopers, though that's what it reminds one of. I don't think this knife ever had a bail. It is an interesting collectible.
Mint value: $800

Model # 11004. *Black grooved bakelite handles. There is an interesting combination of metals with steel top bolsters and steel liners while the bottom bolsters, button and folding guard are nickel silver. The only large Flylocks that I've seen with the bottom bolsters are the folding guard knives.* **Mint value: $1,000**

Letter Openers

Model # 1124LO. *Black/green/orange mottled celluloid handles and brass liners on this 3 ⅜" knife with a letter opener built in. Single spear blade stamped "Flylock" over "REG US PAT OFF" and the back reads "Flylock" over "KNIFE CO" over "B'PORT, CONN". It measures 8 ¾" overall with the knife closed.* **Mint value: $500**

Model # 1122LO. *Green celluloid handles with brass liners. Single spear blade is stamped "Flylock" over "REG US PAT OFF" and back tang reads "FLYLOCK" over "KNIFE CO" over "B'PORT, CONN". This would appear to be simply a single blade knife, but that is not the case. It was actually a letter opener knife that has had the letter opener carefully cut and ground off and these are often passed off as original single blade 3 ⅜" knives, which Flylock never made. I've seen it happen with gold metal handled ones also. Although the knives are altered, they still have some value to collectors.*
Altered value: Up to $200

George Schrade Knife Co. PRESTO Trademark

Brideport, Conn. 1929–1956

George Schrade had patented his Flylock knife in 1918 and was involved in a deal with Challenge Cutlery Corporation of Bridgeport, Conn to manufacture the knives based on his patent. Challenge Cutlery Corp. went out of business in 1928. George was able to start his new business, the George Schrade Knife Company, at 46 Seymour St. in Bridgeport, the same building where the failed Challenge Cutlery Company had been producing his Flylock knives. His son, George M. Schrade, joined him in the business and he acquired equipment from Challenge in exchange for money owed to him. Although he started his business in 1929, at the start of the Great Depression, the business prospered. He marketed the majority of his switchblade line under the name PRESTO. He did sell one model of switchblade with the George Schrade Knife Co. stamp and that was his line of 2 7/8-inch pullball knives. (This measurement includes the ball which activates the blade.)

Since George did not manufacture a 2 7/8-inch double switchblade like his brothers were doing at Schrade Cutlery Co., the 2 7/8-inch pullball was the smallest knife in his line of switchblades. It may well have been the most popular advertising switchblade of its day because they were very inexpensive to manufacture and most of these knives that you find do have advertising on the handles. One interesting fact about this particular model is that many of them were stamped with the wrong patent date. The correct patent dates should be 11-9-37 and 10-10-44. The incorrect stamps read 11-9-27 and seem to be very common. One might assume that the mistake was made at the beginning of production and corrected at a later date, but the strange thing is that the tang stamp went through three changes through the years and two out of three had the wrong date. Apparently it was quite some time before the problem was corrected because there seem to be about as many wrong ones as there are right ones from what I've seen. I hope to solve this mystery and would appreciate any information from my readers that might help me do so. The four variations in the tang stamps that can be found on these

knives are listed above the knives in this section.

These knives were mostly handled in plastic, but many were manufactured with metal handles as well. All of them had a knob at the end, which when pulled released the blade. They were mostly balls that were made in many colors and some were black with a number "8" on them to resemble pool ball. There were some that were square with dots on the sides to look like a die and some were even metal balls. Normally knives are worth more if they are made in smaller numbers and that is partly the case with one aspect of the pullballs. Since the majority of these pullballs have advertising on them one might think that the ones without advertising would be worth more, but that is the exception here. The advertising actually makes these knives double collectibles since there are many collectors of advertising out there, not to mention the adventurous knife collectors who might strive to collect all of the different ones. These facts combine to make the advertising knives worth slightly more than others and considerably more if it happens to have desirable advertising on it. Most of these knives have a thin brass covering over the backspring that will sometimes kink slightly from the spring pressure of a closed blade over time. It is definitely best to store these knives open to help avoid this problem.

Although George didn't bother manufacturing the small 2 7/8-inch double switchblade that his brothers at Schrade Cutlery Co. were making, he did make knives to compete with most of the rest of their switchblade line. There were only subtle differences between the two companies' knives. They were, in fact, so similar that George's brothers brought a lawsuit against him for patent infringement, but since some of their original patents were granted to George, combined with the fact that some were expired, he was able to win the lawsuit and continued to make his knives. George's other switchblade knives were stamped "PRESTO", and were offered in the following eight basic patterns produced with this stamping and they were:

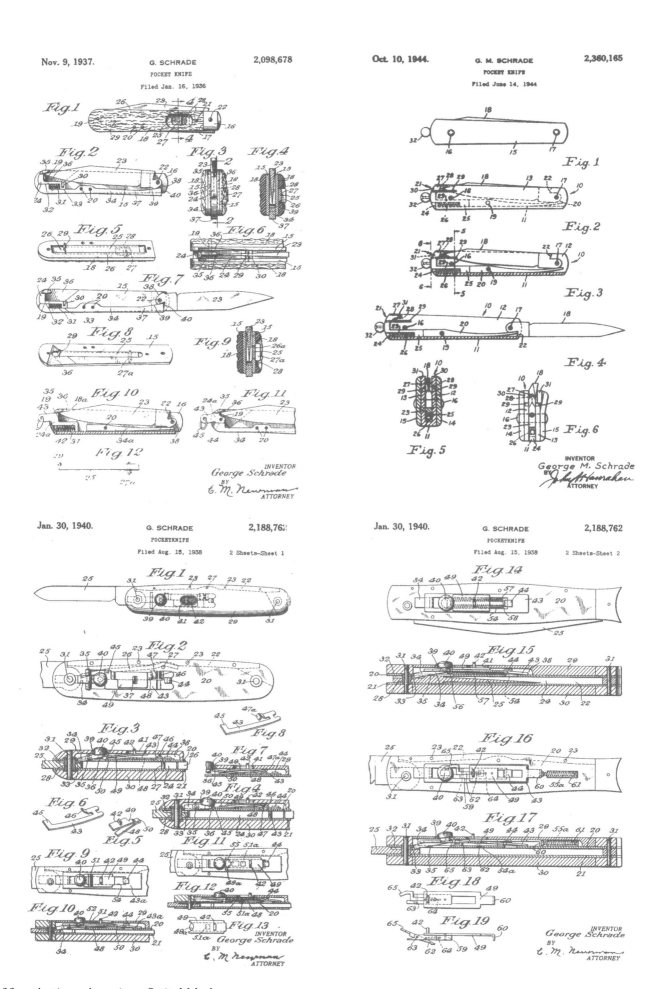

1. 3 ⅜-inch single-blade (jack)
2. 3 ⅜-inch double-blade
3. 3 ⅜-inch single-blade attached to letter opener
4. 4-inch single-blade (fishtail)
5. 4-inch single-blade (bowtie)
6. 4 ⅛-inch single-blade (outdoor knife)
7. 5-inch single-blade (hunter)
8. 5-inch single-blade with folding guard

These basic patterns were made with a variety handle materials, blade types, liner and bolster changes as well as different stampings which would make for a large number of knives to be sought by the adventurous collector! A good representation of this company's switchblade line can be accomplished with only nine basic models, including the pullball.

George also did some switchblade contract work for companies like Remington and Case as well as JCN Co., Shapleigh Hardware and others. Most were stamped with the contract company's name with the exception of Shapleigh Hardware who sold some knives with the "PRESTO" tang stamp. You may find more information on all of these contract knives in their respective chapters.

The earliest of the 4 ⅛" and 5" Presto knives had a distinctive tang stamp in that it was smaller than the later knives and was stamped "PRESTO" over "Pat Pndg". Don't be confused by later versions, which were also stamped "Pat Pndg" with the regular large "PRESTO" stamp. Although these, too, are fairly early in production, made prior to 1940, they are much more common than the earliest small-stamp knives and do not command the higher prices that the small-stamp knives will. More information on the various

Presto tang stamps can be found in the Presto chapter. George Schrade applied for another patent on switchblade knives in 1938 to cover the knives that he was producing. On Jan. 30, 1940 he was granted U.S. patent # 2,188,762 and most of the Presto knives manufactured after 1940 carry this date on the front tang.

George Schrade died on September 9, 1940 and the company continued to operate under the control of his son George M. Schrade and his grandson Theodore. They continued to operate the business until 1956 when Boker of Germany bought them out. Theodore was retained to run the company until 1958 when they closed the business and all of the machinery was auctioned off. It was the end of an era.

Observations	
1.	4 ⅛-inch and 5-inch knives are the most common.
2.	There are many combinations of handles, blades, bolsters and guards on the large knives.
3.	3 ⅜-inch single-blade knives are more common than doubles. (opposite of Schrade Cut Co)
4.	Many Presto knives, and especially contract knives, had copper beryllium springs. Copper in color.
5.	The fixed-guard knives are harder to find than the folding-guard knives.

2 ⅞" pullballs

The knives pictured here have the following in common: They all measure 2 7/8" closed and 5" open including the pullball. They all have clip blades, brass backspring covers and a ball that you pull to open the knife. These knives usually have one of four different marking combinations:

A. *Front:* "G.SCHRADE" in an arch over "B'PORT, CT"
   Back: "PATS" over "11-9-37" over "10-10-44"

B. *Front:* "G.SCHRADE" in an arch over "B'PORT, CT"
   Back: "PATS" over "11-9-27" over "10-10-44"

C. *Front:* "G.SCHRADE" straight line over "KNIFE CO INC" over "B'PORT, CT USA"
   Back: "PATS" over "11-9-27" over "10-10-44"

D. *Front:* "G.SCHRADE" in an arch over "PAT" over "11-9-37"
   Back: "B'PORT, CT"

Red synthetic handles with brass liners and a green ball. Tang markings group C. This knife is in mint condition and in its original box with the original knife paper with instructions on it.
Mint value: $225 with box adds $40 with paper adds $40

Cream colored synthetic handles with brass liners and a metal ball. Tang markings group A. Handles have advertising for the Ludwig Milk Company and the knife is in the original box with the original knife paper. Advertising, box and paper all add to collector interest. **Mint value: $240 with box adds $40 w/paper adds $40**

> **Instructions For Operating**
> **"PULL-BALL" Automatic Knife**
>
> TO OPEN: Pull Ball.
> TO CLOSE: Simply press blade down until blade snaps into lock position.
>
> **Keep Your Knife In Proper Condition**
>
> Do not sharpen blade on grind stone. Sharpen blade on oil stone by holding blade at a slight angle so that it will have a short bevel. Do not lay blade flat on stone when sharpening.
>
> Oil joints of knife occasionally so that blade will open and close smoothly.
>
> **The OSBORNE COMPANY**
> **Clifton, N. J., U. S. A.**
>
> Schrade Patents
> 11-9-37 10-10-44

Black synthetic handles with brass liners and an amber ball. Tang markings group C. Handles have advertising for both the "Dennis Supply Company" and for the "Superior Supply Company". It would seem possible that this was a salesman's sample unless the companies are related, which I have not been able to confirm so the price is for regular advertising knife. **Mint value: $240 Verified salesman's sample adds $50, or more.**

Cream colored synthetic handles with brass liners and black ball. Tang markings group B. Handles have advertising for a chicken hatchery in Tennessee. The back handle says "Baby Chicks". **Mint value: $240**

Black synthetic handles with brass liners and a green ball. Tang markings group C. Advertising is for the Trenton Cracker Company. **Mint value: $240**

Silver metal handles with no liners and a green ball. Tang markings group A. This knife is special because the blade is stainless steel with an "S" stamped on the front tang to indicate this fact. The metal handles tend to bring a bit more, combined with the less common blade add a premium to the value of this knife. **Mint value: $275**

Cream colored synthetic handles with brass liners and a black ball. Tang markings group A. **Mint value: $225**

Group of five pullballs larger than actual size to show more variety.

Graef & Schmidt

New York City, NY.   1881–1952

Two men who immigrated to the United States from Germany in the 1870s started this company. William R. Graef and Carl Schmidt started the company in New York in 1881 as an import/jobber business. Graef & Schmidt occupied several different locations over the years including 29 Warren St., 107 Chambers St., and 114 E 25ᵗʰ St., all in New York City. Their most recognized trademark was "WELKUT" and they imported most of their cutlery from Germany. They were the sole U.S. representatives for J.A. Henckels of Solingen, Germany and they imported many German switchblades over the years, but that's not why they are important to this book. Sometime between 1892 and 1923 they contracted the Press Button Knife Company of Walden, N.Y. to manufacture some of their 4 ⅞-inch Invincible model knives with the Graef & Schmidt tang stamp. I have only had the good fortune to run across one example of this knife in many years of searching, so I must assume that they were made in very limited numbers and are very collectible.

	Observations 4 ⅞-inch Graef & Schmidt Invincible	
1.	Jigged bone handles with nickel silver bolsters and button.	
2.	Circular tang stamp with "Graef" over "Schmidt" with "&" in between.	
3.	Steel liners.	

Clip blade stamped "Graef & Schmidt" back reads "PAT 470605". Jigged bone handles with steel liners and nickel silver bolsters and button. Measures 4 ⅞" closed and 8 ¾" open. The Press Button Knife Co., Walden, NY, made these knives.
Mint value: $1,500

Hatch Cutlery Company

South Milwaukee, Wis.   1891–1925?

W alter Hatch was born in New Haven County, Conn. July 27, 1855 to Levi and Carrie Hatch. He attended the public schools of Naugatuck, Conn. until he was 14 years old and he went to work for Union Knife Company of Naugatuck, not to be confused with Union Cutlery Company of Olean, N.Y. He worked there as a clerk for several years and by the age of 20 he was given management of the company's affairs. He stayed with the company for approximately four years after his promotion and in that time he managed to accumulate a large portion of the stock in the company. He wanted to head west and in 1879, at the age of 24, he sold his stock in Union Knife Co. and moved to Elyria, Ohio. While there he engaged in the manufacture of shears in a partnership with a man referenced in my research by only his last name: Clauss. This partnership lasted for five years before Hatch sold his interest to Clauss and moved to Cleveland. It was around this time that Hatch began having health problems. After regaining his health he became manager of the Cleveland Machine Company. In 1887 the Cleveland Machine Company was consolidated with the Cleveland Drop Forge and Foundry Company of Kensington, Ill. Walter assumed management for the whole company and four years later, with the help of Daniel P. Eells, who was president of the company, bought out the business and decided to move it to Wisconsin.

In 1891 they moved into a factory in South Milwaukee at 1200 Minnesota Ave. They were one of the leading concerns in the country in the manufacture of shears, scissors, razors, tinners' snips, curtain and screw rings as well as pocket cutlery. All of their cutlery products were forged from razor steel and were fully warranted. D.P. Eells was president of the company and Walter Hatch was vice president and treasurer. The factory suffered a devastating fire in 1893 and the company was forced to relocate. Ironically, Walter's house at 1218 Milwaukee Ave was destroyed in a fire on March 2nd of the same year. His residence had previously been the Lakeview Club House, which had been built as a recreation and meeting center, but the idea fizzled and Walter turned it into a home. That year turned out to be a busy one for Walter because it was also in 1893 that he bought the Automatic Knife Company of Middletown, Conn. He continued to manufacture the knives based on Arthur Wilzin's patent of 1889, but changed the markings on the knives from "Aut Knife Co", "Middletown, CT" to "Hatch Cutlery Co", "So Milwaukee, Wis". These knives were displayed at the Columbian Exposition in Chicago in 1893. They continued manufacturing knives at the Middletown factory until 1895, or so, when Walter decided to close that factory. I believe that all the machinery was moved to Buchanan, MI, but I do not know if any of these knives were ever manufactured there.

The factory that Hatch Cutlery Co. occupied after the first one burned was 40 feet by 250 feet and two stories high. There was a separate powerhouse that measured 80 by 80 feet and housed a Corliss 150-horsepower engine that operated the machinery in the factory. It was made by the E.P. Allis Company. They also had a 35-horsepower Westinghouse engine that operated the dynamo providing electricity for the factory and nearby hotels and businesses. The factory was supplied with both arc and incandescent lights. The company employed over 100 people for many years.

The following is an excerpt from a book titleed *South Milwaukee Penned & Brushed*:

> All shears and scissors turned out by the company are coupled with the Hatch patent bolt and washer, invented by W.P. Hatch and a feature which adds much to the superiority of the product. The company has agencies in San Francisco, Indianapolis, West Toronto, Canada and New York City. Its New York office branch is at 97 Chambers Street and is in (the) charge of David Eastman, one of the best

(No Model.)

A. WILZIN.
POCKET KNIFE.

No. 401,093.

Patented Apr. 9, 1889.

Fig.1. Fig.2. Fig.3.

Fig.4. Fig.5.

Fig.6. Fig.7.

WITNESSES:

Phil C. Dieterich.
C. Sedgwick

INVENTOR:
A. Wilzin
BY
Munn & Co
ATTORNEYS.

known men in the cutlery trade in the United States. The company is making the largest line of shears of any works of the kind in the country, including solid steel and a full line of laid shears. The tinners' snips which it produces are endorsed by the trade everywhere as superior to any others in quality and strength. The demand for the company's products at the end of the first six months of its operations so far exceeded its ability to supply that it was having a large amount of work done elsewhere and a speedy enlargement of the works was decided upon.

The last listing I found for the company was in the 1922 city directory, at which point the company was listed as "operating with 100 employees". I wasn't able to find any listings between 1922 and 1935, by which they were out of business.

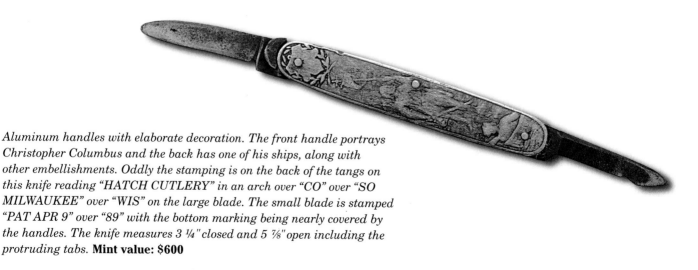

Aluminum handles with elaborate decoration. The front handle portrays Christopher Columbus and the back has one of his ships, along with other embellishments. Oddly the stamping is on the back of the tangs on this knife reading "HATCH CUTLERY" in an arch over "CO" over "SO MILWAUKEE" over "WIS" on the large blade. The small blade is stamped "PAT APR 9" over "89" with the bottom marking being nearly covered by the handles. The knife measures 3 ¼" closed and 5 ⅞" open including the protruding tabs. **Mint value: $600**

Imperial
Knife Company

Providence, RI   1916–Present

Michael Mirando immigrated to the United States from Frosolone, Italy before 1910. Michael had "cut his teeth" in the cutlery business long before coming to the United States. He settled in Winsted, Conn. and got a job with the Empire Knife Co. as a grinder. Within a year he was joined in this country by his parents, Cosmo and Philomena, and by his brother, Felix. Felix also went to work for Empire as both a grinder and polisher.

The brothers left Empire Knife Co. in the fall of 1916 to try to form their own knife company. It's said that they hitchhiked on their way to Providence, R.I. They set up a shop in a loft above a blacksmith shop and began making skeleton watch chain knives to sell to jewelers in Providence and nearby Attleboro, Mass. They named the company Imperial Knife Company. Their father joined them and for a while it was just the three of them turning out knives above the blacksmith shop. Within a year they had eight employees and were turning out approximately 1,000 knives per week.

The Mirandos decided to take on a business partner in 1919. Domenic Fazzano was also born in Frosolone and had been a boyhood friend of the Mirandos. He too had learned the cutlery trade in Italy. He brought this experience combined with business and marketing experience he had gained as president of United Cycle in Hartford, Conn., which was an automobile tire business. Domenic's contributions to the company would prove invaluable, especially with the approach of the Great Depression. By the early 1920s wristwatches began replacing pocket watches and Imperial had to adjust to the market change. They still produced skeleton knives, but now they added plastic handles, which were very inexpensive to produce. With the onset of the Great Depression in 1929 Imperial had to adjust some more to the market change created by the financial ruin. During a time when most knife companies were still handling their knives in jigged bone, pearl, sterling silver, and other expensive materials, Imperial was making low-cost knives

with plastic handles, which could be sold for 25 to 50 cents each compared to those of other manufacturers that sold for $1 or more. Soon after the Depression they developed another low-cost handle material: tin. They patented a stamped tin shell handle that was clipped onto the frame. This eliminated the more expensive and time-consuming pinning At a time when people were spending as little as possible on knives, Imperial was selling them cheap.

To keep up with production demands Imperial purchased a factory on Blount St in Providence. In 1936 they acquired the Hammer Brand trademark from New York Knife Company, which went out of business in 1931, another victim of the depression. By 1940 Imperial had to enlarge their Blount Street facilities and upgraded all of their equipment, which just happened to make them one of the best prepared knife companies in this country for the overwhelming wartime demands created by WWII.

When the U.S. entered the war in 1941, Imperial was manufacturing as many as 100,000 knives a day, but production of civilian knives was restricted during the war and Imperial converted to full wartime production. Imperial produced most of the trench knives used by the Armed Forces. They were involved in the design of the M-4 bayonet and produced the largest quantity of all bayonets purchased by the U.S. government during the war. The Ulster Knife Company of Ellenville, N.Y. also received a large order for military knives, but they were not equipped to handle it by themselves so they enlisted the help of Imperial. Imperial would produce and assemble the rough knives and then ship them to Ulster for finishing. Imperial received the "E" award of excellence from the U.S. government for their wartime effort and production.

Somewhere between 1942 and 1945 Imperial merged with Ulster Knife Company owned by Albert and Henry Baer. They formed the Imperial Knife Associated Companies Inc. In 1946 they purchased Schrade

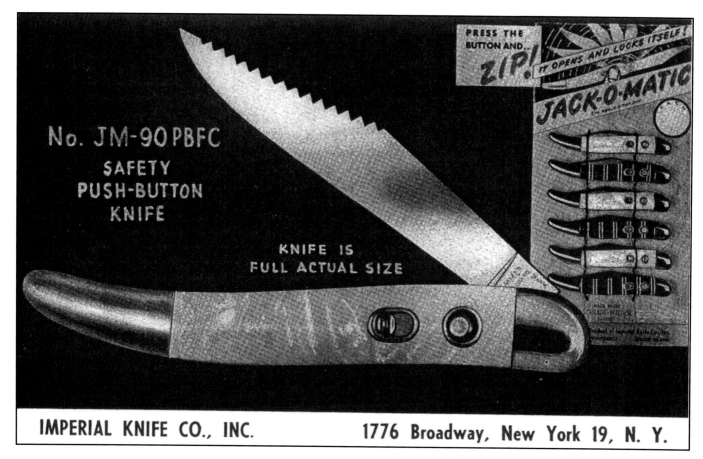

Cutlery Company of Walden, N.Y. and renamed it Schrade Walden Cutlery Corporation. The Schrade Walden division was moved from Walden, N.Y. to Ellenville, NY in 1958, coincidentally, the same year that Congress enacted the ban on interstate commerce of switchblade knives.

On July 28, 1949 Michael Mirando of Imperial applied for a patent for the shell-handled switchblade knife. The patent was not granted until April 12, 1955 and it was patent number 2,705,832. This is the patent for the Hammer Brand and Imperial toothpick switchblade knives that measure 4 ¼ inches closed and are most often seen with candystripe or cracked ice celluloid wrapped handles. They were also produced in several different color combinations and also with finger guards. It is also the patent for the Hammer Brand utility or serpentine switchblade that measures 3 ½ inches closed and is most commonly seen with cracked ice celluloid wrapped handles. Unlike the toothpick models, candystripe handles are very rare on the serpentine knives. They, too, were produced in a variety of colors. The third model produced under this patent is the Imperial Jack-o-matic Junior, or Mini as they are often called. This knife is the smallest U.S.-made switchblade; measuring just 2 ¼ inches closed and is most commonly found with cracked ice handles. These were also produced with a variety of different colors. Models with handles other than cracked

ice are very hard to find and are highly collectible. The unusual colored knives are extremely popular with collectors because of their rarity and uniqueness and will command much higher prices than the cracked ice or candystripe knives. Production on all of these knives started around 1950 and continued until the ban in 1958. The early toothpick-style knives were stamped Hammer Brand and had either brass liners or coated steel liners that looked like brass. The serpentine, or utility knives were all stamped Hammer Brand and most had steel liners. The toothpicks manufactured in the late 1950s were mostly stamped Imperial and had steel liners. These later toothpicks had either candystripe or cracked ice handles and some of the last ones had an orange/gold variation on the candystripe handles, which is also very rare and collectible since production was stopped shortly after it began. I believe they were all manufactured in Providence, R.I., but the display card for the Hammer Brand toothpick says "Made under Schrade-Walden Patents" near the bottom so it could have been a joint project between the two divisions of Imperial Knife Associated Companies. Most of Imperial's records were apparently lost after the Rhode Island plant was shut down so I've been unable to find definitive information on this.

Schrade Walden Cutlery Corp., a division of Imperial Knife Associated Companies, stopped production of their switchblade knives in Walden, N.Y. in 1957 according to company representatives. After 1957 the only switchblade production by Imperial Knife Associated Companies was done at the Imperial plant in Rhode Island.

There are, at least, four different models of switchblades that were produced at the Imperial plant in Rhode Island. They are as follows:

1. 2 ¼-inch closed Jack-o-matic Junior, (Mini) stamped "Imperial"
2. 3 ½-inch Serpentine or Utility stamped "Hammer Brand"
3. 4 ¼-inch Toothpick model stamped either "Hammer Brand" or "Imperial"
4. 4 ¼-inch toothpick with finger guards stamped "Hammer Brand" or "Imperial"

Some of the toothpick models were made with a fish scaler on the top of the blade, model JM-90 PBFC, which adds to their value. Again, many of these knives were made in unusual and very interesting color combinations Those knives are much harder to find and therefore command higher prices. I am fortunate to be able to feature many of these rare colors in this

book. Please keep in mind that though many different colors are pictured, they are still very rare and the knives featured here represent many years of avid collecting! The knives with cracked ice celluloid handles outnumber the rare color knives by at least 25 to 1. The most uncommon knife with an Imperial tang stamp that I've come across is a 2 ⅞-inch double with celluloid handles. The one featured in this book has cracked ice celluloid handles and spear/file blade combination. It also has advertising on it for Senator Pastore, who was a close friend of Felix Mirando Sr., one of the original founders of Imperial. Through research I found out that these knives were most likely manufactured at Schrade Walden by request of Imperial Knife Co. and stamped with the Imperial marking as though it were a regular contract knife. Regardless of exactly when and where they were made, these knives are extremely rare and collectible. I have heard that there may be some 3 ⅜-inch doubles with the Imperial stamp also, but I've never actually seen one.

In 1985 all aspects of the company's U.S. operations were combined under one roof in Ellenville, NY and the name of the company was changed to Imperial Schrade Corporation and they are still going strong today.

2 ⅞" double

Cracked ice celluloid handles with brass liners. Spear/file blade combination marked "Imperial" over "PROV, R.I." on tang of spear and back stamped "US PAT 2304601". The file blade is unmarked. More information on this knife can be found in the accompanying text. This knife is very rare. **Mint value: $600**

2 ¼" Jack Jr. or mini

The knives pictured here have the following in common: They all measure 2 ¼" closed and 3 ¾" open. All have celluloid wrapped hollow tin shell handles that are held on by tabs bent over the brass liners. All have spear blade stamped "Imperial" over "USA" and the back is marked "P2170537" over "2281782". Any color other than Cracked Ice is a rare color for this model. The Imperial model number for all of these knives is JM-96 PB.

Cracked Ice celluloid handles with shackle and original keychain. This is the most common handle color for this model. **Mint value: $225**

From Left to Right: Burgundy pearl and black mottled celluloid covered metal handles with shackle and original keychain. **Mint value: $300** *Maroon pearl and cracked ice celluloid covered metal handles with shackle and keychain. This knife is very unusual since the blade is slightly different than normal and has a different shackle, not to mention the unusual color. I suspected that it had been tampered with, but upon close inspection it would appear that the blade is original to the knife which makes me suspect that it's possibly a prototype knife made by Imperial during development of the JM-96 PB model. I have confirmed that the handle color was used by Imperial, but cannot confirm that it is a prototype. If I could confirm this the knife would be worth twice as much, maybe more.* **Mint value: $300** *Blue pearl and green mottled celluloid covered metal handles with shackle and original keychain.* **Mint value: $300** *Grey pearl streaked celluloid covered metal handles with shackle and original keychain.* **Mint value: $300** *Copper & Cream celluloid covered metal handles with shackle and original keychain.* **Mint value: $300** *Firebrick celluloid covered metal handles with shackle and original keychain.* **Mint value: $300**

3 ½" Utility Jack

The knives pictured here have the following in common: Clip blade stamped "Hammer Brand" with the picture of an arm and hammer and to the right "USA". The back is marked with patent numbers "2170537" over "2281782" with a "P" to the left of them. They measure 3 ½" closed and 6 ¼" open. All colors other than Cracked Ice are rare in this model and will command higher prices. The Imperial model number for these knives is JM-98 PB.

Cracked ice celluloid covered metal handles with brass liners. This is the most common color. **Mint value: $275**

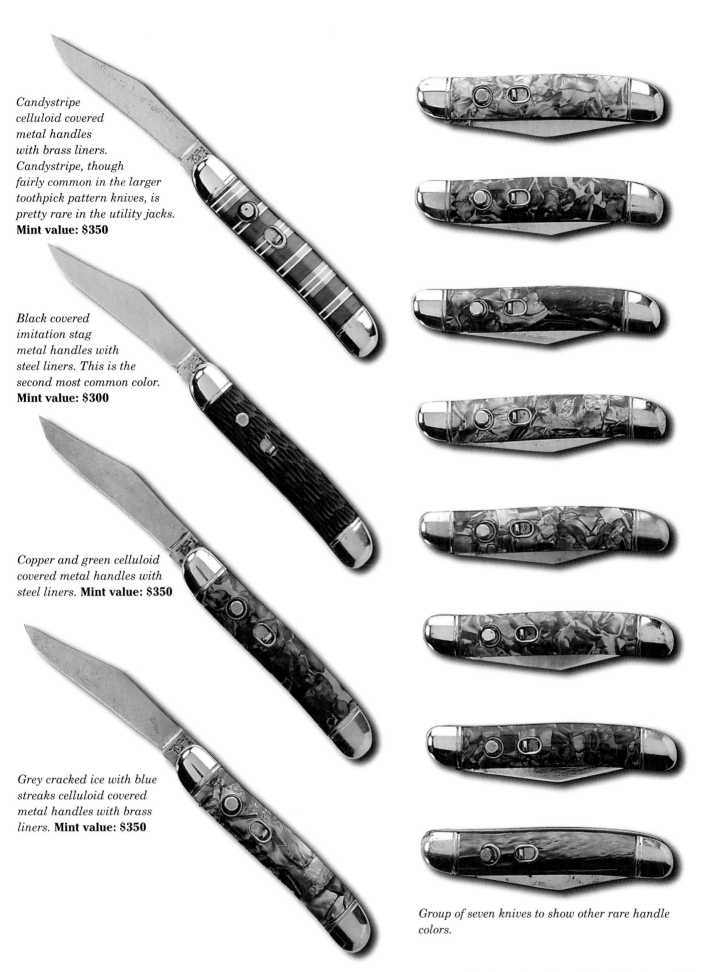

Candystripe celluloid covered metal handles with brass liners. Candystripe, though fairly common in the larger toothpick pattern knives, is pretty rare in the utility jacks.
Mint value: $350

Black covered imitation stag metal handles with steel liners. This is the second most common color.
Mint value: $300

Copper and green celluloid covered metal handles with steel liners. **Mint value: $350**

Grey cracked ice with blue streaks celluloid covered metal handles with brass liners. **Mint value: $350**

Group of seven knives to show other rare handle colors.

4 ¼" Toothpicks

The knives pictured here have the following in common: They all have a clip blade and measure 4 ¼" closed and 7 ⅝" open. Most are stamped "Hammer Brand" with a picture of an arm holding a hammer and "USA" to the right of that, unless otherwise stated. All of the back tangs are marked "2170537" over "2281782" with a "P" to the left of them. Cracked Ice is the most common color for this knife and all others valued slightly higher.

Model # JM-90 PBC. Tang stamped "Imperial" with a crown dotting the small "i" over "PROV. USA". Candystripe celluloid covered metal handles with plated steel liners. **Mint value: $260**

Tang stamped "Imperial" with a crown dotting the small "i" over "PROV. USA". Rarer fixed-guard handles are covered with candystripe celluloid wrap and it has steel liners. **Mint value: $300**

Model # JM-90 PBC. Hammer Brand with candystripe celluloid covered metal handles with brass liners. Most of the candystripe knives have perpendicular stripes. Note that the stripes are slightly diagonal on this knife, which seems to be rarer and possibly older. **Mint value: $275**

Model #JM-90 PBC. Hammer Brand with cracked ice celluloid covered metal handles with brass liners. This is the most common color. **Mint value: $250**

Hammer Brand with fixed-guard handles covered with cracked ice celluloid and it has brass liners. Common color, but guards add. **Mint value: $290**

Hammer Brand with fixed-guard handles covered with green jade celluloid and it has brass liners. This is a rare combination with unusual color plus the guards. **Mint value: $375**

Model # JM-90 PBC. Hammer Brand with copper and jade mottled celluloid covered metal handles and brass liners. **Mint value: $325**

Model #JM-90 PBFC. Hammer Brand with gold streaked celluloid covered metal handles and brass liners. Rare color combines with fish-scaler blade. **Mint value: $350**

JM-90 PBC. Tang stamped "Imperial" with a crown dotting the small "i" over "PROV. USA". Gold/orange candystripe covered metal handles and steel liners. This appears to be a foil, not celluloid wrap, over these handles. I would guess that they got away from celluloid near the end of production in the late 1950s and did not manufacture many of these before production was halted in 1958. They are very rare. **Mint value: $400**

Display Cards

I have used the same card with different knives on it in five of these pictures in order to achieve a better effect and more interesting display of the knives. All of these knives most likely would have been displayed and sold on a card just like this back in the 1950s so it seemed fitting. The original card is shown with the accompanying original box in one of the photos as well as 12 mint knives just as they would have come from the factory. The card and box show some wear, but considering how rare they are, it doesn't detract much from the value.

* These cards are so rare and especially with original knives on them, combined with the fact that it is nearly impossible to find a truly mint set since you're dealing with several knives plus the card, prompted me to make an exception and list their values as Near Mint. If you had a truly Mint set there are many collectors who would pay much more than the values that I have listed here.

JACK-O-MATIC display card from the 1950s with six Hammer Brand toothpick knives held in place by an elastic cord. These knives all have rare handle colors.
Near Mint value card with knives: $2,350* w/ box adds $150
Mint value card alone: $400

Left to Right: JACK-O-MATIC display card with six Hammer Brand toothpicks with fixed-guard handles and rare handle colors. **Near Mint value card with 6 knives: $2,650* w/ box adds $150 Mint value card alone: $400** #JDC3: JACK-O-MATIC display card with six toothpick knives, some Hammer Brand and some Imperial, with rare handle colors. **Near Mint value card with 6 knives: $2,400* w/ box add $150 Mint value card alone: $400** #JDC4: JACK-O-MATIC display card with six toothpick knives, some Hammer Brand and some Imperial, with rare fish-scaler blades. **Near Mint value card with 6 knives: $2,175* w/ box add $150 Mint value card alone: $400**

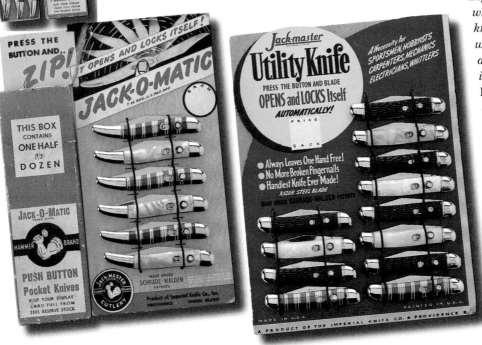

Left: JACK-O-MATIC display card with 12 Hammer Brand toothpick knives and the accompanying box which holds six of the knives. These are all the more common cracked ice and candy stripe handles. **Near Mint value card with 12 knives: $3,400* w/ box add $150 Mint value card alone: $400**

Right: Jackmaster Utility Knife display card with 12 Hammer Brand serpentine utility knives. This card was mint and had never had knives on it when I got it, but I could not resist displaying the knives this way. **Near Mint value card with 12 knives: $4,100* Mint card alone: $500**

JCN Co.
Jewelry & Cutlery Novelty Co.

North Attleboro, Mass.   1937–1948

P.J. Cummings operated the Jewelry Cutlery Novelty Company was located in North Attleboro, Mass. from approximately 1937 to 1948. The company's connection to switchblade knives was through the George Schrade Knife Company of Bridgeport, Conn. JCN Co. contracted them to make pullball switchblades with a JCN Co. tang stamp. Most of the pullball switchblades made by the George Schrade Knife Company had celluloid or plastic handles, but interestingly, the knives made for JCN Co. all seem to have metal handles and a small shackle to make attachment to a watch chain or key chain an easy task. Some were even plated with real 12K gold, like the knife in the original box, pictured here. Most of these metal-handled knives seem to have a pattern stamped into the metal and are quite attractive. Metal or metal-colored pullballs are also common with the JCN Co. knives. I've even seen one with part of the top edge of the blade grooved to act as a nail file. As far as I know this is the only switchblade model JCN Co. ever sold and I suspect they were only made for a few years prior to 1944.

These knives were made in smaller quantities than the other pullballs made by George Schrade Knife Company. With the more expensive materials and the limited quantities, these knives very collectible and often harder to find than other similar switchblades.

	Observations
1.	Most, if not all, JCN Co. pullballs have metal handles.
2.	Many have a metal or metal-colored ball on the end.
3.	Should have a small shackle on the blade end of the knife to attach to a chain.
4.	Most have a pattern stamped into the handles.
5.	Can be found with nail file grooved into top edge of blade.
6.	Most have a patent date of 11-9-37 stamped on the tang.

2 ⅞" pullballs

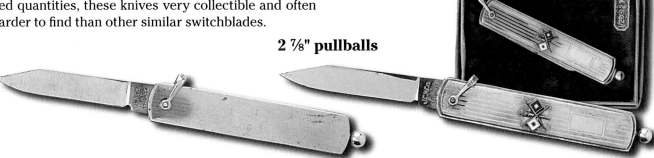

Left to Right: Clip blade stamped "J.C.N. Co" over "PAT" over "11-9-37" and the back is blank. 12K gold-plated handles with signet for engraving initials and a shackle to connect to a chain. It has a metal ball. The shackle is marked "J&CN Co" and the knife measures 5"open. Most of the gold plating has worn off this knife, which would affect the value. **Mint value: $325**
Clip blade stamped "J.C.N. Co" over "PAT" over "11-9-37" and the back is blank. 12K Gold plated handles with crossed flag symbol and shackle to connect to a chain. It has a metal ball. The shackle is marked "J&CN Co" and the knife measures 5"open. Knife is in the original box, which enhances the value. **Mint value: $375 w/box adds $50 w/ original knife paper add $50**

KA-BAR
Trademark of Union Cutlery Co.
Olean, NY.   1923–Present

Brothers Wallace R. and Robert E. Brown started a cutlery jobber business in Little Valley, N.Y. in 1898. They eventually moved to Olean, N.Y. around 1911 and changed their name to Union Cutlery Company. They manufactured cutlery under several different names over the years, but probably their most famous trademark was "KA-BAR", which was adopted in 1923. The story goes that they received a letter from a customer about killing a bear with one of their knives and his poor spelling lead to the name. The KA-BAR stamp has gone through some changes over the years and is still used today as "Kabar," but the stamping that we're interested in was used by the Brown brothers between 1923 and 1951. The trademark was so popular that the company name was changed to KaBar Cutlery Company around 1951. The tang markings were also changed at that time. Please note the subtle change in the stamping. The one that is on the switchblade knives is in capitol letters with a hyphen. They stopped using this stamp shortly after 1950, but the KaBar name is still in use today in one form or another. The company was sold to Cole National Corp. in 1966 and has changed hands since then.

Several interesting American switchblades can be found with "KA-BAR" stamped on the tang. In fact, four basic models were made with several variations on the handle materials including jigged bone, stag, celluloid and black jigged Bakelite. There were also variations in the releases. These models are as follows:

1. 4 ½-inch lever-release
2. 4 ¾-inch Grizzly (extremely rare and looks like a cross between a Grizzly and Union Cut Co. "Dog's Head")
3. 5 ¼-inch Baby Grizzly
4. 5 ½-inch Grizzly

If the 4 ¾-inch Grizzly had been made in greater quantities, collectors may have been more aware of its existence, and it would have earned the name Baby Grizzly. Instead the more popular 5 ¼-inch knife got the name because it was still smaller than the biggest Grizzly in the line. Though slightly different in appearance, the Grizzlies all share a common characteristic; a large metal spring that is exposed and runs full length on the backside of the knife. This spring keeps pressure on the release button. Some collectors believe that these knives were never intended to open to the full open position automatically. I suspect they came to this conclusion because most of the Grizzlies you run across have weak springs and do not open properly. The one featured in this section operates perfectly and the blade smartly snaps into the full open position when the button is pressed. I must admit that is a bit tricky

Stag handles with brass liners and nickel silver bolsters and button. This is the "unknown Grizzly" and measures approx. 4 ¾" closed and approx. 9" open and is stamped "KA-BAR" over "USA" on the front tang and back is blank. On a rarity scale this knife is a "9+ out of 10". **Mint value: $6,000**

to operate and takes a bit of practice to get it to operate perfectly. It works the best when held with both hands putting a bit of pressure on both the top and bottom bolsters when you press the button. It is strong enough to open against gravity and will throw the blade up if held in the vertical position. The lever-released knives can be found with levers in two basic shapes with slight variations. They can be found with square levers (actually rectangular) or teardrop levers. Both can be seen on the knives pictured in this section.

The most common handle material for KA-BAR switchblades seems to be stag. You may occasionally find some with jigged bone and even less often find one handled in celluloid. Some were made with translucent yellow celluloid and some of the lever knives can be found with black jigged celluloid. I feel that the celluloid, partly because of the attractive appearance and partly because of the rarity, enhances the value. Celluloid is a softer and more unstable handle material than others used on these knives, and does not normally fair as well over time, making a nice example harder to find. KA-BAR knives, especially the switchblades, are very popular with collectors and will command very high prices.

Also see: Keenwell Brown & Union Cutlery Company chapters for related information.

	Observations
1.	KA-BAR switchblades are most often found with stag handles.
2.	Baby Grizzlies are harder to find than the bigger version
3.	Many of the knives you will find have weak springs, though some just need lubrication to work properly. I recommend a wax-based lubricant.
4.	Celluloid handled KA-BAR switchblades are the hardest to find.

Grizzlies

*Model # 2179. Stag handles with brass liners and nickel silver bolsters and button. Commonly referred to as the "Grizzly", it's large clip blade is stamped "KA-BAR" over "USA" and back reads "PAT" over "Union Cut Co". Many originally had the following etching on the blade "Grizzly" over "PAT PENDING". They may be found with other etches as well. This is one of the largest American made switchblades measuring 5 ½" closed and 10" open. **Mint value: $3,000***

*Model # 21107. Stag handles with brass liners and nickel silver bolsters and button. Commonly referred to as the "Baby Griz" this knife measures a mere 5 ¼" closed and 9 ¼" open. The clip blade is stamped "KA-BAR" over "USA" and the back is blank. Stampings may vary on these knives and I don't know if the blades were etched since I've never seen one with etching. This pattern is very hard to find. **Mint value: $3,800***

Model # 61105. . *Stag handles with brass liners and nickel silver bolsters and release lever. Square release lever with grooves used in leter years. Sabre-ground clip blade stamped "KA-BAR" and back is blank. The knife measures 4 ½" closed and approx. 8" open. Bone is less common than stag on this knife so it adds a small premium.* **Mint value: $2,600**

Model # 61105. *Handles appear to be jigged black bone with brass liners and nickel silver bolsters and release lever. Square release lever with grooves used in leter years. Sabre-ground clip blade stamped "KA-BAR" and back is blank. The knife measures 4 ½" closed and approx. 8" open.* **Mint value: $2,600**

Model # 21105. *Stag handles with brass liners and nickel silver bolsters and release lever. Teardrop release lever typical of early production knives. Sabre-ground clip blade stamped "KA-BAR" and the back is marked "Union Cut Co" over "Olean, NY USA". Knife measures 4 ½" closed and approx. 8" open.* **Mint value: $2,500**

Model # 51105. *Jigged black celluloid handles with brass liners and nickel silver bolsters and release lever. Teardrop release lever typical of early production knives. Sabre-ground clip blade stamped "KA-BAR" and the back is marked "Union Cut Co" over "Olean, NY USA". Knife measures 4 ½" closed and approx. 8" open. Celluloid handles are much less common than stag on these knives.* **Mint value: $2,750**

Keen Kutter
Trademark of E.C. Simmons Hardware & Shapleigh Hardware

St. Louis, MO.   1870–1960

Keen Kutter was the trademark first used by E.C. Simmons Hardware Company of St. Louis, Mo. E.C. Simmons started his business around 1870 and the company eventually became one of the largest hardware companies in the U.S., gaining control of other companies along the way. One of the companies that they controlled was the Walden Knife Company of Walden, N.Y., who manufactured switchblades under the name Press Button Knife Company. In 1922 Winchester Arms Company merged with E.C. Simmons and it was decided to shut down the Walden plant and move all knife production to New Haven, Conn. in September of 1923. This merger dissolved in 1929 and the companies went their separate ways. In 1940 the Shapleigh Hardware Co., also of St. Louis, acquired E.C. Simmons. At some point the Schrade Cutlery Company of Walden, N.Y. was contracted to make the Keen Kutter switchblades and they continued to make them until Shapleigh discontinued their switchblade line. There were five basic Keen Kutter patterns made by the Press Button Knife Co. between 1892 and 1923, and they were:

1. 3 ³⁄₈-inch double   Model # 100PB
2. 3 ⁵⁄₈-inch double   Model # 115PB
3. 4-inch single   Model # 500PB
4. 5-inch single   Model # 1000PB
5. 5-inch single with folding guard   Model # 1005WG

Please note that the lengths used here are the same lengths listed in the Keen Kutter catalog from the 1920s and are not all accurate. All model numbers are for knives with imitation stag (jigged bone) handles. I don't know if all of the knives manufactured by Press Button Knife Company for E.C. Simmons were marked "Keen Kutter". I have seen some with the tang stamped "Simmons Hardware" and I believe some, if not all of the main blades were etched with "Keen Kutter".

Schrade Cutlery Company made six basic patterns of Keen Kutter knives sometime between 1920 and 1958, and they were:

1. 2 ⁷⁄₈-inch double   Model # KS311
2. 3 ³⁄₈-inch double   Model # KS310
3. 4-inch fishtail   Model # KS102
4. 4-inch bowtie   Model # KS103
5. 4 ¼-inch single   Model # KS110
6. 4 ⁷⁄₈-inch single   Model # KS104

The knives over 4 inches long closed were referred to as "Outing and Scouting Knives" in the catalogs. Although there were variations in handle materials and blades with most of these patterns, there are just 11 basic patterns to collect. The knives made by the Schrade Cutlery Company typically had "Keen Kutter"

etched on the front of the main blade as well as having "Keen Kutter" and the Keen Kutter symbol stamped on the tang. All of these knives are hard to find and are highly collectible. The knives made by Press Button Knife Company are the most rare.

	Observations
1.	2 ⅞-inch double only made with black/pearl celluloid handles and is very rare.
2.	3 ⅜-inch doubles had either jigged bone or celluloid handles with Butter & Molasses being the most common.
3.	4-inch fishtail most commonly found with Butter & Molasses celluloid handles.
4.	4 ¼-inch knife scarcer than the 4 ⅞" knife, but both very rare!

Both of the knives pictured here have their clip blade stamped "KEEN" over "KUTTER" inside of the Keen Kutter symbol as pictured in the text. Both back tangs are stamped "US PATS" over "Dec 21, 09" over "Sept 13, 10" over "June 6, 16".

Jigged bone handles with steel liners and bolsters. Blade should have "KEEN KUTTER" etched on front side. Measures 4 ¼" closed and 7 ⅜" open and is very rare. **Mint value: $1300**

Jigged bone handles with steel liners and bolsters. Blade should have "KEEN KUTTER" etched on front side. Measures 4 ⅞" closed and 8 ¾" open and is very rare. **Mint value: $1200**

Keenwell Brown Mfg Co.

Olean, NY   1926–1939

Wallace R. Brown and his brother Robert Emerson Brown started a cutlery jobber business in Little Valley, N.Y. in 1898. They began manufacturing razors under the name Union Razor Company after buying the Tideoute Cutlery Co. in 1902. They changed their name to Union Cutlery Co in 1909 and shortly thereafter moved their operations to Olean, N.Y. in 1911. Interestingly, the Brown brothers manufactured their cutlery under several different names over the years including: Union Razor Co, Brown Brothers Knife Company, Olean Cutlery Co, Union Cutlery Co, KA-BAR Cutlery Co, Olcut and others. The best-known switchblades they manufactured were made under the names KA-BAR and Union Cut Co.

There was another, lesser known, company name used by the Browns to produce switchblades: Keenwell Brown Mfg. Company. Robert E. Brown patented at least three different switchblade designs between 1925 and 1931. I suspect that Keenwell Brown Mfg. Co. was set up to market cutlery designed by Robert as his own little pet project. Robert's switchblade patents were U.S. Pat # 1,584,165 of May 11, 1926, U.S. Pat # 1,701,027 of Feb 5, 1929 and U.S. Pat # 1,810,999 of June 23, 1931. I haven't been able to confirm that all of these patents went into production, but I do know the last one did. This last patent was used to manufacture switchblade knives in the 1930s and I've had the good fortune to see two of them. They have an unusual appearance with both a button and a lever. The button is actually the safety and the lever moves the backspring to release the blade. This knife tends to be a bit temperamental in locking closed and opening. I suppose this design weakness might have contributed to a lack of popularity and ultimately to the knife's demise. This particular model measures 5 ¼ inches closed and 9 ¼ inches open.

I believe at least two different switchblade patterns were manufactured under the Keenwell name, but I only have this one example in the book. I hope to come across some examples of the other designs one day, but for now all I can include is a picture of one model and copies of the original patents for the others. On a rarity scale of one to 10, Keenwel switchblades are a 10, so keep your eyes open and your fingers crossed. See also: KA-BAR and Union Cut Co. sections.

	Observations Keenwell Brown 5 ¼ inches	
1.	Smooth yellow celluloid seems to be the handle of choice.
2.	Patent number is stamped on the back of the tang.
3.	Brass liners and nickel silver bolsters, button and release.

Clip blade is stamped "KEENWELL" over "BROWN MFG. CO" over "OLEAN, NY" and the back is marked "PAT 1810999". Knife measures 5 ¼" closed and approx. 9 ¼" open. Beautiful translucent yellow celluloid handles with brass liners and nickel silver bolsters, button and release lever. Extremely rare knife. **Mint value: $7,500**

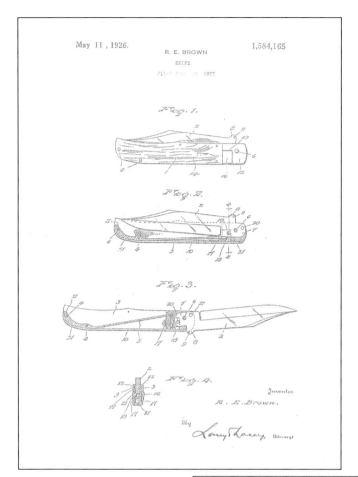

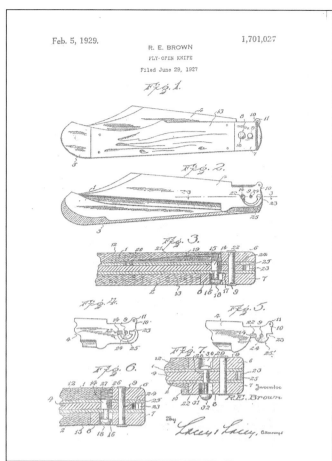

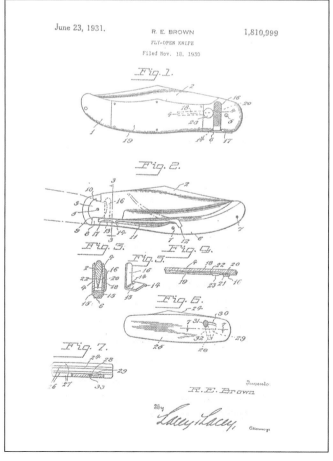

Korn's–Patent
George W. Korn

New York, NY

George W Korn was born in Breslau, Poland on May 22, 1846. He immigrated to the United States somewhere around 1880 and at first he settled in Buffalo, but later moved to New York City. In 1881 he was working with August Weck, the same year he patented his buttonhole scissors. In the next few years he worked with Weck and Hermann Heinrichs on other cutlery inventions. Sometime prior to 1890 he was also associated with the Cattaraugus Cutlery Company as a traveling salesman, which would explain the Cattaraugus stampings on some of his razors. George stayed in New York for the rest of his life. I believe that he also worked for the cutlery jobber Alfred Field for a while. George made his mark on the American switchblade industry when he received two separate patents for what he called "Fly-Openers." His first patent was granted on March 13, 1883 and was only the second switchblade patent ever issued in the United States. It was U.S. Pat # 273,858 and I do not know if any knives were ever manufactured based upon this patent. The second patent was granted the following year on Oct. 21, 1884 and was U.S. Pat # 306,839. The second patent shows the bolster with graceful guards, which have become a sort of signature feature on most Korn's Patent switchblade knives. Unfortunately there doesn't seem to be any information to indicate exactly where the knives were made or how many were ever produced. The only advertising that I've ever seen for the knives was from an old catalog for G.W. Claflin & Co., 54 & 56 Duane St, New York, N.Y. from 1886. That means that they were being marketed in 1886, four years before George started the George W. Korn Razor Mfg. Co. of Little Valley, N.Y. and six years before George Schrade patented his first switchblade knife.

There are two theories about where and how these knives were manufactured. The most generally accepted theory is that they were manufactured in Germany and imported into the United States. Since it was prior to 1891 they would not been required to have "Germany" stamped on the knives. I've heard arguments both

for and against this theory. Taking into consideration how scarce these knives are and that they were obviously hand-assembled with great skill, I think it is also feasible that George set up a small shop somewhere in New York and produced the knives himself. Most likely he would have employed some skilled cutlers to help him. One argument for this theory is that a few custom-made knives have surfaced including one designed for left-handed operation which makes it seem more likely that they were hand-crafted here in the states, rather than ordered from overseas. I've seen no evidence that the knives were ever produced in any great numbers; in fact they are extremely rare. Until some proof is furnished, these will have to remain theories. I would appreciate any information that my readers might be able to provide on this subject. Feel free to contact me through my website which is listed in the front of this book.

The G.W. Claflin ad stated that the knives were made in two sizes, a small one with no finger guards for normal use and a larger knife with guards for hunters. The smaller knife measures approximately 4 inches closed and the larger knife measures approximately 5 inches closed. They were made with stag, gutta percha, mother of pearl and possibly some other handle materials. The ones handled in gutta percha were usually elaborately engraved with hunting scenes, etc. On the rare occasions that the Korn's Patent knives do surface, they are usually the 5-inch Hunter model with the distinctive Korn signature guards. I was lucky enough to find an extremely rare version of an extremely rare knife to feature in this book. These knives are operated by applying pressure to the front bolster with your thumb. The bolster pivots slightly lifting a pin out of a hole in the blade and the spring then throws the blade open and the pin drops into another hole to lock the blade in the open position. Of the few Korn knives that I've had the pleasure of viewing, this is the only one that I've ever seen which has a safety. This safety predates George Schrade's safety patent by about 10 years. The design is simple. The small oval tab that you see at the base of the front bolster slides, ever so slightly, toward the handle and the tab protrudes over the handle slightly, preventing the bolster from pivoting. This rarity among rarities definitely adds to the value. I have personally seen one without a safety that was in rough condition sell for over $3,000 recently. The blade was rusty, tip protruded from handle when closed and it had other problems as well. I believe that it would have brought more under the right circumstances.

I suspect that the Korn knives were manufactured from approximately 1884 until 1900, when he started the razor company. Korn took on a partner in the razor company, E.E. Kelley. They manufactured razors, including contract pieces for companies like W.R. Case & Sons, Sears, Roebuck & Co., Cattaraugus and others. George died on June 7, 1919 and Kelley acquired control of the company and was president until 1925 when the company closed its doors.

I am very proud to be able to include two of the Korn's Patent knives in this book. Although one of them is in very rough condition, it is still a very desirable collectible and most collectors who love these old knives would be happy to display it in their collection. That may help you understand just how special these knives really are.

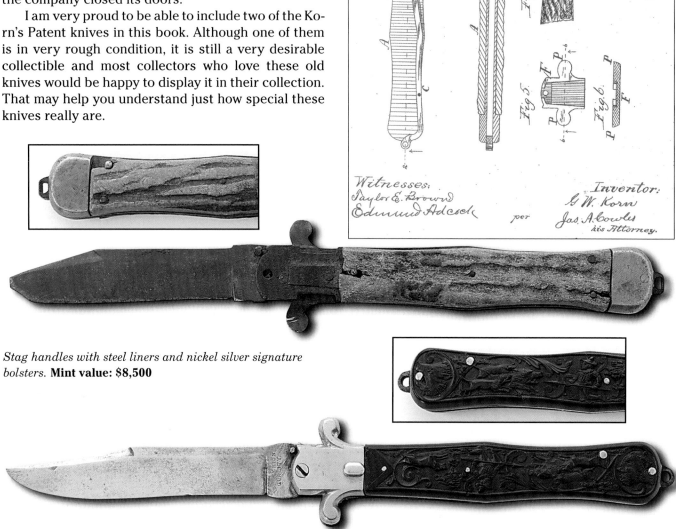

Stag handles with steel liners and nickel silver signature bolsters. **Mint value: $8,500**

Black gutta percha handles with elaborate boar hunting scenes on both sides and nickel silver signature bolsters with nickel silver sliding safety. With the safety this knife on a rarity scale rates at least 9 out of 10. **Mint value: $9,000**

L.L. Bean Inc.

Freeport, Maine   1912–Present

Leon Leonwood Bean started a mail order retail company in 1912. He called it L.L. Bean. The company went from a modest start with $400 in borrowed money and a single self-designed product to one of the largest mail order businesses in the United States. The address in one of their 1938 catalogs has them at 222 Main Street, Freeport, Maine. Although they never manufactured any knives, L.L. Bean contracted Schrade Cutlery Company of Walden, N.Y. to manufacture two different models of switchblade knives. The more common of the two is a 3 ⅜-inch single-blade with butter and molasses celluloid handles, which they listed in their catalog as "ivorloid" handles. This little knife came with a custom leather knife purse into which the knife fit snugly. It is stated in the catalog that this was L.L. Bean's favorite knife. The other model was the 4 ⅞-inch Hunter's Pride model with a clip blade and folding guards. The blade on this knife was etched with "Hunter's Pride" from the factory. These can be found with jigged bone handles that were used on knives made prior to 1947, black jigged celluloid which was used from 1947 to 1956, or black jigged Delrin handles, which were used on knives made between 1956 and 1958. Oddly the bone-handled version had brass liners. Normally the large-frame knives made by Schrade Cutlery Co. had steel liners, so the brass must have been a special request by L.L. Bean. I do not know if the synthetic-handled knives had brass or steel liners. Even though I say that the smaller single-blade is the more common of the two, they are still by no means easy to find. These were not made in great numbers and to find a nice one is no easy task. They command much higher prices than their Schrade Cutlery Company counterparts.

Clip blade is stamped "L.L. BEAN INC." over "FREEPORT, M.E." and the back is marked "US PATS" over "Dec 21, 09" over "Sept 13, 10" over "June 6, 16". Knife measures 3 ⅜" closed and 5 ⅞" open. Butter & Molasses celluloid handles with brass liners. **Mint value: $700**

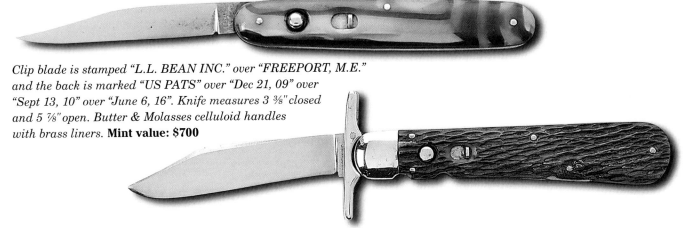

Clip blade is stamped "L.L. BEAN INC." over "FREEPORT, M.E." and the back is marked "US PATS" over "Dec 21, 09" over "Sept 13, 10" over "June 6, 16". Commonly referred to as a "Hunter's Pride" this knife has jigged bone handles, brass liners and nickel silver bolsters, button and folding guards. It measures 4 ⅞" closed and 8 ¾" open. Later versions had synthetic handles and are worth slightly less. **Mint value: $1,200**

Norvell-Shapleigh Hardware Co.

St Louis, MO   1902–1920

The AF Shapleigh Hardware Company of St Louis, MO went through many changes over the years. One of the most noteworthy changes came in 1902 when the company ownership changed hands after the passing of the company's founder A.F. Shapleigh. A man named Saunders Norvell bought the company and changed the name to Norvell-Shapleigh Hardware Company. He became president of the company in 1907. It was around this time that Norvell-Shapleigh Hardware Company contracted the Schrade Cutlery Company of Walden, NY to manufacture switchblades for them to Shapleigh Hdwr Co.. By 1920 the company name was changed to Shapleigh Hardware Company and the tang stampings on the contract knives were also changed around this time to the Shapleigh Hardware Company.

Schrade manufactured at least three different patterns stamped Norvell-Shapleigh and those were:
1. 3 ⅜" double
2. 3 ¾" double
3. 3 ¾" double with two large blades, separate springs, extra liner and full bolsters

It would seem likely that they also would have made some 4 ¼" and 4 ⅞" single blade patterns with the Norvell-Shapleigh tang stamp, but if so they are very hard to find and I've never actually seen one.

The 3 ⅜" doubles were handled in celluloid in a variety of colors. I don't know if they used any other handle materials on these, but bone and pearl would be likely possibilities. Some had nickel silver tip bolsters and some even had a file blade instead of a pen blade as the secondary. The other patterns that I've seen with this tang stamp are both 3 ¾" doubles, but there is enough difference to justify listing them separately. All three patterns are pictured in this book. One of these 3 ¾" knives is also the most interesting Norvell-Shapleigh switchblade that I've come across. It is a double and one blade is a clip, while the other is a spey blade. It has jigged bone handles and full nickel silver bolsters. What makes it really unique, besides the blade configuration, is that it has an extra brass liner between the blades and each blade has its own separate spring instead of sharing a common spring as most doubles do. This knife is thicker and heavier than other 3 ¾" doubles and is of high quality construction. It is a scarce and interesting old American switchblade! Please see the chapter on the Shapleigh Hardware Company for more information.

3 ⅜" doubles

Black celluloid handles with brass liners. Pen blade "NORVELL" over "SHAPLEIGH" over "ST. LOUIS" and the back is marked "US PATS" over "Feb 13, 06" over "Feb 26, 07". **Mint value: $550**

Woodgrain celluloid handles with brass liners. Pen blade stamped "NORVELL" over "SHAPLEIGH" over "ST. LOUIS" and the back is marked "US PATS" over "Feb 13, 06" over "Feb 26, 07". **Mint value: $550**

Tortoise celluloid handles with brass liners. Pen blade stamped "NORVELL" over "SHAPLEIGH" over "ST. LOUIS" and the back is marked "US PATS" over "812601" over 845130". These markings indicate that this knife was made prior to 1908, which makes it one of the earliest Schrade Cut Co switchblades. This enhances the collector value. **Mint value: $650**

Black celluloid handles with tip bolsters and brass liners. Pen blade stamped "NORVELL" over "SHAPLEIGH" over "ST. LOUIS" and the back is marked "US PATS" over "Feb 13, 06" over "Feb 26, 07". **Mint value: $575**

Jigged bone handles and brass liners on this 3 ¾" double switchblade. Clip/pen bade combination. Clip blade has an interesting "swedge" grind and is stamped "NORVELL" over "SHAPLEIGH" over "ST. LOUIS" on the front and "SCHRADE CUT. CO" over "WALDEN, NY" on the back. The pen blade has the same front stamp as the clip blade, but the back is marked "US PATS" over "Feb 13, 06" over "Feb 26, 07". **Mint value: $700**

Jigged bone handles with full nickel silver bolsters and three brass liners on this 3 ¾" double switchblade. Clip/Spey blade combination with brass liner between the blades and separate springs for each blade. Clip blade "NORVELL" over "SHAPLEIGH" over "ST. LOUIS" and back stamped "US PATS" over "Feb 13, 06" over "Feb 26, 07". The spey blade has same front stamp, but back stamped "SCHRADE CUT. CO" over "WALDEN, NY". This particular knife is in desperate need of repairs, but it is so rare because of the blade combination and liners, that to have one in any condition a collector is fortunate. **Mint value: $900**

Press Button Knife Company
A Division of Walden Knife Company

Walden, NY — 1892–1923

George Schrade was a machinist by trade, which makes his interest in switchblade knives understandable. He became interested in developing a design for a spring-activated knife and in 1892 he patented his first design. After an unsuccessful attempt at manufacturing the knives himself in a small shop in New York City, he accepted an offer from Edward Whitehead of the Walden Knife Company. Whitehead was intrigued with George's knife and invited him to come to Walden where George would oversee the manufacture of his knives. Walden bought an interest in the knives and set up a division just for the switchblades. A corporation was later formed and named The Press Button Knife Company of Walden, N.Y., a Corporation of West Virginia. The Press Button Knife Company knives were manufactured in nine basic patterns:

1. 2 ⅞-inch double (Ladies knife)
2. 2 ⅞-inch single (High School Girl) Extremely rare.
3. 3 ⅜-inch double (Pen knives)
4. 3 ¹¹⁄₁₆-inch double (Mechanics)
5. 4-inch single (Business or Farmers)
6. 5-inch single (Invincible or Sportsman's)
7. 5-inch single with folding guard (Victor)
8. 5-inch fixed guard (Guardian)
9. 4 ⅝-inch One Armed Man Knife. With a curved blade and a three-tined fork on the end. This knife was designed to be a cutting and eating utensil for people with one arm.

Sears, Roebuck & Co. purchased three different models of the Press Button Knife Co. knives for sale in at least one of their catalogs around the turn of the century.

a. *3 ⅜-inch double in bone — Sears model # 28R1326
b. *4-inch Business — Sears model # 28R1320
c. *4 ¾-inch Invincible — Sears model # 28R1324

*measurements according to the Sears catalog

Probably the rarest Press Button Knife Co switchblade is a knife designed for high school girls. It is a 2 ⅞-inch single-blade switchblade that I believe was handled in celluloid. I don't know if this knife even made it to production, but if it did they must not have manufactured them for very long because they are extremely rare. Many of the 2 ⅞-inch and 3 ⅜-inch doubles were handled in sterling silver. Some had a simple raised design on the silver while others

The Walden Knife Company, Walden, NY

were more elaborate with pictures and information. Some of the themes that you may come across are a St. Augustine, Florida commemorative, one that has a Gothic face, or tribal. If anyone knows more about the Gothic face, or its significance, I would love to hear about it. Another one that is often referred to as "Old Man Winter" is actually a Satyr, which is a mythological cross between a goat and a man. The creature's beard and attached design do make it resemble an old man with cold air blowing out of his mouth, hence the name. I see no harm in calling it "Old Man Winter" if you prefer, I just wanted to present the facts. I believe the Satyr was only done on the 3 ⅜-inch doubles. Another theme that you may find on the 2 ⅞-inch knives a commemoration of Ponce de Leon with his embossed bust on the sterling silver handle. Other themes that you may find on the 3 ⅜-inch doubles include a George Washington knife which has George Washington's bust and the Capitol Building on the front and a bust of Martha Washington and the Whitehouse on the back and one commemorating the Railroad through the Florida Keys.

Besides commemoratives there were also a lot of advertising knives made and some were even handled in Sterling silver. One of the more common has the Satyr on one side and "Compliments of the Home Insurance Co. NY" on the other. Many also had advertising etched on the blades, one example is pictured in this section. Celluloid handles provided a great place to display advertising and a high percentage of the 3 ⅜-inch doubles were advertising knives. Some of the things you'll see advertised are: Hoff's Extract, Post Telegram, Coffee, White Mountain Refrigerators and many others. There is even a celluloid-handled double to commemorate the St. Louis World's Fair of 1904.

The larger 3 ¹¹⁄₁₆-inch doubles were supposedly made with a seven different blade combinations, but these knives are so rare it's hard to believe. From what I've observed the 3 ⅜-inch doubles outnumber the 3 ¹¹⁄₁₆-inch doubles at least 25 to 1, and that's most likely a low estimate. This pattern was apparently only handled in jigged bone, which Press Button Knife Co referred to as American Stag. An interesting feature found on these knives is a "half moon" groove cut into the handles near one of the blades, usually a spey blade. These grooves are designed for practicality, not decorative purposes, since it is actually a thumb groove designed to give more leverage and control while castrating animals, etc. Again, this model is very rare so don't pass on it if you're lucky enough to find one.

Two of the largest switchblades that Press Button Knife Co. made measured 4 inches and 4 ⅞ inches, respectively. They are most often found with American Stag (jigged bone) handles, nickel silver bolsters and a

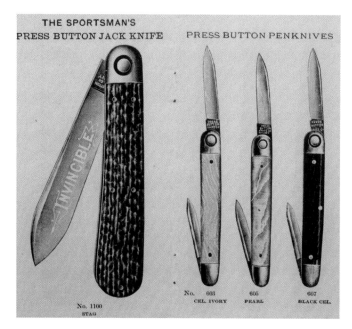

clip blade. Some were also made with spear blades in both sizes and all of these blades were etched at the factory. One of the rarest patterns of the larger Press Button knives was called the Guardian and it had finger guards built into the bolsters. Production on this pattern didn't start until around 1914 and was short lived. These knives are very hard to find.

The smaller pattern measured 4 inches closed and was etched "Business" and the larger which measured 4 ⅞ inches was etched "Invincible" on the front of the blade. The larger knife with folding guards was etched "The VICTOR." Some of the Invincibles were also handled in ebony, a very dark wood. I believe that these were the only American switchblades to have wood handles. Some were also made under contract for other companies and can be found with different tang stamps including Graef & Schmidt, Elliot Langley, Torrey, Simmons Hdwre and others. They also made knives etched "KEEN KUTTER" for Simmons Hardware, but I do not know if any had that tang stamp. These knives are all very rare and highly collectible.

Press Button Knife Co. also manufactured one of the most recognized, and unusual, switchblade knives in American history. That is the "One arm man knife" pictured in this section. It was designed as a tool for the handicapped that could be both a cutting and an eating utensil. The handles curve almost into a "J" to accommodate the unusual curved blade with three fork tines on the end It is easily opened and closed with one hand and balances quite well. They worked so well, in fact, that most of the knives saw heavy use and because of food and other foreign particles that got left on the blades, most of the blades ended up corroded or broken. Many of these knives also had an etching on the blade that was usually for the AA Marks Company, who apparently contracted Press Button

Knife Co. to make them with their markings. If you're lucky enough to find one of these wonderful knives, I strongly suggest you add it to your collection and be prepared for it to become a focal point. They fascinate even people who aren't interested in knives.

George Schrade stayed in charge of production until 1903 when he sold his interest in the Press Button knife to the Walden Knife Co. and left to form a company with his brothers J. Louis and William Schrade. At some point a tang stamp change was made. I have come across a very small number of the 4 ⅞-inch Invincible model knives that have a tang stamp of "Walden Knife Co., NY" instead of the usual "Press Button Knife Co" over "Walden, NY". It seems likely that the "Walden Knife Co., NY" stamp was used at the beginning of production and the "Pressbutton Knife Co." stamp came after, making these the oldest. Another oddity, which occurred after George left Walden Knife Co., is that they made some 3 ⅜-inch double switchblades with sliding safeties. These models are extremely rare and had been thought to be only prototypes, but I believe they were actually produced for sale in very limited numbers. The patent for this safety was granted to George L. McVey who was assignor to the Press Button Knife Company of Walden, N.Y. He applied for U.S. patent # 901,253 on April 30, 1908 and it was granted on October 13, 1908. Press Button Knife Co. was in business for nearly 15 years after the patent was granted so it seems odd that there weren't more of these knifes produced. My guess would be that the tiny tab sitting in a little notch in the handle, right next to button, was not very "user friendly" and they determined that it was not worthwhile to continue manufacturing them with the safeties. The other likelihood would be that they didn't bother to develop the safety modification until the earl 1920s and they went out of business before it got into full production. Whatever the scenario, this is one hard-to-find little switchblade and I am proud to be able to feature two of them in this book. One of them is in rough shape, but they are so rare that to own one in any condition you would have to be very lucky.

The Walden Knife Company became a subsidiary of Simmons Hardware Company of St. Louis, MO around 1911. Five models of the switchblade knives produced by the company were marked with "Keen Kutter", which was a trademark of Simmons, and they were sold through their catalogs. Simmons merged with Winchester Arms Co. in 1922 and it was decided to close the Walden Knife Co. factory and move all knife production to New Haven, Conn. in September of 1923. That marked the end of production for the Press Button Knife Company.

2 ⅞" doubles

The knives pictured here have the following in common: The measure 2 7/8" closed and 5 ⅝" open. All have the following markings: Interestingly all of the blades are stamped the same. Front tang stamped "PRESS" over "BUTTON" over "KNIFE CO" over "WALDEN" over "NY" and the backs are stamped "U.S. PAT" over "470605".

Model # 300. Jigged bone handles with brass liners and spear/pen blade combination.
Mint value: $600

Model # 300SS. Sterling silver handles and nickel silver liners. Handles have a face embossed on the front handle along with some gothic decorations on both the front and back handles. I have not been able to figure out the significance of the face, if any? It is an interesting knife regardless. **Mint value: $625**

Model # 300SS. Sterling silver handles and nickel silver liners. Handles have embossed scenery of "St. Augustine, Florida Settled 1565" on the back handle and a tower, native Floridian and a palm tree on the front. Spear/pen blade combination.
Mint value: $650

Model # 302. Tortoise celluloid handles with brass liners and spear/pen blade combination.
Mint value: $575

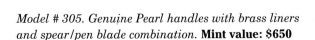

Model # 305. Genuine Pearl handles with brass liners and spear/pen blade combination. **Mint value: $650**

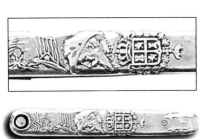

Two more sterling doubles to show more handle variety. One is a basic raised dot pattern and the other is a Ponce de Leon commemorative.

3 ⅜" doubles

The knives pictured here have the following in common: They measure 3 ⅜" closed and 6 7/8" open. Both blades have the same markings of "PRESSBUTTON" over "KNIFE CO" over "WALDEN, NY" and the back is stamped "US PAT" over "470605" unless otherwise noted.

Model # 202. Tortoise celluloid handles with brass liners and spear/file blade combination. **Mint value: $575**

Model # 102 with safeties. Tortoise celluloid handles with brass liners and spear/pen blade combination. This knife is very unique in that it has sliding safeties which until recently was virtually unknown in the knife collecting world. This knife is extremely rare. **Mint value: $1,200**

Model #102. Tortoise celluloid handles with brass liners and spear/pen blade combination. **Mint value: $525**

Model # 200 with safeties. Imitation stag handles with brass liners and spear/file blade combination. Don't be fooled because I was fortunate enough to find two of these rare safety knives to include in this book. They were unheard of until recently in the knife world and are extremely rare. **Mint value: $1,500**

Model # 100. Imitation stag handles with brass liners and spear/pen blade combination.
Spear blade deeply etched with "JESSOP'S". **Mint value: $575**

Model # 105. Genuine pearl handles with brass liners and spear/pen blade combination.
Mint value: $600

Model # 103. Ivory celluloid
handles with brass liners and
spear/pen blade combination.
There are no patent numbers
stamped on this knife. **Mint
value: $500**

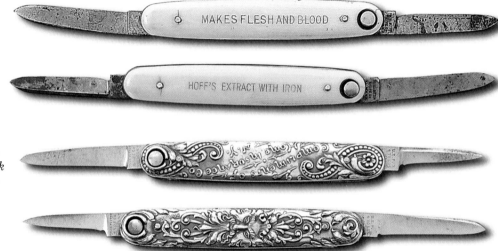

Model # 110SS. Sterling Silver
handles with nickel silver liners.
The knife has a Satyr on the back
handle and "Compliments of the
Home Insurance Co. NY" on the
front. They are often found with
the Satyr on both handles.
Mint value: $575

Model #103. Ivory celluloid handles with brass liners and spear/pen blade combination.
Patent numbers are stamped on the front of both blades and backs are blank. The knife
is not stamped Press Button Knife Co. which makes it an oddity and adds slightly to the
value. I suspect that it is one of the first doubles made by the company. **Mint value: $650**

Model # 110SS. Sterling Silver
handles with nickel silver liners.
Spear/pen blade combination
on this George Washington
commemorative. Embossed
George Washington bust on the
front along with a picture of
the Capitol Bldg and the back
features Martha Washington and
the Whitehouse. This is a very
rare historical commemorative.
Mint value: $700

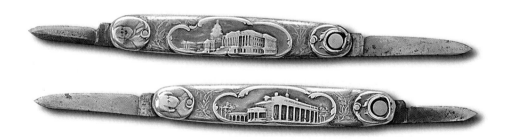

Model #110SS. Sterling Silver embossed design handles with nickel silver bolsters. Spear/cutting manicure blade combination. **Mint value: $575**

Model # 110SS. Sterling Silver embossed design handles with nickel silver liners. Spear/pen blade combination. No patent number stampings on this knife. Personalization does not detract if nicely done. **Mint value: $550**

3 ¹¹⁄₁₆" double

Model # 115. Imitation stag handles with brass liners and clip/spey blade combination. Blades stamped "PRESS BUTTON" over "KNIFE CO" over "WALDEN, NY" on the front and backs are blank. Measures 3 ¹¹⁄₁₆" closed and 7 ⅞" open. Knife has a thumb groove near the spey blade end. These were most often referred to as a "Mechanic's jack". **Mint value: $900**

Larger singles

Model # 510. Imitation stag handle with nickel silver bolsters and iron liners. Clip blade stamped "PRESS BUTTON KNIFE CO" over "WALDEN, NY" and the back is blank. Measures 4" closed and 6 ⅞" open. Originally had etching on the blade that said "BUSINESS". These knives were heavily used and it is rare to find one with a full blade. **Mint value: $1,050**

Model # 1000. Imitation stag handle with nickel silver bolsters and iron liners. Clip blade stamped "PRESS BUTTON KNIFE CO" over "WALDEN, NY" and the back is blank. Measures 4 ⅞" closed and 8 ¾" open. Originally had etching on the front of the blade that said "INVINCIBLE". Since these knives were too large to comfortably carry in a pocket many did not see heavy use and it's easier to find one with a full blade in this larger size. **Mint value: $950**

Model # 1007. Ebony wood handles with nickel silver bolsters and iron liners. Clip blade stamped "PRESS BUTTON KNIFE CO" over "WALDEN, NY" and the back is blank. Measures 4 ⅞" closed and 8 ¾" open. Originally had etching on the front of the blade that said "INVINCIBLE". Ebony is much rarer than imitation stag. This example is in rough shape, but at least shows the handles. I believe this was originally a spearpoint blade that someone has altered. **Mint value: $1,100 If blade was spearpoint the mint value would be $1,500**

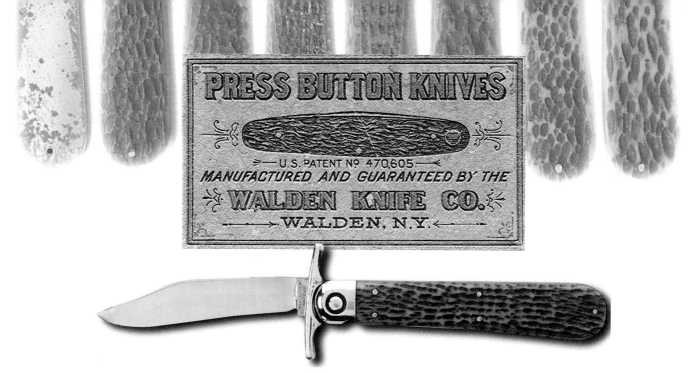

Model # 1005. Imitation stag handles with nickel silver bolsters and guards and iron liners. Clip blade stamped "PRESS BUTTON KNIFE CO" over "WALDEN, NY" and the back is stamped "US PAT" over "470605". Measures 4 ⅞" closed and 8 ¾" open. Originally had etching on the blade that read "The Victor". This knife is very popular with collectors. **Mint value: $1,200**

Imitation stag handles with nickel silver fixed-guard bolsters and iron liners. Clip blade stamped "PRESS BUTTON KNIFE CO" over "WALDEN, NY" and back is blank. Measures 4 ⅞" closed and 8 ¾" open. Originally had etching on the blade that read "GUARDIAN". I believe this pattern wasn't made until 1914 and apparently wasn't made for long because they are very rare. **Mint value: $2,500**

Aluminum embossed handles with nickel silver bolsters and iron liners. Unusual curved blade with fork tines is designed for people with one good arm as a cutting/eating tool. Blade stamped "PRESS BUTTON KNIFE CO" over "WALDEN, NY" and back is blank. Measures 4 ⅝" closed and 8 ¾" open. Many of these had etching on the blade if made under contract and they work and display great. This is one hard to find knife. **Mint value: $1,250**

"WALDEN" over "KNIFE . Co" over "N.Y" is the unusual stamping on this clip blade. The back tang is stamped "U.S. PAT" over "470,605". Imitation stag handles with nickel silver bolsters and iron liners. Measures 4 ⅞" closed and 8 ¾" open. This is a very rare knife because of the tang stamp. **Mint value: $1,500**

PRESTO Trademark of
George Schrade Knife Co.

Bridgeport, Conn.   1929–1956

The George Schrade Knife Company of Bridge-port, Conn. used the Presto brand name for most of their switchblade line. After a 10-year collaboration with Challenge Cutlery Corporation of Bridgeport, Conn. to produce his Flylock knives ended, George Schrade proceeded to go it on his own and he formed the George Schrade Knife Company. He was able to start his new business at 46 Seymour St. in Bridgeport, the same building where the failed Challenge Cutlery Corporation had been producing his Flylock knives. He acquired equipment from Challenge in exchange for money owed to him. Although he started his business in 1929, at the start of the Great Depression, the business prospered. He did sell one model of switchblade with the George Schrade Knife Co. stamp. It was his line of 2 ⅞-inch pullball knives. George's other switchblade knives were all stamped "Presto" and there were eight basic patterns produced with this stamping:

1. 3 ⅜-inch single-blade (jack)
2. 3 ⅜-inch double-blade
3. 3 ⅜-inch single-blade attached to letter opener
4. 4-inch single-blade fishtail
5. 4-inch single-blade bowtie
6. 4 ⅛" single-blade (sportsman)
7. 5-inch single-blade (hunter)
8. 5-inch single-blade with folding guard

These basic patterns were made with variations in handle materials, blade type, liner and bolster variations as well as different stampings, which make for a large number of t knives for the adventurous collector. A good representation of this company's switchblade line can be accomplished with only nine basic models including the pullball.

Several different stampings can be found on these knives. On the earliest 4 ⅛" and 5" knives the"PRESTO" stamp is smaller than the later versions and also says "PAT PEND-G". This stamp was used in the early 1930s.

The next stamp that was used was a larger "PRESTO" that was still accompanied by the "Pat Pnd-g" stamp. They dropped the "Pat Pnd-g" stamp by 1940 when George received his last switchblade patent covering the manufacture of these knives. After 1940 the stamp was changed to "PRESTO" over "PAT. JAN 30-40". Another stamping used was "PRESTO" over "MADE IN USA". I know that this stamp was used on some of the knives they sold to Shapleigh Hardware, but I don't know if it was used specifically for those knives. It's fairly common and my guess would be that it was simply a stamping used later in production. The back tangs are usually stamped "G. Schrade" over "Bport, Conn" or similar stamping. The earliest "small stamp" is the rarest and most desirable will command higher prices.

One observation I've made is that much of the cel-luloid used by this company seems to be more suscep-tible to deterioration than that used by competitors. It's very rare to find any Presto candystripe handles in perfect condition. Certain color combinations are worse and the problems are most common with the doubles. There seem to be a couple of exceptions. One of which is the Onyx celluloid, which was used quite a bit by them. For some reason this color seems to hold up better. One must take this into consideration when pricing these knives, since it means that there are going to be fewer "colorful" Presto celluloid double switchblades in existence as the years pass. Therefore, the ones that do hold up are worth more money. An-other important fact is that more single-blade 3 ⅜-inch switchblades were made by Presto than the doubles; this also enhances the value of nice Presto celluloid doubles. The opposite is true of Schrade Cutlery Com-pany who produced far more doubles than singles in this size, so their singles will command higher prices because they are much harder to find. For some rea-son Schrade Cutlery Co. celluloid seems to hold up bet-ter than that used by Presto. I believe this is because Schrade Cutlery Co. allowed their celluloid to cure and shrink more before making handles out of it. Please see the chapter on Remington for related information.

When you start getting into the larger knives there is some confusion about which ones were actually military paratrooper knives and which were not. All of these knives that have a bail are thought to be paratroopers, but I do not believe that is true. I am sure that the 4 ⅛-inch model with black wormgroove synthetic handles and a bail were indeed military-issue paratrooper knives because I've seen them still in the wrapper with military papers. I also believe that some of the bone-handled knives with bail were WWII vintage paratroopers. A possible factor is that shortages of materials as the war dragged on resulted in some substitutions of handle materials and possibly even some military-issue knives without a bail. I do not have proof of this, but I have it on pretty good authority.

In years following the war there was a lot of public interest in the paratrooper knives, which prompted George Schrade and a couple of other manufacturers to make a civilian version of the knife. I believe that the 4 ⅛-inch and 5-inch Presto knives with painted metal handles and a bail were some of these civilian versions. Although this fact reduces their interest to military collectors, there is still plenty of interest in them and they are still quite collectible. Some of these metal-handled knives were sold through Shapleigh Hardware catalogs.

Please see the chapters on the George Schrade Knife Company, Remington and Case for related information on this subject.

3 ⅜" singles

The knives pictured here have the following in common: They measure 3 ⅜" closed and 6" open. All have clip blades and brass liners.

Model # 610. Onyx celluloid handles. Blade stamped "PRESTO" over "PAT PEND-G" and back marked "G. SCHRADE" in an arch over "P'PORT, CT". **Mint value: $375**

Jigged bone handles. Blade stamped "PRESTO" over "MADE IN USA" and back marked "G. SCHRADE" in an arch over "B'PORT, CT". Bone handles are popular with collectors and enhance value. **Mint value: $450**

Smooth metal handles. Blade stamped "PRESTO" over "PAT. JAN 30-40" and back marked "GEO. SCHRADE" over "KNIFE CO INC" over "B'P'T, CONN". **Mint value: $400**

Coffee & cream swirl celluloid. Blade stamped "PRESTO" over "PAT. JAN 30-40" back marked "G. SCHRADE" in an arch over "B'PORT, CT". Attractive handles enhance value slightly. **Mint value: $475**

Black painted metal handles formed to resemble stag. Blade stamped "PRESTO" over "PAT. JAN 30-40" back marked "G. SCHRADE" in an arch over B'PORT, CT". These handles are hard to find. **Mint value: $500**

3 ⅜" doubles

The knives pictured here have the following in common: They measure 3 ⅜" closed and 7 1/16" open. Spear/pen blade combination with spear stamped "PRESTO" over "PAT. JAN 30-40" over "MADE IN USA" and the back is blank. Pen blade stamped "G. SCHRADE" in an arch over "KNIFE CO" over "B'PORT, CT" unless otherwise stated.

Onyx celluloid handles with brass liners. This is the most common color. **Mint value: $500**

Jigged bone handles with brass liners. Bone is popular with collectors and slightly enhances value. **Mint value: $550**

Jigged bone handles with brass liners and bail on pen blade end. Spear blade stamped "PRESTO" over "MADE IN USA" back blank. Pen blade stamped "G. SCHRADE" in an arch over "B'PORT, CT". Stamp may vary. Extremely rare Girl Scouts switchblade. Spear blade originally etched "GIRL SCOUTS" with their symbol between the two words and "GS" inside the symbol. The unusual jigging pattern and bail are dead giveaways even if the etch is gone from the blade. **Mint value: $1,000**

Smooth metal handles with brass liners. **Mint value: $450**

Burgundy & black mottled celluloid handles with brass liners. Spear blade stamped "PRESTO" over "PAT. PEND-G" back blank. Pen blade stamped "G. SCHRADE" in an arch over "B'PORT, CT". Presto colorful-celluloid is a factor in the value. **Mint value: $525**

Candystripe celluloid handles with brass liners. Candystripe celluloid is popular among collectors because of its beauty. Unfortunately the candystripe cell used by Presto is more prone to deterioration so it's rare to find them in mint condition so the value is enhanced. **Mint value: $700**

Blue & silver streaked celluloid handles with brass liners. Presto celluloid is a factor in the value. **Mint value: $525**

3 ⅜" letter openers

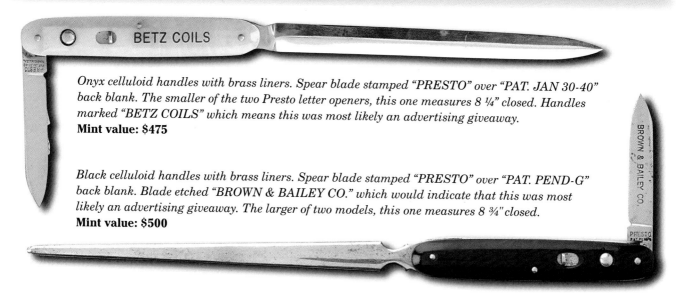

Onyx celluloid handles with brass liners. Spear blade stamped "PRESTO" over "PAT. JAN 30-40" back blank. The smaller of the two Presto letter openers, this one measures 8 ¼" closed. Handles marked "BETZ COILS" which means this was most likely an advertising giveaway.
Mint value: $475

Black celluloid handles with brass liners. Spear blade stamped "PRESTO" over "PAT. PEND-G" back blank. Blade etched "BROWN & BAILEY CO." which would indicate that this was most likely an advertising giveaway. The larger of two models, this one measures 8 ¾" closed.
Mint value: $500

4" fishtails

The knives pictured here have the following in common: All measure 4" closed and 7 ¼" open. All have a clip blade.

Model # 5500. Bowtie with Green Candystripe handles, nickel silver top bolster with finger guards and brass liners. Clip blade stamped "PRESTO" over "PAT. JAN 30-40" over "MADE IN USA" back reads "GEO. SCHRADE" over "KNIFE CO. INC" over "B'P'T, CONN". This is an extremely rare color. **Mint value: $850**

Model # 6000. Fishtail with Candystripe celluloid handles and brass liners. Blade stamped "PRESTO" over "PAT. JAN 30-40" over "MADE IN USA" back reads "GEO. SCHRADE" over "KNIFE CO." over "B'P'T, CONN". Candystripe handles enhance collector value. **Mint value: $750**

Model # 6000. Fishtail with Grey Swirl celluloid handles and steel liners. Blade stamped "PRESTO" over "PAT. JAN 30-40" over "MADE IN USA" back reads "G. SCHRADE" in an arch over "B'PORT, CT".
Mint value: $500

Jigged bone handles with brass liners. Blade stamped "PRESTO" over "PAT. JAN 30-40" over "MADE IN USA" back reads "GEO. SCHRADE" over "KNIFE CO INC" over "B'P'T, CONN". Bone handles enhance value.
Mint value: $650

Model # 5500. Bowtie with Brown Swirl celluloid handles, nickel silver bolsters and brass liners. Blade stamped "PRESTO" over "PAT. JAN 30-40" over "MADE IN USA" back reads "GEO. SCHRADE" over "KNIFE CO, INC" over "B'P'T, CONN". Rare bolster configuration adds to value. **Mint value: $625**

Model # 6000. Fishtail with Maroon Swirl celluloid handles and brass liners. Blade stamped "PRESTO" over "PAT. JAN 30-40" over "MADE IN USA" back reads "G. SCHRADE" in an arch over "B'PORT, CT". **Mint value: $500**

Model # 6000. Fishtail with Red celluloid handles and brass liners. Blade stamped "PRESTO" over "MADE IN USA" back reads "G. SCHRADE" in an arch over "B'PORT, CT". Red is a popular color with collectors. **Mint value: $500**

Model # 4000. Fishtail with Tortoise celluloid handles, nickel silver bolsters and steel liners. Blade stamped "PRESTO" over "PAT. PEND-G" back reads "G. SCHRADE" in an arch over "B'PORT, CT". **Mint value: $575**

Model # 6000. Fishtail with Coffee & Cream celluloid handles and steel liners. Blade stamped "PRESTO" over "PAT. JAN 30-40" over "MADE IN USA" back reads "G. SCHRADE" in an arch over "B'PORT, CT". **Mint value: $525**

Model # 4500. Fishtail with Brown Swirl celluloid handles, nickel silver top bolsters and steel liners. Blade stamped "PRESTO" over "PAT. JAN 30-40" over "MADE IN USA". Scarce bolster configuration adds to value. **Mint value: $600**

Model # 5000. Bowtie with Blue cell handles, nickel silver bolsters and brass liners. Blade stamped "PRESTO" over "PAT. JAN 30-40" over "MADE IN USA". **Mint value: $625**

4 ⅛" singles

The knives pictured here have the following in common: All measure 4 1/8" closed and 7 1/8" open. All have steel liners. They are stamped with one of the five following marking combinations.

A. "PRESTO" over "PAT. PEND-G" back "G. SCHRADE" over "B'PORT, CT". This is the rare, early Small Stamp.
B. "PRESTO" over "PAT. PEND-G" back "G. SCHRADE" over "B'PORT, CT". Regular size.
C. "PRESTO" over "PAT. JAN 30-40" over "MADE IN USA" back "GEO. SCHRADE" over "KNIFE CO. INC" over "B'P'T. CONN".
D. "PRESTO" over "MADE IN USA" back "G. SCHRADE" over "BRIDGEPORT" over "CONN".
E. "PRESTO" over "MADE IN USA" back "GEO. SCHRADE" over "BRIDGEPORT" over "CONN".

Jigged bone handles with steel bolsters and bail. Clip blade markings group B. Often referred to as a paratrooper knife, but I have not confirmed this. Has high collector interest. **Mint value: $625**

Jigged bone handles with steel bolsters. Clip blade markings group A. This is a pretty rare knife because of the early small stamp marking. You can also tell that it's older by the jig pattern. Even more scarce in this size than the 5" knife. **Mint value: $800**

Jigged bone handles with steel bolsters. Hawkbill blade markings group C. Rare to find the hawkbill blade with jigged bone handles. **Mint value: $700**

Black wormgroove plastic handles with steel bolsters and bail. Clip blade markings group C. These definitely were military issue as a paratrooper knife which adds interest as a double collectible. **Mint value: $625**

Black wormgroove plastic handles with nickel silver fixed-guard bolsters. Clip blade markings group C. The fixed guard knives are pretty rare and black seems to be harder to find than brain.
Mint value: $700

Black painted metal handles formed to look like stag with bail. Clip blade markings group E. Although this knife is commonly referred to as a paratrooper, I believe it to be the civilian version. **Mint value: $475**

5" singles

The knives pictured here have the following in common: All measure 5" closed and 8 3/4" open. All have clip blade and steel liners. All have one of the following five marking combinations:

A. "PRESTO" over "PAT. PEND-G" back "G. SCHRADE" over "B'PORT, CT". This is the rare, early Small Stamp.
B. "PRESTO" over "PAT. PEND-G" back "G. SCHRADE" over "B'PORT, CT". Regular size.
C. "PRESTO" over "PAT. JAN 30-40" over "MADE IN USA" back "GEO. SCHRADE" over "KNIFE CO. INC" over "B'P'T. CONN".
D. "PRESTO" over "MADE IN USA" back "G. SCHRADE" over "BRIDGEPORT" over "CONN".
E. "PRESTO" over "MADE IN USA" back "GEO. SCHRADE" over "BRIDGEPORT" over "CONN".

Jigged bone handles and steel bolsters. Blade markings group A. It's easy to tell that this is an early knife because of the rare "small stamp" on the tang. If compared to a regular Presto stamp the difference becomes obvious. **Mint value: $750**

Jigged bone handles and steel bolsters. Blade markings group B. **Mint value: $600**

Brain wormgroove plastic handles and steel bolsters. Blade markings group C.
Mint value: $550

Wormgroove bone handles and steel bolsters. Blade markings group B. This is a rare handle because of the light color and worming groove bone. I've only seen two of them.
Mint value: $700

Black painted metal handles formed to resemble stag with bail. Blade markings group D. I believe this to be a civilian model of the military paratrooper. Usually found with much of the paint rubbed off from use. This example most likely repainted. **Mint value: $450**

Brain wormgroove plastic handles with nickel silver fixed-guard bolsters. Blade markings group C. Knives with the fixed-guard bolsters are very scarce which enhances the value.
Mint value: $800

5" folding guard knives

Black wormgroove plastic handles with nickel silver bolsters and folding guards.
Blade markings group C. Very collectable knife.
Mint value: $750

Brain wormgroove plastic handles with nickel silver bolsters and folding guards.
Blade markings group C. The folding guards have high collector interest. The brain handles are slightly more common.
Mint value: $700

Jigged bone handles handles with nickel silver bolsters and folding guards.
Blade markings group C. Very collectable knife.
Mint value: $750

Boxes

Presto knife box which measures 4 ¾" x 3 ⅞" x 1 ⅜". It is marked ½ DOZ #2000 JS. Original boxes and advertising add interest to a collection and are quite valuable. These items were most often thrown away and those that were not are obviously quite fragile so few mint examples still exist. **Mint value: $250**

Presto knife box which measures 3 ⅝" x 2 ⅜" x 1 ¼". It is marked ½ DOZ #610. This box held 3 ⅜" single switchblades. **Mint value: $250**

Presto knife box which measures 4 ¾" x 3 ⅞" x 1 ⅜". It is marked ½ DOZ #6000 Stag. This box held jigged bone fishtail switchblades. Few of these boxes have survived the test of time.
Mint value: $250

Queen Cutlery Company

Titusville, PA   1918–Present

Queen Cutlery Company got its start in 1918 when several employees of the Schatt & Morgan Cutlery Company decided to start their own firm. They began making knives under contract for other companies right away and didn't even register a name for the company for four years. In 1922 they registered the name Queen City Cutlery Company Inc. and the business was going strong. Schatt & Morgan, on the other hand, was heading downhill and finally closed its doors in 1930. In 1932 Queen bought out the defunct company and moved their operations into the old Schatt & Morgan factory where they had been employees 14 years earlier. During the 1940s many companies were experimenting with different grades of stainless steel in an attempt to improve quality. Stainless steel is harder to work with and many grades will not hold a good sharp edge, but Queen discovered 440C stainless, which does hold a good edge, and they decided to use it for their blades and springs. Public opinion of stainless steel at that time was low because of the problems with keeping it sharp so Queen came up with and registered the name "Queen Steel" which was stamped on many of their knives. In 1945 the company name was changed to Queen Cutlery Company.

Queen, being a competitive company and not wanting to miss out on any areas of the pocketknife market, decided to get into the switchblade market. In 1948, Eric C. Erickson, one of the company's original founders, applied for a patent for a switchblade knife which he had designed. On November 14, 1950 he was granted U.S. patent # 2,530,236 for his design. Queen manufactured two versions of the Model 25 Jet push-button knife. One had a sliding safety and the other did not. Closed, the knife measures 5 inches and is a toothpick pattern with one end of the knife tapering down almost to a point. It is generally accepted that these knives were only made with black jigged plastic handles, but I've seen a few handled in candystripe celluloid, like the one featured in this book, that sure look good enough to be original. I haven't been able

No. 25 Jet Push Button Pattern with Safety Lock — Our own exclusive patented knife. Something brand new! Opens like a jet plane takes off. Double bolster, nickel silver finish with brass linings. Sturdily constructed. One heavy duty large clip blade 3-15/16 inches long. 5 inches long when closed.

to find any proof yet, though I've been searching. It certainly seems possible that some could have been made at the factory, either near the end of production, special order, or possibly just by an employee with extra time on his hands. Regardless, the candystripe celluloid is very popular with collectors and I've seen one of these sell for over $700 on an online auction where the black-handled ones would only bring $400 or so right now.

It is common to find these with proud blades (tip sticking out when closed) and they do not lock in the open position, but otherwise they work pretty well. There are a couple of different tang stamp varia-tions that you may run into. They should all have a big "Q" with dots and a crown over it. Many are also found with the stamp "Pat Pending" on the back tang. These knives are still not well known and I believe that most collectors undervalue them, but the knives will increase in value as collector interest increases. You should try to find one with a safety and one without if you want to have a good representation of the Queen switchblades in your collection. If you happen to run across one in candystripe celluloid you'll probably be very tempted to add that one to your collection also. It is a very attractive knife!

Candystripe celluloid handles with nickel silver bolsters and brass liners. Clip blade stamped with a "Q" with a crown over it and back reads "Pat Pending". Normally handled in black jigged plastic, this knife has gorgeous candystripe handles. Though possibly not original, they still add collector interest to the knife. No safety.
Mint value: $600

Black jigged plastic handles with nickel silver bolsters and brass liners. Clip blade stamped with a "Q" with a crown over it and back reads "Pat Pending". This knife features a sliding safety. **Mint value: $450**

R.C. Kruschke

Duluth, MN   1881–1921

Rudolph C. Kruschke was interested in switchblade knives at the time that they were just beginning to be manufactured in the United States. He was an entrepreneur who lived in Duluth, Minn. and he started a jewelry and pocket watch repair business there on Lake Ave in 1881. By 1889 he had expanded his business and moved to 16 West Superior where he opened a jewelry, music and gun store. It was around this time that he was joined in his business by his brother, Louis, a gunsmith. By 1891 the business had changed slightly to a jeweler, sporting goods and gunsmith/dealer. It was also in 1891 that he filed for a patent for his own switchblade design. On October 27, 1891 he was granted U.S. Pat # 462,141. This was only the ninth switch blade patent ever granted in the United States and it was just before George Schrade filed for his first switchblade patent. By 1899 his business shifted slightly again and he was listed as the proprietor of the City Gun Store. His products were listed as guns, revolvers, ammunition and sporting goods of all kinds, cutlery, etc. It was also in 1899 that Kruschke introduced the Brilliant Searchlight, which he invented and manufactured. He also dabbled in bicycle repair and locksmithing into the early 1900s.

I only know of one switchblade knife that Kruschke ever sold and it was not based upon his patent. I have included a copy of his patent for you to see. I believe that his "Northwestern" knife was actually made in Germany by Robert Klass Company as I have seen knives that looked nearly identical that were marked as Klass knives. In 1896 a man named Max Klass opened an office at 298 Broadway, New York, N.Y. Klass was an importer for the Robert Klass factory in Germany. This importer was in business for many years and it is my guess that they supplied R.C. Kruschke with knives bearing his name. I hope to discover that Kruschke actually did have some knives manufactured based upon his patent. There should be, at least, a prototype or two out there somewhere that would have been used for the patent process. If any of you happen to find one of them I would love to hear about it.

I was lucky enough to find an original advertisement for the R.C. Kruschke "Northwestern" knife in a sporting magazine from 1909 and have included a copy in this book. Unfortunately I do not have one of the original knives to feature. I have had opportunities to buy a couple of them in the past, but at the time I felt the $1,500 price tags were a bit high. Looking back now, that price doesn't seem so bad. Unfortunately we all pass up on opportunities we later regret. My experiences have taught me to be more open minded about prices of antique switchblades and since making that change I have had fewer regrets.

The City Gun Store finally ended up at 402 West Superior St and Rudolph was president of the company until he passed away on May 11, 1918. His son George A. Kristy was also involved in the business as secretary and treasurer among other things. He stayed on and helped his mother with the business for a few years before moving to Chicago to manage the Brilliant Search Light Company that his father started. The last listing found for City Gun Store in the Duluth City Directory was in 1921 and it listed his wife as the proprietor.

This advertisement was found in a sporting magazine from 1909 and features not only the Kruschke Northwestern knife, but also the Brilliant Search Light. They sure seem like bargains now don't they!

R. C. KRUSCHKE.
CLASP KNIFE.

No. 462,141.   Patented Oct. 27, 1891.

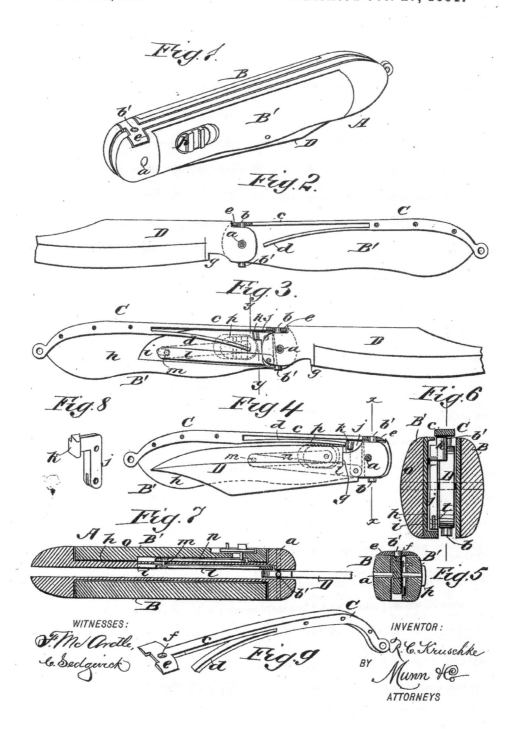

The NORTHWESTERN CLASP KNIFE

Remington

Bridgeport, Conn.   1816–Present

Eliphalet Remington started Remington Arms Company back in 1816. Remington was strictly an arms and munitions company until WWI, when they started making bayonets for the war effort. By the end of WWI Remington was geared up for production, but was lacking in orders. The taste of manufacturing edged weapons during the war planted an idea in the minds of management and Remington made its first pocketknives in 1920 at theplant in Bridgeport, Conn. Controlling interest in the company was sold to the DuPont Company in 1929.

Remington made hundreds of different patterns of pocketknives in the 1920s and 1930s. Outside of the switchblade world they are probably best known for their Bullet knives, which have become very collectable and valuable. It seems only natural that since the factory was located in Bridgeport, Conn., the same city where the George Schrade Knife Company was located, that they would contact George when they decided to add switchblades to their line of knives. The George Schrade Knife Company made all of Rem-ington's switchblade knives under contract. They made seven basic patterns:

1. 2 ⅞-inch pullball   #R17
2. 3 ⅜-inch single   #R8055
3. 3 ⅜-inch double   #R8065 (celluloid),
    #R8063 (jigged bone)
4. 4-inch fishtail   #R655
5. 4-inch bowtie   #R645
6. 4 ⅛-inch single   #R2303
7. 5-inch single   #R2403

Other than a few prototype knives that might be floating around, these seven patterns with just a few handle variations represent the entire Remington switchblade lineup. Remington remained in the knife manufacturing business until 1940 when they sold their entire cutlery division and materials to Pal Blade Company whose headquarters were at 595 Madison Ave, New York, N.Y. Coincidentally, Remington's executive offices were also in New York City at 25 Broadway.

See also: G. Schrade Knife Co. and Presto section.

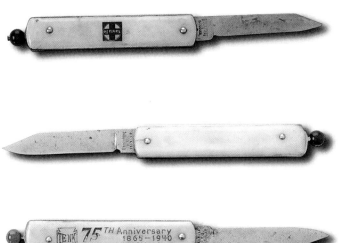

White plastic handles with brass liner and backspring cover and black ball. Clip blade stamped "Remington" over "PAT 11-9-37" back reads "Quick Point" over "St. Louis". Advertising on the handles is "Santa Fe" inside a blue cross, inside a white circle, inside a blue box. Most likely was an advertising giveaway. Rare marking adds to the value.
Mint value: $450

Model # R17. White plastic handles with brass liner and backspring cover and black "8" ball. Clip blade stamped "Remington" over "PAT 11-9-37" back reads "R17".
Mint value: $350

Model # R17. White plastic handles with brass liners and backspring cover and red ball. Clip blade stamped "Remington" over "PAT 11-9-37" back reads "R17". Handles have advertising for TENK Hardware of Quincy, IL and mentions their 75ᵗʰ anniversary. **Mint value: $375**

Model # R8055. Onyx celluloid handles with brass liners. Clip blade stamped "Remington" back reads "R8055". Blade originally etched "Remington Master Knife" on front. **Mint value: $650**

Model # R8063. *Stag handles with brass liners. Remington called them stag, but they were really jigged bone. Spear/pen blade combination. Spear blade stamped "Remington" back reads "R8063". Pen blade stamped "Remington" on the front and back is blank. Spear blade etched "Remington Master Knife" on front. Measures 3 ⅜" closed and 7 ¹⁄₁₆" open. Jig pattern on bone is pretty distinctive, although Presto did use it on some of their own knives also. **Mint value: $750**

Model # R8065. *Horn Pyralin handles with brass liners. Spear/pen blade combination. Spear blade stamped "Remington" back reads "R8065". Pen blade stamped "Remington" and back is blank. Master blade etched "Remington Master Knife" on the front. Measures 3 ⅜" closed and 7 ¹⁄₁₆" open. **Mint value: $700**

Model # R645. *Candystripe Pyralin handles with nickel silver fixed guard bolsters and brass liners. Clip blade stamped "Remington" back reads "R645". This bowtie measures 4" closed and 7 ¼" open. Candystripe handles are extremely rare and very popular with collectors. **Mint value: $1,500**

Model # R2303. *Stag handles with steel bolsters and liners. Clip blade stamped "Remington" back reads "R2303". Blade etched "Remington Master Knife". Measures 4 ⅛" closed and 7 ⅛" open. This size was more heavily used than the 5" model which makes it very hard to find one with an unsharpened blade. **Mint value: $1,400**

Model # R655. *Horn Pyralin handles with nickel silver bolsters and brass liners. Clip blade marked "Remington" back reads "R655". This fishtail measures 4" closed and 7 ¼" open. This example is damaged on the front so I included a picture of the back handle. **Mint value: $900**

Model #R2403. *Stag handles with steel bolsters and liners. Clip blade stamped "Remington" back reads "R2403". Blade etched "Remington Master Knife". Measures 5" closed and 8 ¾" open. **Mint value: $1,300**

*Terms used by Remington to describe the handles in their literature.
   i.   Pyralin- Celluloid
   ii. Horn Pyralin- Horn celluloid
   iii. Stag- Jigged bone

Russell Automatic Knife Co.

Chicago, IL   1891–1895

The Russell Automatic Knife Company existed in Chicago, Ill. from 1891 to 1896. The offices were located at 1204 Ashland and the factory had a view of Lake Michigan from 1133 School Street. Charles F. Haines was the president and C.M. Weaver was the secretary. As far as I know they only produced one model of switchblade knife, which was designed and patented by Albert H. Russell of Kansas City, Mo. This switchblade measured just over 3 inches closed and had a large oval button in the handle that released the blade. I suspect that this company was started with high hopes for exposure at the 1893 Columbian Exposition in Chicago. Many companies put their wares on display at the exposition and the exposure they got there actually "made" or "broke" many of them. Apparently it didn't go well for the Russell Automatic Knife Co. because they went out of business shortly after the expo and Russell switchblades are near the top of the list of extremely rare knives. Ironically, the patent was applied for on Jan. 24, 1893 and U.S. Patent # 552,928 was granted on Jan. 14, 1896, which was **after** they went out of business. If you're ever lucky enough to find one I'd say that a Russell in fair condition would be worth in excess of $1,000 and a nice one would be in excess of $5,000. Mint: much more!

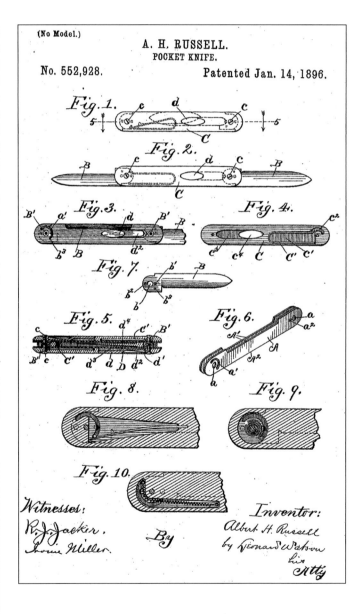

Observations 3 ⅛-inch single blade knife	
1.	Oval shaped release button.
2.	Metal handles, most likely aluminum.
3.	On the rarity scale it is a 10 of 10

Schrade Cutlery Company

Walden, NY   1904–1946

In 1904 George Schrade sold his remaining control of the Press Button Knife Co. to the Walden Knife Company of Walden, N.Y., where the knives were being made. Along with two of his brothers, Jacob Louis Schrade and William Schrade, he started the Schrade Cutlery Company. Up until this time most knife companies had been dependent upon moving water to power their machinery, which explains why most early companies were located along streams or rivers. With the introduction of electricity and other means of powering the machinery, many companies were now able to operate wherever they pleased and George and his brothers pleased to operate at the end of Main Street in Walden, N.Y. On Feb. 13, 1906 George was granted U.S. Patent # 812,601 for a switchblade knife design. This was his second recorded switchblade patent. He received his third switchblade patent on Feb. 26, 1907 and it was U.S. Patent # 845,130. These patents were the foundation for switchblade production at Schrade Cutlery Co. and the most significant thing about them was the introduction of a safety to keep the knife from opening accidentally.

Interestingly, the knives pictured in these two patents appear totally different than the knives that were produced from them. The first patent shows a knife similar in appearance to his first patent of 1892, for which he had recently sold his rights. It shows the release button on the end of the knife just like it is on the Press Button Knife Co. knives. What they did use from this patent was the sliding safety, which moves back and forth between the handle and the liner, though the safety featured in the patent looks much different than the one actually used. The next patent has two things that are significant about it. A spring-actuated trigger (button) rocks on a pivot resting in supports and secured to the lining of the knife. Second it has a finger at the end of the trigger (button) that enters slots in the base of the blade allowing locking and release of the blade. Both of these features can be found in the Schrade Cutlery Co. switchblades. Both of the patents

featured a spring fastened by a rivet to throw the blades open.

These two patents were the foundation for the Schrade Safety Knife. It is possible to more accurately date some of the earliest Schrade Cutlery Co. switchblades because of changes in the patent information stamped on the blades. Some of the earliest Schrade Cutlery Co. switchblades, which were made between 1904 and 1907, were stamped with the two patent numbers "812,601" & "845,130" on the small blade. Schrade switchblades that were made between 1907 and 1910 were mostly stamped "US PATS" over "Feb 13, 06" over "Feb 26, 07". Schrade switchblades made between 1910 and 1916 were stamped "US PATS" over "Feb 13, 06" over "Feb 26, 07" over "Sept 13, 10". Schrade switchblades manufactured between 1916 and 1946 were stamped "US PATS" over "Dec 21, 09" over "Sept 13, 10" over "June 6, 16". Though these patent dates will help you to date many of the knives, it is not 100% accurate. Some parts may not have been used up right away and therefore some of the earlier dated blades may be found on knives that were assembled at a later time, but for the most part it is pretty accurate. The tang stamp on the larger switchblades was actually smaller prior to 1910, than on the later knives. Comparing the stamps on the 4 7/8-inch knives in this section shows this difference.

George Schrade sold his interest in the company shortly after 1910 and traveled to Europe with his son George M. Schrade. Most of Schrade Cutlery Company's switchblade patents after this time were granted to William and J. Louis, with J. Louis receiving most of them. By 1916 there was no longer any trace of George's patents on Schrade Cutlery Co. knives. Oddly, one of the three patent dates that are found on most of Schrade's switchblades was granted to someone else. United States Patent # 943,990 was granted to J.A. Nell on Dec 21, 1909. Through research I have linked J.A. Nell to the Walden Knife Company around 1900, so I suspect that he either made the move with George when he left

Walden Knife Co., or more likely, that he was later persuaded to join the team at Schrade Cutlery Company. Whatever the case, his patent proved useful to Schrade Cutlery Co. and is found on the majority of the Schrade switchblades made between 1916 and 1946

Schrade Cutlery Co. continued to prosper and in 1917 they opened another factory in Middletown, N.Y. and the fourth Schrade brother, Joseph, was put in charge. J. Louis and William had a joint switchblade patent on Sept 13, 1910. It was U.S. Pat # 969,909. J. Louis was granted U.S. Pat # 1,185,725 on June 6, 1916. Shortly after that George Schrade returned to the United States from Germany and wasted no time in designing and patenting another switchblade knife, the Fly Lock on March 5, 1918. Since George had sold his interest in Schrade Cutlery Co. before leaving for Europe, he had to find someone else to help him manufacture his new knife. (See Flylock Knife Co. section for more info)

With the onset of the Great Depression, Schrade Cutlery Co. felt the pinch and was forced to shut down the Middletown factory in 1932. Shortly after that J. Louis was granted his next switchblade patent #1,931,360 on Oct 17, 1933. J. Louis received his final switchblade patent on Dec 8, 1942. It was US Pat # 2,304,601. These last two patent dates do not show up on any of the Schrade Cutlery Co. switchblades, but the number from the last patent, 2,304,601 does show up on some Schrade Walden knives, including the back tang of some fishtails and on some doubles.

Schrade Cutlery Co. manufactured a large variety, as well as a large number, of switchblades between 1904 and 1946. In all there are 10 different switchblade patterns, with many variations in blades, handles, bolsters and liners. The 10 basic patterns are:

1. 2 ⅞-inch double
2. 3 ⅜-inch single
3. 3 ⅜-inch double
4. 3 ¾-inch single
5. 3 ¾-inch double
6. 4-inch fishtail
7. 4-inch bowtie
8. 4 ¼-inch single
9. 4 ⅞-inch single
10. 4 ⅞-inch single with folding guards

You would have a good representation of Schrade Cutlery Company switchblades with one of each of these 10 patterns. To try to collect every variation they made would be nearly impossible since there are hundreds of variations on these 10 patterns. I'm still working on compiling a complete list, but it may be impossible since some were made in very small numbers some one-of-a-kind knives were also produced. Many of these rare variations are hidden away in private collections and will seldom be seen by others. I am currently working to compile a list of Schrade switchblade models that is as complete as possible, in hopes that I will have the opportunity to include it in another book on these knives.

Over the years Schrade Cutlery Co. used bone with several slightly different jig patterns. One of the most distinctive is the one used on knives made prior to 1911, which I refer to as their Zigzag pattern. I have tried to include knives with as many different jig patterns as I could so that you can see the differences and become more familiar with them. As near as I can tell there were at least six different jig patterns used on the knives marked Schrade Cutlery Co. and a couple of more on their contract knives. Probably the most common one was the Peachseed pattern, which gets its name from its appearance. It looks very similar to the outside of a dried peach seed. This pattern is seen on knives made after 1916. Though the jig patterns themselves don't have a large affect on the value, they do

WORKS AT WALDEN, N. Y.

KEY TO NUMBERING SYSTEM

(a). The first figure of a number indicates the number of blades in the knife, as follows:—

    1 represents a 1 blade knife
    2 represents a 2 blade knife (both blades in one end)
    3 represents a 3 blade knife (3 blades in one end)
    7 represents a 2 blade knife (1 blade in each end)
    8 represents a 3 blade knife (2 blades in one end and
        1 blade in the other end)
    9 represents a 4 blade knife (2 blades in each end)

(b). The second and third figures of a number indicate the pattern or style of knife:

    Example! In No. 2013 the second and third figures indicate our Easy Opener Pattern as per the cut in this catalogue. In No. 7113 the second and third figures indicate our Sleeveboard Pattern as per the cut in this catalogue.

(c). The last figure of a number indicates the kind of handle, as follows:—

1—Cocobola	4—Celluloid	7—Stained Bone
2—Ebony	5—White Bone	8—Buffalo Horn
3—Bone Stag	6—Mother of Pearl	9—Miscellaneous

(d). The kind or color of celluloid handles is indicated by a letter or letters after the fourth figure (which is always No. 4 for celluloid handles.) as follows:

    7434C, indicates Cocobola Celluloid, etc.

The following is a list of celluloid colors, with letters indicating same, in alphabetical order:—

AC—Assorted Colors	J—Red-White-Amber Striped
AP—Abalone Pearl	K—Brown Lined Cream
B—Black (Ebony)	M—Marine Pearl
BLUE—Blue Pearl	MB—Mottled Blue
BP—Black Pearl	MR—Mottled Red
BRNZ—Bronze	O—Onyx
C—Cocobola	P—Smoked Pearl
GL—Goldaleur	PP—Persian Pearl
GP—Golden Pearl	S—Tortoise Shell
G—Green Pearl	US—Red-White-Blue Striped
H—Black and White Striped	W—(White) Ivory
HORN—Horn	X—Mottled Green

(e). Miscellaneous handles are indicated by a letter or letters after the figure 9, as follows: 7439GSIL, indicates a nickel silver handle, etc.

KEY TO NUMBERING SYSTEM (Continued)

The following is a list of miscellaneous handles, with letters indicating same:—

BR—Solid Brass	GS—Genuine Stag
GM—Gun Metal	GSIL—Nickel Silver
GOLD—12 Karat Gold Plate	SS—Sterling Silver

(f). A fraction at the end of a number indicates the kind of blade substituted for a spear pocket blade, as follows:—

    Example! No. 2157¼ would indicate our regular No. 2157 with a Spey blade substituted for Spear blade. No. 2173¾ would indicate our regular No. 2173 with a Clip blade substituted for Spear blade, etc.

The following is a list of fractions used:—

¼—Spey Pocket	¾—Clip Pocket
½—Sheepfoot Pocket	⅞—Razor Point Pocket

(g). Patterns which are made up in Shadow, Tip and Bolster styles are indicated as follows:—

    A Shadow knife is a knife with the handles extending to the ends of the inner metal linings and has neither small nickel silver tips, bolsters or caps.
    To indicate a knife with nickel silver tips add the letter T to the shadow number. Example: 7113 indicates a shadow Sleeveboard knife, No. 7113T equals the same knife but with nickel silver tips.
    To indicate a bolster knife, add the letter B. Example: No. 7113B equals the same knife with bolsters or caps added.
    The above only applies on the knives that are made in this way, such as Sleeveboard patterns, Senator patterns, etc.

(h). "S" prefixed to a number indicates a *Special* combination or finish.

(i). "SS" prefixed to a number indicates a knife with Stainless Steel Blades and Springs.

(j). "CHAIN" or "CH" added to a number indicates a knife with a chain.

(k). "EO" added to a number indicates an Easy Opener knife, that is usually manufactured without Easy Opener notch hollow.

(l). "LB" added to a number indicates the substitution of a Leather Borer or Punch for a cutting blade.

(m). "SHACKLE" or "SHACK" added to a number indicates a knife with a shackle, which is used to attach knife to watch chain.

(n). "B" prefixed to a number indicates a knife with brass linings that is usually manufactured with steel linings.

(o). "F" prefixed to a number indicates a knife with nail file blade that is usually manufactured with cutting blades.

---

play a part, and some of the earlier patterns are harder to find and create extra collector interest. The Zigzag is my personal favorite.

One question that keeps popping up in the knife collecting world has to do with a name that is found on the handles of many switchblade knives. Anyone who's been collecting Schrade doubles for very long has probably seen the name "Bruce H. Seabright" on the handle of a knife. Nobody seemed to know who he was or why his name seems to be on so many old switchblades. I knew I had to try to solve this mystery, so I tracked down Bruce H. Seabright, the son of the man in question. It turns out that Bruce H. Seabright Sr. owned a car dealership in Wheeling, W.V. in the 1940s, '50s and '60s. He sold GMC trucks, Cadillacs and Oldsmobiles, mainly. He believed in "word of mouth" advertising and he liked to give his customers something useful with his name on it to help accomplish this. Apparently he was fond of switchblades.

This name can also be found on Schrade Walden and Presto doubles with a couple of variations. One variation also has "Cincinnati 1252-145" and I've also seen "Exchange 1452-1453" which I would guess are phone numbers from the 1930s and 1940s when these knives were made.

The last Schrade Cutlery Co. switchblades were made around 1946, when the Schrade Cutlery Company was sold and became the Schrade Walden Cutlery Company. The last Schrade Walden switchblades were made in 1957 with the exception of MC1 paratrooper knives made for the U.S. Government. Camillus took over this contract around 1960. In 1958 all operations and equipment were moved to Ellenville, N.Y. In 1985 the name of the company was changed to Imperial Schrade Corp. and all operations were combined under one roof in Ellenville, N.Y. Though Schrade Cutlery Company is gone, Imperial Schrade is still going strong today.

2 ⅞" doubles

The knives pictured here have the following in common: All measure 2 ⅞" closed and 6" open. Spear/pen blade combination unless otherwise noted. Spear blade stamped "SCHRADE" over "CUT. CO." over "WALDEN, NY" back is blank. Pen blade stamped "US PATS" over "Dec 21, 09" over "Sept 13, 10" over "June 6, 16". All have nickel silver liners.

Model # 7444STG. Stagged celluloid handles. **Mint value $475**

Model # F7444W. Ivory celluloid handles. Letters "ORA" on front handle. **Mint value $475**

Model # 7444AC. Blueberries & cream celluloid handles. Very attractive handles are popular with collectors. **Mint value $525**

Model # F7444D. Green pearl & black mottled celluloid handles. Spear/file blade combination. **Mint value: $550**

Model # 7444E. Marine pearl & black mottled celluloid handles. **Mint value: $475**

Model #7444K. Brown lined cream butter and molasses celluloid handles. **Mint value: $450**

Model # 7444M. Marine pearl celluloid handles. Not to be confused with genuine pearl, which is more valuable. I have placed the two next to each other for easy comparison. **Mint value: $500**

Model # 7444X. Green mottled celluloid handles. **Mint value: $450**

Model # 7449GSil. Nickel silver handles with Deluxe scroll pattern. **Mint value: $500**

Model # 744SS SHAC. Sterling silver handles with Deluxe scroll pattern and shackle. **Mint value: $550**

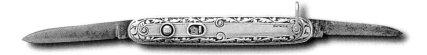

3 ⅜" singles

The knives pictured here have the following in common: All measure 3 ⅜" closed and 5 ⅞" open. Clip blade stamped "SCHRADE" over "CUT. CO." over "WALDEN, NY" back reads "US PATS" over "Dec 21, 09" over "Sept 13, 10" over "June 6, 16".

Model # 1404 3/4 B. Black celluloid handles with brass liners. Single blade 3 ⅜" models are scarce.
Mint value: $600

Model # 1404 3/4 H. Smoked pearl celluloid handles with brass liners. **Mint value: $600**

Model # 1404 3/4 H. Black & white striped celluloid handles with brass liners.
Mint value: $600

Model # 1404 3/4 K. Brown lined cream butter and molasses celluloid handles with brass liners.
Mint value: $600

3 ⅜" doubles

The knives pictured here have the following in common: All measure 3 ⅜" closed and 7 1/8" open. Spear/pen blade combination unless otherwise noted. Spear blade stamped "SCHRADE" over "CUT. CO." over "WALDEN, NY" back is blank. Small blade stamped "US PATS" over "Dec 21, 09" over "Sept 13, 10" over "June 6, 16" unless otherwise noted. Brass liners unless otherwise noted.

Model # 7404AC. Green & pink mottled celluloid handles. Blade etched "M.A. Steel"
Mint value: $475

Model # F7444W. Ivory celluloid handles. Letters "ORA" on front handle. **Mint value $475**

Model # 7444AC. Blueberries & cream celluloid handles. Very attractive handles are popular with collectors. **Mint value $525**

Model # F7444D. Brown stagged handles. Spear/file blade combination. **Mint value: $550**

Model # 7444E. Black stagged celluloid handles. **Mint value: $475**

Model #7444K. Brown lined cream celluloid handles. **Mint value: $450**

Model # 7444M. Marine pearl celluloid handles. Not to be confused with genuine pearl, which is more valuable. I have placed the two next to each other for easy comparison. **Mint value: $500**

Model # 7446. Genuine pearl handles. Often called Mother of Pearl, these handles are highly sought after by collectors. Very rare handles on this model. **Mint value: $700**

Model # 7444X. Faux woodgrain celluloid handles. **Mint value: $450**

Model # 744SS SHAC. Black mottled celluloid handles. **Mint value: $450**

Model # 7404W. Ivory celluloid handles. Pen blade stamped "US PATS" over "Feb 13, 06" over "Feb 26, 07". Knife made prior to 1910. **Mint value: $475**

Model # 7404PP. Persian pearl celluloid handles. Pen blade stamped "US PATS" over "Feb 13, 06" over "Feb 26, 07" over "Sept 13, 10". Knife made prior to 1916. Rare and interesting color enhances value. **Mint value: $500**

Model # 7404AC. Brown & cream swirl celluloid handles. Attractive and unusual handles add slightly to value. **Mint value: $475**

Model # 7404X. Green mottled celluloid handles. **Mint value: $450**

Model # 7404W. Ivory celluloid handles. Blade etched "Clydesvale Steel".
Mint value: $475

Model # 7404BLUE. Blue pearl celluloid handles with advertising for McKenna Brass & Mfg Co Inc of Pittsburgh, PA on the front handle and Shields Automatic Bottling Machine on the back. Pen blade stamped "US PATS" over "Feb 13, 06" over "Feb 26, 07" over "Sept 13, 10". Advertising adds to the value. **Mint value: $475**

Model # 740SSD. Deluxe sterling silver handles with nickel silver liners. **Mint value: $600**

Model # 7406. Genuine Mother of Pearl handles. Pen blade stamped "US PATS" over "Feb 13, 06" over "Feb 26, 07" over "Sept 13, 10". Knife made prior to 1916. Value enhanced by age and genuine pearl handles. **Mint value: $700**

Model # 7406T. Genuine Mother of Pearl handles and nickel silver tip bolsters. Pen blade stamped "US PATS" over "Feb 13, 06" over "Feb 26, 07". Knife made prior to 1910. Value enhanced by age, pearl and tip bolsters. **Mint value: $750**

Model # 7404AC. I believe this to be a salesman's sample. Different colored woodgrain celluloid handles on each side with nickel silver tip bolsters. One side is burgundy and the other is green. Pen blade stamped "US PATS" over "Feb 13, 06" over "Feb 26, 07". Value enhanced because of added interest. **Mint value: $650**

Model # 7404C. Cocobola celluloid handles with advertising for Red Cut Superior Tobacco. **Mint value: $500**

Model # 7404D. Green pearl & black celluloid handles. **Mint value: $475**

Model # SS7404K. Brown lined cream celluloid handles, commonly called Butter & Molasses. This knife is special because it has stainless steel blades and most Schrade blades are carbon steel. The back tangs of both blades are stamped "Stainless" over "Steel". I would estimate the ratio between stainless and none stainless doubles at about 75 to 1. **Mint value: $750**

Model # 7409GSil. Nickel silver handles with Deluxe scroll pattern. Another name for it is German silver. One way to tell the difference between nickel silver and sterling is to check the liners. Nickel silver handled knives have brass liners. Also sterling knives should be stamped on the handle "Sterling Silver". **Mint value: $550**

Model # 7404W. Ivory celluloid handles with advertising for Dolly Varden Chocolates. Pen blade stamped "US PATS" over "Feb 13, 06" over "Feb 26, 07". Interesting vintage advertising combined with ivory cell handles enhances value. **Mint value: $550**

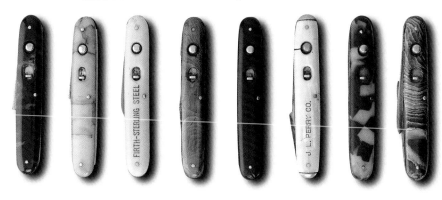

Group of eight knives to show more handle variety.

3 ¾" singles

Model # 1504 3/4 K. Brown lined cream celluloid handles with brass liners. Clip blade stamped "SCHRADE" over "CUT. CO." over "WALDEN, NY" back reads "US PATS" over "Dec 21, 09" over "Sept 13, 10" over "June 6, 16". Single blade knife in this size is much harder to find than a double with ratio of about 15 to 1. **Mint value: $700**

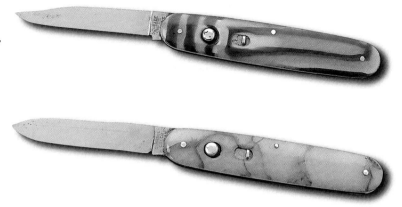

Model # 1504AC. Dreamsicle celluloid handles with brass liners. Spear blade stamped "SCHRADE" over "CUT CO" over "WALDEN, NY" back reads "US PATS" over "Feb 13, 06" over "Feb 26, 07". Single blade knives with clip are rare, but with a spear blade is even rarer. **Mint value: $800**

3 ¾" doubles

The knives pictured here have the following in common: All measure 3 ¾" closed and 8 ⅛" open. All have brass liners. All main blades stamped "SCHRADE" over "CUT CO" over "WALDEN, NY" back blank. All secondary blades stamped with one of three patent date combinations which are:
- A. "US PATS" over "Feb 13, 06" over "Feb 26, 07"
- B. "US PATS" over "Feb 13, 06" over "Feb 26, 07" over "Sept 13, 10"
- C. "US PATS" over "Dec 21, 09" over "Sept 13, 10" over "June 6, 16"

Model # 7503 3/4. Bone stag handles with clip/pen blade combination. Pen blade markings group A. **Mint value: $600**

Model # 7503T. Bone stag handles with nickel silver tip bolsters and spear/pen blade combination. Pen blade markings group B. **Mint value: $625**

Model # 7503. Bone stag handles with spear/pen blade combination. Pen blade markings group A. **Mint value: $600**

Model # 7503 3/4 B. Bone stag handles with full nickel silver bolsters and clip/pen blade combination. Pen blade markings group C. The full bolsters are very popular with collectors and will bring a small premium. **Mint value: $700**

Model # 7504STG. Stagged celluloid handles with spear/pen blade combination. Pen blade markings group C. Schrade didn't start using these handles until the late 1940s so they are hard to find. **Mint value: $575**

*Model # 7504GP. Golden pearl
celluloid handles with spear/pen
blade combination. Pen blade
markings group A.* **Mint value: $550**

*Model # 7504 3/4 S. Tortoise
celluloid handles with clip/pen
blade combination. Pen blade
markings group B.*
Mint value: $575

*Model # 7504AC. Horn celluloid
handles with clip/pen blade
combination. Pen blade
markings group C.*
Mint value: $575

*Model # 7504AC. Dreamsicle
celluloid handles with spear/pen
blade combination. Pen blade
markings group C.*
Mint value: $550

*Model # 7504P. Smoked pearl
celluloid handles with nickel silver
tip bolsters and spear/pen blade
combination. Pen blade markings
group B.* **Mint value: $575**

*Model # 7506B. Genuine Mother
of Pearl handles with full nickel
silver bolsters. Spear/pen blade
combination. Pen blade markings
group C.* **Mint value: $850**

*Model # 7504WS. Number represents two
different knives because this knife has
two different handles. I believe it to be a
salesman's sample. Front handle is Ivory
celluloid and back handle is Tortoise
celluloid with nickel silver tip bolsters on
both. It has been handled a lot, but the
blades don't show any wear. Spear/pen
blade combination. Pen blade markings
group B.* **Mint value: $700**

*Model # 7504 3/4 K. Brown lined
cream celluloid handles with clip/
pen blade combination. Pen blade
markings group C.*
Mint value: $550

*Model # 7504J. Candystripe celluloid
handles with spear/pen blade
combination. Pen blade markings
group C. Candystripe handles
enhance value quite a bit on this
knife.* **Mint value: $800**

*Group of 12 knives
to show more
handle variety.*

4" fishtails

The knives pictured here have the following in common: All measure 4" closed and 7 3/16" open. Clip blade stamped "SCHRADE" over "CUT CO" over "WALDEN" back stamped "US PATS" over "Dec 21, 09" over "Sept 13, 10" over "June 6, 16". All have brass liners.

Model # G1514K. Brown lined cream celluloid handles and nickel silver bolsters on this bowtie.
Mint value: $575

Model # G1514C. Cocobola celluloid handles and nickel silver bolsters on this bowtie. **Mint value: $575**

Model # 1514STG. Stagged handles with no bolsters on this fishtail.
Mint value: $600

Model # 1514C. Cocobola celluloid handles and nickel silver bolsters on this fishtail. **Mint value: $525**

Model # 1514G. Green pearl celluloid handles and nickel silver bolsters on this fishtail. Attractive handles add interest to this knife.
Mint value: $550

Model # 1514AC. Grey pearl celluloid with red splotches and nickel silver bolsters on this fishtail. **Mint value: $525**

4 1/4" singles

The knives pictured here have the following in common: All measure 4 1/4" closed and 7 3/8" open, approximately. All have clip blades that are stamped "SCHRADE" over "CUT. CO." over "WALDEN, NY" on the front. The back of the tang has one of three different set of patent dates and they are as follows:

A. "US PATS" over "Feb 13, 06" over "Feb 26, 07"
B. "US PATS" over "Feb 13, 06" over "Feb 26, 07" over "Sept 13, 10"
C. "US PATS" over "Dec 21, 09" over "Sept 13, 10" over "June 6, 16"

Model # 1553 ¾. Bone stag handles with steel bolsters and liners. Back tang markings group C. This size knife tended to see more use over the years than the larger 4 ⅞" model which was too big to carry in your pocket comfortably. Therefore they got sharpened more and often used until worn out. It is much harder to find a mint example of this knife than the larger version.
Mint value: $750

Model # 1554 ¾ STG. Stagged celluloid handles with steel bolsters and liners. Back tang markings group C. Due to its late introduction, this handle material, on this knife, is not as common as jigged bone handles. This knife is much harder to find than the later Schrade Walden version. **Mint value: $650**

No picture: Model # 1553. Same as above only it has a spear blade instead. Clip bladed knives outnumber the spear bladed ones by at least 25 to 1. These are very hard to find. **Mint value: $950**

4 ⅞" singles

The knives pictured here have the following in common: All measure 4 ⅞" closed and 8 ¾" open, approximately. All have clip blades that are stamped "SCHRADE" over "CUT. CO." over "WALDEN, NY" on the front. The back of the tang has one of three different set of patent dates and they are as follows:

A. "US PATS" over "Feb 13, 06" over "Feb 26, 07"
B. "US PATS" over "Feb 13, 06" over "Feb 26, 07" over "Sept 13, 10"
C. "US PATS" over "Dec 21, 09" over "Sept 13, 10" over "June 6, 16"

Model # 1543 ¾. Bone stag handles with steel liners and bolsters. Back tang markings group A. This knife was made prior to 1911. The jig pattern on the bone is quite distinctive on the earlier knives and this one has a zigzag appearance to it. These earlier patterns are harder to find than the post 1916 ones. **Mint value: $725**

Model # 1543 ¾. Bone stag handles with steel liners and bolsters. Back tang markings group A. Jig pattern on the bone is quite distinctive on the earlier knives and I have included this knife to show another early variation. **Mint value: $700**

Model # 1543 ¾. Bone stag handles with steel liners and bolsters. Back tang markings group B. This knife was most likely made between 1910 and 1916 and you can see another early variation on the jig pattern. **Mint value: $700**

Model # 1543 ¾. Bone stag handles with steel liners and bolsters. Back tang markings group C. This is a post-1916 model and you will observe yet another jig pattern. This is a "tight" Peachseed pattern. **Mint value: $650**

Model # 1543 ¾. Bone stag handles with steel liners and bolsters. Back tang markings group C. This is a post-1916 model and it also has a Peachseed jig pattern, but you will notice that the pattern is "looser" than the previous knife. **Mint value: $650**

Model # 1613 ¾. Bone stag handles with steel liners and bolsters. Back tang markings group C. "Schrade Hunting Knife" is etched on the sabre-ground clip blade. Handles have the "loose" Peachseed jig pattern. The unique blade combined with bone handles makes this knife very popular with collectors. **Mint value: $800**

Model # 1544 ¾ STG. Stagged celluloid handles with steel liners and bolsters. Back tang markings group C. Schrade switched over to the imitation stag celluloid handles not long before they became Schrade Walden in 1946. Due to this fact there are not a lot of these knives that are stamped Schrade Cut Co. around which adds to their collector interest and value. **Mint value: $700**

Model # 1544 ¾ BM. Buttermilk celluloid handles with nickel silver bolsters and steel liners. Back tang markings group C. Most of the large Schrades were made with bone handles and the ones handled in celluloid are very hard to find and will command high prices. Originally etched "Forest King." **Mint value: $1000**

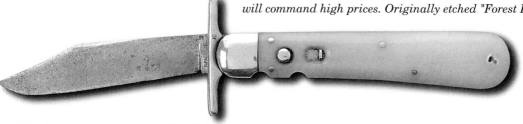

Model # G1544 ¾ BM. Buttermilk celluloid handles with nickel silver bolsters and guards and steel liners. Back tang markings group C. Blade originally etched "Hunter's Pride". This is a great combination with the folding guards and the rarer celluloid handles and is one of my personal favorites. **Mint value: $1,200**

Model # G1544 ¾ M. Marine pearl celluloid handles with steel bolsters and liners. Back tang markings group C. Blade originally etched "Hunter's Pride". This is one of the most sought after Schrade switchblades. The handles are gorgeous and combined with the folding guards it really is a rare combination. **Mint value: $1,300**

Model # G1544 ¾ STG. Stagged celluloid handles with steel bolsters and liners and nickel silver guards. Back tang markings group C. Blade originally etched "Hunter's Pride". Most of the knives you see that look like this will have a Schrade Walden tang stamp. Schrade Cut Co didn't start using this black jigged handle material until the 1940s so they were only produced for a short time.
Mint value: $800

Model # G1543 ¾. Bone stag handles with nickel silver bolsters and guards and steel liners. Back tang markings group C. Blade originally etched "Hunter's Pride". Though jigged bone handles are very popular with collectors, the fact that bone is the most common handle used on this pattern makes it one of the least valuable. **Mint value: $850**

Model # 1544 ¾ AC. Yellow translucent celluloid handles with nickel silver bolsters and steel liners. Back tang markings group C. Blade etched "FOREST KING". I believe that this color of celluloid is even rarer on this pattern than the Buttermilk or Marine pearl. **Mint value: $950**

Miscellaneous

These rare switchblade related items are a wonderful addition to any collection. These items add interest to the knives and make wonderful displays. Since it doesn't seem likely that you'd ever find these items in unused condition I have opted to list their values in good used condition.

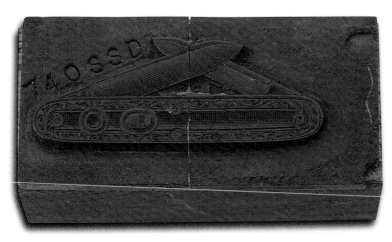

Original printing block used for catalog and other advertising. This block features a Schrade Cut Co. model # 740SSD switchblade. **Used value: $100**

*Original printing block used for catalog
and other advertising. This block features
a Schrade Cut Co. model # 1553 ¾
switchblade.* **Used value: $100**

*Original printing block used for catalog
and other advertising. This block features
a Schrade Cut Co. model # 1514 fishtail
switchblade.* **Used value: $100**

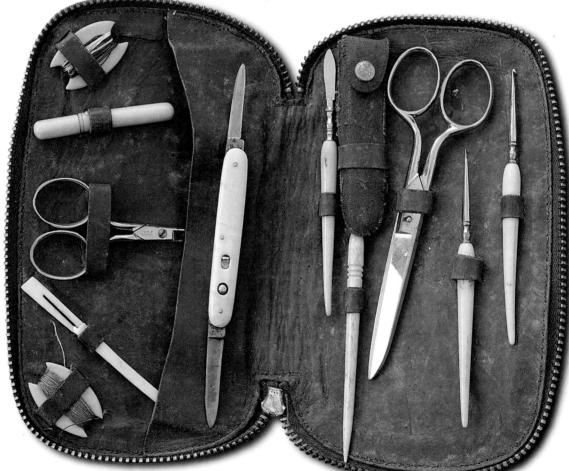

*Old sewing kit with
ivory handled tools
and a Schrade model
7444M switchblade
in an authentic
leather purse. It
would appear that
this kit has been
together for over
75 years.*
Used value: $350

Schrade Walden Cutlery Corp

A division of: Imperial Knife Associated Companies Inc.

Walden, NY & Ellenville, NY   1946–Present

World War II helped to set the stage for the coming together of Ulster Knife Co. and Imperial Knife Co., who had combined forces to meet the needs of the U.S. Government during the war. Ulster was able to secure orders for knives, but supplies were being rationed during the war and being a small company they had trouble getting enough materials to make them. Imperial was a much larger company and they were able to acquire the materials that Ulster needed, so it was only natural that the ambitious Baer brothers made a deal to work with Imperial to fill their orders. In 1942 the two companies joined to form the Imperial Knife Associated Companies Inc. The collaboration proved fruitful and in 1946 Albert Baer, then President of the firm initiated the purchase of Schrade Cutlery Company of Walden, N.Y. They renamed this company Schrade Walden Cutlery Corp. and continued manufacturing knives in the Walden plant until 1958 when that plant was shut down and all operations were moved to Ellenville, N.Y. The manufacture of switchblades had already stopped before this move. The last year that Schrade Walden manufactured switchblades was 1957.

The switchblade product line was altered slightly after Schrade Cutlery Co. became Schrade Walden Cutlery Co. The new line included eight basic patterns that were made in Walden between 1946 and 1957. Those are as follows:

1. 2 7/8-inch double — model 744 and 745
2. 3 3/8-inch double — models 740, 741 & 742
3. 3 3/4-inch double — model 750
4. 4-inch fishtail — models 150 & 151
5. 4-inch bowtie — model 152
6. 4 1/8-inch single — model 155
7. 4 7/8-inch single — model 154
8. 4 7/8-inch Hunter's Pride — model 153 with folding guards.

The 2 7/8-inch doubles made by Schrade Walden seem to outnumber the larger 3 3/8-inch model. The most common handles for this pattern seem to be metal with the elaborate DeLuxe scroll pattern. They made these using three different metals. Many were made with sterling silver handles and have this stamped on the handles. Many were made with nickel silver handles and can usually be identified by the liners. The sterling handled knives have nickel silver liners and it appears that most, if not all, of the nickel silver-handled knives in this size have brass liners. The third metal used has a different look to it than the two silvers and I believe that it is stainless steel, but I have not been able to confirm this yet. It looks like aluminum, but it is magnetic so it would seem likely that it is stainless steel. The liners are nickel silver on this knife also.

You will encounter two different stampings on most of the Schrade Walden switchblades. The earliest one is "SCHRADE" over "WALDEN" over "NY", which was used from 1946 until about 1950 when they added "USA" after "NY". So the other stamp is "SCHRADE" over "WALDEN" over "NY, USA". You'll also find "Stainless" on some of the paratrooper switchblades.

The 3 3/8-inch doubles, as previously mentioned, were made in lesser numbers and limited color variety. Most of these that you will come across will be handled in butter and molasses celluloid, stagged celluloid or silver. This makes the assorted colors more collectable since they are scarce. One thing that seems unusual is most of these knives only have one stamp on the front tang of the main blade and no other markings. You may find some of the pen blades stamped "Schrade Walden". Another thing that shows up in random places is "US PAT" over "2304601", which was J. Louis Schrade's last patent. There are also some knives that have Schrade Cutlery Co. patent dates including "June 6, 16" stamped on the back. These most often show up on 2 ⅞-inch doubles and 4-inch fishtails. This might be explained if we assume that they were thrifty and did not want to waste any leftover parts from Schrade Cutlery Co. Meaning that any Schrade Walden knives with these Schrade Cutlery Co. patent dates were probably made around 1947, or so. Seems like a fair conclusion, but it is only an educated guess at this point and not a proven fact.

In 1956 Schrade substituted Delrin for the black jigged celluloid they commonly referred to as "stagged" handles. Unfortunately the Delrin is more prone to shrinkage and the majority of them ended up shrinking and cracking by the pins before the material stabilized. The earlier black jigged celluloid handles did not shrink as much or crack as easily as the Delrin. Delrin was used for less than two years on the switchblade knives before production was stopped. Even though many of the Delrin handles that you come across on these knives will be cracked, they are still quite collectible because there are not a lot of them around and it is an important knife to those collecting all handle materials or variations.

In 1957 Schrade Walden stopped production on switchblade knives. At that point all remaining switchblade production within Imperial Knife Associated Companies was now at the Imperial plant in Providence, R.I. There seem to be a few Schrade Walden models floating around that have an Imperial tang stamp. There is a 2 ⅞-inch model featured in this book and I've heard from other collectors that they've also been seen in a 3 ⅜-inch double. I've spoken with experts at Imperial Schrade and the only explanation that they could come up with was that a limited number of these knives were likely made at Schrade Walden by request of Imperial Knife Co. Felix Mirando of Imperial Knife Co. was friends with a Senator named Pastore, whose name is on the knife that I have featured in this book. It would seem likely that Felix, as a favor, ordered the knives for his friend. I'm anxious to see other examples of this oddity and I hope that some of you readers will let me know if you come across any.

In 1985 the name of the company was changed to Imperial Schrade Corp. and all operations were combined under one roof in Ellenville, N.Y. See also: Schrade Cut Co. and Imperial Knife Co. sections.

The knives pictured here have the following in common: All measure 2 ⅞" closed and 6" open. All are spear/pen blade combination unless otherwise stated. Spear blade stamped "SCHRADE" over "WALDEN" over "NY, USA" and back is blank. Pen blades blank unless otherwise noted.

Model # 745. Brown lined cream celluloid handles with nickel silver liners.
Mint value: $425

Model # 745. Coffee & cream celluloid handles with brass liners. The pen blade is stamped "US PAT" over "2304601". Some added interest because of color and stamp.
Mint value: $450

Model # 744. Sterling Silver handles with Deluxe scroll pattern with nickel silver liners and shackle for attaching to chain.
Mint value: $550

Model # 744. Nickel Silver handles with Deluxe scroll pattern and brass liners. Nickel silver often looks gold in color when photographed, especially in low light.
Mint value: $500

Model # 744. Stainless steel handles with Deluxe scroll pattern and nickel silver liners. This one has a spear/file blade combination which enhances value. **Mint value: $500 without file blade $450**

3 ⅜" doubles

The knives pictured here have the following in common: All measure 3 ⅜" closed and 7 ⅛" open. Spear/pen blade combination with spear stamped "SCHRADE" over "WALDEN" over "NY, USA" back is blank. Pen blade has no markings unless otherwise noted. All have brass liners.

Model # 741. Brown lined cream celluloid handles. **Mint value: $475**

Model # 742. Stagged celluloid or Delrin handles. **Mint value: $500**

Model # 741. Abalone pearl celluloid handles. **Mint value: $550**

Model # 741. Coffee & cream celluloid handles. **Mint value: $525**

3 ¾" doubles

The knives pictured here have the following in common: All measure 3 ¾" closed and 8 ⅛" open. Main blade stamped "SCHRADE" over "WALDEN" over "NY, USA" back blank. The pen blade is not marked unless otherwise noted. All have brass liners.

Model # 750. Stagged celluloid or Delrin handles. Clip/pen blade combination. Pen blade is stamped "US PATS" over "Dec 21, 09" over "Sept 13, 10" over "June 6, 16". The stagged handles are less common than other handles on this pattern. **Mint value: $650**

Model # 750. Green pearl celluloid handles. Spear/pen blade combination. Striking color enhances some collector interest in this knife. **Mint value: $625**

Model # 750. Golden pearl celluloid handles. Clip/pen blade combination.
Mint value: $625

4" fishtails

The knives pictured here all have the following in common: All measure 4" closed and 7 ⅜" open. Clip blade which is stamped "SCHRADE" over "WALDEN" over "NY" back reads "US PAT" over "2304601" unless otherwise noted. All have brass liners.

Model #150. Stagged celluloid or Delrin handles and nickel silver bolsters. This is the second variation in stampings before they added "USA" and before they switched to Delrin. **Mint value: $550**

Model #150. Stagged celluloid or Delrin handles and nickel silver bolsters. In addition to the tang stamp listed above, this knife also has "USA" after "NY. **Mint value: $550**

Model #151. Brown lined cream celluloid handles with nickel silver bolsters. **Mint value: $500**

Model # 151. Blueberries & cream celluloid handles with nickel silver bolsters. Back tang stamped "US PATS" over "Dec 21, 09" over "Sept 13, 10" over "June 6, 16". **Mint value: $500**

Model # 151. Red, black & grey mottled celluloid handles with nickel silver bolsters. Back tang stamped "US PATS" over "Dec 21, 09" over "Sept 13, 10" over "June 6, 16". **Mint value: $500**

Model #150. Stagged celluloid or Delrin handles. Back tang stamped "US PATS" over "Dec 21, 09" over "Sept 13, 10" over "June 6, 16". **Mint value: $525**

PROTOTYPE. Jigged bone handles with nickel silver bolsters and brass liners. RARE spear blade is not finished and is stamped "SCHRADE" over "WALDEN" over "NY, USA" off center. I have a letter that authenticates this knife as a prototype that came from the Research and Development Deptartment at Schrade. It is rough and unfinished as one might expect from a prototype pattern that never made it to the production stage. This knife is one of a kind and it's hard to place a value on it, but it is obviously of great interest to collectors. I believe there are collectors who would pay more than $2,500 for it.

The knives pictured here have the following in common: All measure 4 ¼" closed and 7 ⅜" open. Clip blade stamped "SCHRADE" over "WALDEN" over either "NY" or "NY, USA". Back tangs are blank.

Model # 155. Stagged celluloid or Delrin handles with steel bolsters and liners. This is the later stamping with "NY, USA". **Mint value: $525**

Model # 155. Stagged celluloid handles with steel bolsters, liners and bail. This is earlier stamp with only "NY". It is commonly referred to as a paratrooper. **Mint value: $575**

Model # 155. Stagged celluloid or Delrin handles with steel bolsters, liners and bail. This is the later stamp of "NY, USA". It is commonly referred to as a paratrooper. **Mint value: $575**

Smooth red celluloid handles with nickel silver bolsters and folding guards and brass liners. Knife has the earlier "NY" stamping. The blade is etched "Craftsman 9450". Obviously a contract knife made for Sears. This knife has high collector interest. **Mint value: $850**

Smooth orange celluloid handles with nickel silver bolsters and folding guards and brass liners. Knife has the later "NY, USA" stamping. I believe this blade was originally etched "Paratrooper" and was manufactured for the civilian market. **Mint value: $800**

Model # MC1 paratrooper. Orange jigged synthetic handles with steel liners and bail. Clip/shroud cutter combination with clip blade marked "SCHRADE" over "WALDEN" over "NY, USA" and also stamped "Stainless". Shroud cutter unmarked. **Mint value: $225**

Stagged synthetic handles with steel liners and bail. Clip blade stamped "SCHRADE" over "WALDEN" over "NY, USA" back stamped "Stainless". Unusual to find this style in single blade with black handles. **Mint value: $450**

4 ⅞" singles

The knives pictured here have the following in common: All measure 4 ⅞" closed and 8 ¾" open. Clip blade stamped "SCHRADE" over "WALDEN" over either "NY" or "NY, USA".

Model # 154. Stagged celluloid or Delrin handles with steel bolsters and liners. Later "NY, USA" stamping with back tang blank. **Mint value: $550**

Model # 154. Stagged celluloid or Delrin handles with steel bolsters and liners. Early "NY" stamping and back tang marked "154". Model number means it could be a salesman's sample, but I have not confirmed it so the price is for regular knife. **Mint value: $550**

Model # 153. Stagged celluloid or Delrin handles with steel bolsters and liners and nickel silver guards. Blade etched "Hunter's Pride" with the later "NY, USA" stamping and back is blank. The majority of these knives seem to have steel guards. **Mint value: $650**

Schrado

George Schrade Knife Company

Bridgeport, Conn.	1929–1956

Schrado appears to be an altered stamping used by the George Schrade Knife Company of Bridgeport, Conn. Since the knives also have German markings of "D.R.G. M." it seems likely they were manufactured for export to Germany. It is obvious that the knives were made at the George Schrade Knife Company because they are identical to their other 3 3/8-inch doubles. The first knife I found has only the Schrado and D.R.G.M. markings, but the second one actually has the G. Schrade markings on the small blade, which made this mystery very easy to solve. I would doubt that many, if any, were sold here in the United States. Most likely all but a few made it to Germany, so any that do show up here should be very collectible. I feel fortunate to be able to feature two of these knives here in this book. I suspect that there may be other variations on this stamping, possibly just the DRGM with no Schrade or Schrado markings.

Some collectors may not be interested in these knives because of the markings, but they were made in the United States, which makes them American knives. I also feel that the marking variations add much to their collector interest and I'm sure most of you will agree. The "o" is such a subtle change from Schrade that I'm sure many go undetected because they are mistaken for Schrade Cutlery Co. doubles. Hopefully now collectors will keep a closer watch for them and maybe more will start to surface, but for now they are quite scarce. It is my suspicion that the knives were made prior to WWII, which would put the dates of manufacture between 1929 and 1940, but I have not been able to confirm this.

Blue mottled celluloid handles with brass liners. Spear/pen blade combination with spear blade stamped "SCHRADO" over "D.R.G.M." back blank. Pen blade stamped "G. SCHRADE" in an arch over "B'PORT, CT" back blank. Measures 3 ⅜" closed and 7 1/16" open. **Mint value: $625**

Coffee & cream celluloid handles with brass liners. Spear/pen blade combination with spear blade stamped "SCHRADO" over "D.R.G.M." back blank. Pen blade stamped the same as spear blade. Measures 3 ⅜" closed and 7 1/16" open. **Mint value: $600.**

Shapleigh Hdw Co.

Diamond Edge Trademark

St. Louis, MO   1843–1960

I have abbreviated the title of this chapter to mimic the actual tang stamps of these knives. A.F. Shapleigh was the founder of this company. Although the company got its start in the 1840s, it wasn't until 1863 that it took on the name A.F. Shapleigh Hardware Company. The famous "Diamond Edge" trademark was introduced in 1864 and was used on both cutlery and tools. Over the years the company went through several name changes, but only one change is noteworthy for switchblade collectors. In 1902 the name was changed after A.F. Shapleigh passed away. Saunders Norvell, who had built his reputation in the hardware business at the E.C. Simmons Hardware Company, bought the Shapleigh Hardware Company and the name was changed to Norvell-Shapleigh Hardware Company. Norvell became president of the company in 1907. Sometime between 1904 and 1907 Norvell-Shapleigh Hardware Co. contracted Schrade Cutlery Co. of Walden, N.Y. to manufacture switchblade knives with the Norvell-Shapleigh tang stamping. Schrade manufactured at least two basic models for Norvell. I've seen some 3 ⅜-inch doubles as well as some 3 ¾-inch doubles, but there may also be some 4 ¼-inch or 4 ⅞-inch singles as well. Around 1920 the company name was changed to Shapleigh Hardware Company, which is the other name that is interesting to switchblade collectors. Around this time more models were added to Shapleigh's switchblade line. The knife patterns that bore the "Shapleigh Hdw Co" stamp were as follows:

1. 2 ⅞-inch double
2. 3 ⅜-inch double
3. 4-inch single (fishtail)
4. 4-inch single (bowtie)
5. 4 ¼-inch single (sportsman)
6. 4 ⅞-inch single (hunter)
7. 4 ⅞-inch single with folding guard (Hunter's Pride)

These knives also bore the Diamond Edge trademark and had a diamond with the letters "D-E" inside of it stamped on the front tang. Many of the master blades were also etched "Diamond Edge" with a "D-E" inside of the diamond. There were more than 20 variations made on these seven basic patterns, with different handle materials and blade combinations. In 1940 Shapleigh bought E.C. Simmons Hardware Company, also of St. Louis, and at that time they acquired the "Keen Kutter" trademark which they continued to use as a second line to their "Diamond Edge" products. Schrade Cutlery Co. also manufactured switchblade knives with the "Keen Kutter" markings. They made five basic models with these markings and more information on these can be found in the Keen Kutter section of this book.

In the 1940s switchblades were very popular and Shapleigh did their best to offer a large variety of knives to their customers. They even bought knives from George Schrade's company and featured them in their catalog. In the 1942 catalog they offered these as a third line of switchblades after their Diamond Edge and Keen Kutter lines. These knives were stamped "PRESTO Made in USA" and were manufactured by the George Schrade Knife Co. of Bridgeport, Conn. The Presto models featured in the catalog were as follows:

1. 4-inch single (fishtail)
2. 5-inch single with "Imitation Stag metal handles with Flintex finish"

This second model is often mistakenly called a MKII Paratrooper knife because of its resemblance to that knife as well as some confusion among collectors. I don't know if metal-handled Presto knives were ever produced under contract to the U.S. Government, but I'd imagine many of them did see actual military service one way or another.

Shapleigh hardware closed its doors when the business was liquidated in 1960. See also: Norvell Shapleigh and Keen Kutter sections.

3 ⅜" doubles

The knives pictured here have the following in common: All measure 3 ⅜" closed and 7 ⅛" open. Spear/pen blade combination with spear blade stamped "Shapleigh" over a diamond with "D-E" inside. "HDW" and "CO" underneath the diamond and back is blank. The spear blade was originally etched "DIAMOND EDGE" with a diamond between the words and "D-E" inside the diamond. Pen blade stamped with one of three sets of patent dates:

A. "US PATS" over "Feb 13, 06" over "Feb 26, 07"
B. "US PATS" over "Feb 13, 06" over "Feb 26, 07" over "Sept 13, 10"
C. "US PATS" over "Dec 21, 09" over "Sept 13, 10" over "June 6, 16"

Dreamsicle celluloid handles with brass liners. Pen blade markings group B. **Mint value: $575**

Cocobola celluloid handles with nickel silver bolsters and brass liners. Pen blade markings group A.
Mint value: $600

Model # B30. White grained celluloid ivory handles with nickel silver tip bolsters and brass liners. Pen blade markings group B. **Mint value: $600**

Model # B22. Sterling silver handles with Deluxe scroll pattern and nickel silver handles. Pen blade markings group C. **Mint value: $650**

Model # B19. Genuine pearl handles with brass liners. Pen blade markings group A. **Mint value: $700**

Model # B19. Genuine pearl handles with nickel silver tip bolsters and brass lines. Pen blade markings group A.
Mint value: $725

Model # B24. White grained celluloid (ivory) handles with brass liners. Knife has Spear/spey blade combination. Both blades have "SHAPLEIGH" over a diamond with "D-E" inside over "HDW" and "CO" backs blank. There are no patent dates on this knife. **Mint value: $675**

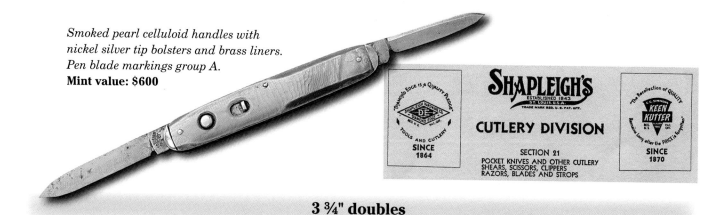

*Smoked pearl celluloid handles with
nickel silver tip bolsters and brass liners.
Pen blade markings group A.*
Mint value: $600

3 ¾" doubles

*Model # B44. White grained celluloid handles with full nickel silver bolsters and brass liners.
Clip/pen blade combination with above markings and group C patent markings.*
Mint value: $650

*Bone stag handles with full nickel silver bolsters and brass liners. Spey/leather punch blade
combination with above markings and group A patent markings. I don't know if this knife had
blade etch originally. Leather punch, full bolsters and bone handles combine to make a highly
collectable knife.* **Mint value: $950**

Larger knives

The knives pictured here have the following in common: Clip blade stamped "Shapleigh" over a diamond with "D-E" inside with "HDW" and "CO" underneath the diamond. The back is stamped "US PATS" over "Dec 21, 09" over "Sept 13, 10" over "June 6, 16". The blade was originally etched "DIAMOND EDGE" with a diamond between the words and "D-E" inside the diamond. Pen blade stamped with one of three sets of patent dates:

*Model # A9. Bone stag handles with steel
bolsters and liners. Measures 4 ¼" closed
7 ⅜" open.* **Mint value: $900**

*Model # A11. Bone stag handles with
steel bolsters and liners. Measures 4 ⅞"
closed and 8 ¾" open.* **Mint value: $800**

*Model # A10. Bone
stag handles with nickel silver
guards and steel bolsters and
liners. Measures 4 ⅞" closed
and 8 ¾" open.* **Mint value: $1,000**

Union Cutlery Company

Olean, NY

Wallace R. Brown and his brother Robert Emerson Brown started a cutlery jobber business in Little Valley, N.Y. in 1898. They operated under the names Brown Brothers and Union Razor Company. In 1902 they purchased the Tidioute Razor Company of Tidioute, Penn. They proceeded to manufacture razors and knives with stampings of "Union Razor Company" and "Tidioute Razor Company". The company name was changed in 1909 to "Union Cutlery Company" and in 1911 they began the move to Olean, N.Y. They were in production in Olean by 1912 and apparently decided that one company wasn't enough. Union Cutlery Company and Olean Cutlery Company were both owned by W.R. Brown and both located on the 400 block of Ninth Street in Olean. Some other names that the Brown brothers manufactured under are: Keenwell Brown, KA-BAR, Olcut, Viking and others.

They made switchblades with three markings on them: Union Cutlery Company, Keenwell Brown Mfg. and KA-BAR. Some of their switchblades have both the KA-BAR and Union Cutlery Co. stamps on them. There are two different switchblade models featured in this section with the Union Cutlery Company stamp on them, one being a lever-release and the other is a backspring-release with the famous Dogshead shield embedded in the jigged bone handle.

1. 4 ½-inch lever-release with stag handles
2. 4 ⅝-inch dogshead with bone stag handles (jigged bone)

I have not seen any of these knives stamped "Union Cut Co" on the front tang with handles other than those listed, but they could have been made with others. They manufactured knives based on the second pattern under contract for Aerial Cutlery Mfg. Co. of Marinette, Wis. in the 1920s. These knives were ordered without handles and some were not even assembled and sold as parts. Aerial was famous for the "picture knife" handles, which used clear celluloid over pictures, art and advertising to make knives that were quite popular around the turn of the 20th century. Aerial installed their own handles on these switchblades using celluloid and two different grades of stag on their model number K112 Sportsman's knife.

Through my research it became obvious that Wallace was more the businessman and Robert was more the knifeman and inventor. Robert had several knife patents over the years including at least three separate patents for switchblade knives. Union Cutlery Company began using the KA-BAR trademark in 1923 and it proved to be extremely popular. It was, in fact, so popular that the company name was changed to Kabar Cutlery in 1951. In 1966 the company was sold to Cole National Corporation of Cleveland, Ohio. The Union Cutlery Company name was revived in 1975 and has been used on commemorative and special-issue knives. The company again changed hands in 1996 when the Alcas Cutlery Company of Bradford, PA purchased them. The Union Cutlery Co. and Kabar names are still in use.

(Please see KA-BAR and Keenwell Brown sections for related information.)

Model # 21105. Stag handles with nickel silver bolsters and lever and brass liners. Measures 4 ½" closed and 8" open. Sabre-ground clip blade stamped "UNION CUT CO" in an arch over "OLEAN, NY".
Mint value: $2,600

Utica Cutlery Company

Utica, NY   1910–Present

This section will probably come as a surprise to most collectors, but it does merit inclusion in this book. The Utica Cutlery Company was founded in 1910 at 820 Noyes St, Utica, N.Y., which was formerly occupied by the Utica Burial Case Company. Jacob Agne was the first president of the new company and most of the officials and board members were longtime residents of Utica. Early production was limited to pocketknives. In 1921 Utica expanded their factory and product line to include fixed-blade knives and household cutlery, which they still make today. In 1929 they came out with a very unique knife called the "Pocket Pard" which had stainless steel blades and 14K gold-filled bolsters, shield and shackle and it retailed for $7.50, which was pretty much unheard of for a pocketknife at that time. Ulster took an active role in producing trench knives, bayonets and even gun parts for the war effort during WWII and later during the Korean War. Utica earned the Army-Navy "E" Award for excellence for their wartime efforts. In 1937 Utica registered the trademark name "Kutmaster" which was used with most of their pocketknives since that time.

What makes Utica Cutlery Company interesting to collectors of switchblade knives is their connection to the first patent in the United States for a lever-release switchblade knife in 1913. Carl W. Tillmanns, who was also associated with Camillus Cutlery Co., was one of the founders of Utica Cutlery Co. On April 24, 1912, less than two years after Utica began manufacturing knives, Carl applied for a patent for a lever-release spring-activated knife. United States Patent # 1,075,519 was granted to Carl Tillmanns on Oct.14, 1913 and he was listed as an assignor to Utica Cutlery Co. of Utica, NY. I have included a copy of the original patent so you will have an idea what the knife might look like. I have never actually seen one of these knives and I do not know if they ever made it into production. If they did make it to production, they must have been made in very small numbers because they are obviously quite rare. Since they had to make a model for the patent, there should be a prototype or two floating around somewhere. I know I'm not going to stop looking for one

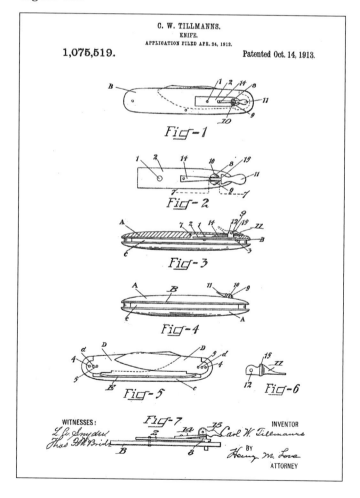

Wade & Butcher
Contracted by: Schrade Cut Co

Sheffield, England   1912–1920

The Butcher family was making razors in England as early as 1730. Robert Wade and William Butcher formed Wade & Butcher of Sheffield in 1818. Around 1830 the company name was changed to W&S Butcher Sheffield, but the Wade & Butcher stamping was still used on much of their cutlery. Another trademark for Wade & Butcher that is often found on their cutlery is a picture of an arrow and cross. The reason that this company is important to this book is that sometime in the early 1900s they contracted Schrade Cutlery Co. of Walden, NY to make some switchblade knives for them. I've only seen two patterns of switchblades with the Wade & Butcher markings and those are the 3 ⅜-inch double and the 4 ⅞-inch single-blade hunter. The large single-blades were

handled in jigged bone and the doubles were done in celluloid, for the most part. It is a bit confusing for collectors since many of these contracted knives are actually stamped "Forged in Sheffield England." The only way that there can be truth in this is if the blades were actually forged in England and shipped to the United States to be used by Schrade Cutlery Company, but this doesn't seem likely. I believe that the majority of the knives were contracted between 1912 and 1920 and they were definitely made right here in the good old USA! These knives are quite hard to find. I'd guess this could be partly due to the fact that most were probably exported to England combined with the short period that they were manufactured. These are very desirable old American-made switchblades.

Bone Stag handles with steel bolsters and liners. Clip blade stamped "WADE &" over "BUTCHER" back is marked "US PATS" over "Dec 21, 09" over "Sept 13, 10" over "June 6, 16".
Mint value: $1,400

Ivory celluloid handles with brass liners. Spear/pen blade combination. Spear blade stamped "WADE &" over "BUTCHER" over a circle, an arrow and a cross. The back is stamped "FORGED IN" over "SHEFFIELD" over "ENGLAND". The back of the pen blade has these markings also, but the front reads "US PATS" over "Feb 13, 06" over "Feb 26, 07" over "Sept 13, 10". The steel may have been forged in Sheffield, but these knives were made in the good old USA. These are an 8 of 10 on the rarity scale. **Mint value: $775**

Blade Illustration Guide
Flylock & Challenge

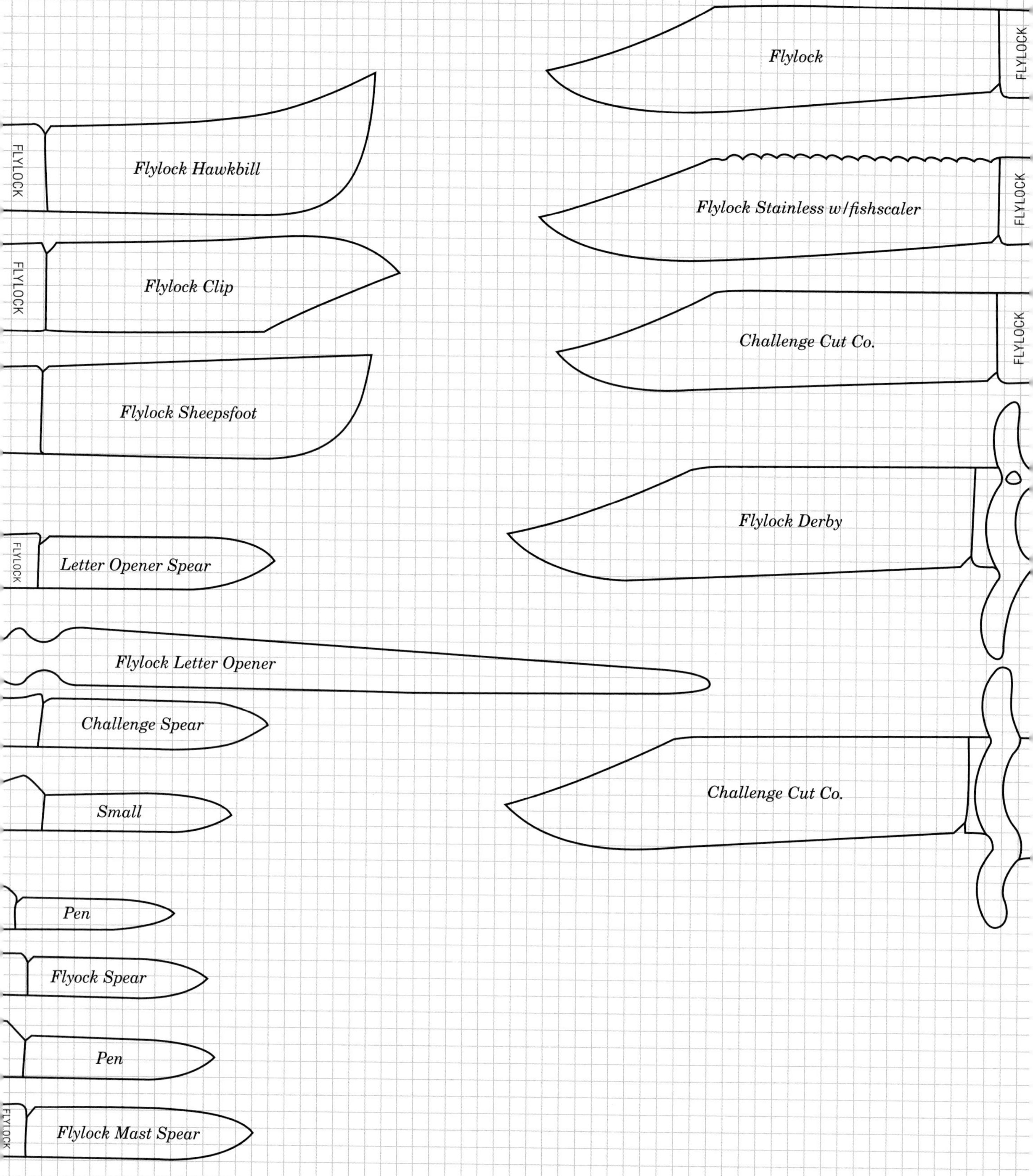

Flylock

FLYLOCK

Flylock Hawkbill

FLYLOCK

Flylock Stainless w/fishscaler

FLYLOCK

Flylock Clip

FLYLOCK

Challenge Cut Co.

FLYLOCK

Flylock Sheepsfoot

Flylock Derby

Letter Opener Spear

FLYLOCK

Flylock Letter Opener

Challenge Spear

Challenge Cut Co.

Small

Pen

Flyock Spear

Pen

Flylock Mast Spear

FLYLOCK

Remington/CASE

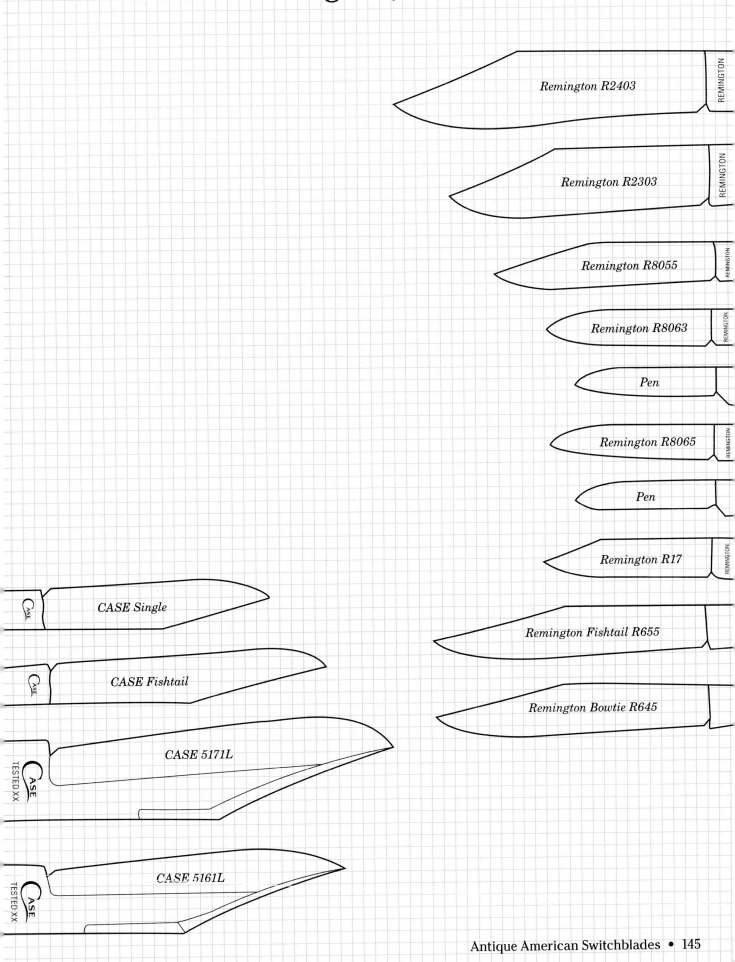

Remington R2403

REMINGTON

Remington R2303

REMINGTON

Remington R8055

REMINGTON

Remington R8063

REMINGTON

Pen

Remington R8065

REMINGTON

Pen

Remington R17

REMINGTON

CASE Single

CASE

CASE Fishtail

CASE

Remington Fishtail R655

Remington Bowtie R645

CASE 5171L

CASE
TESTED XX

CASE 5161L

CASE
TESTED XX

Edgemaster, Imperial & Hammer Brand

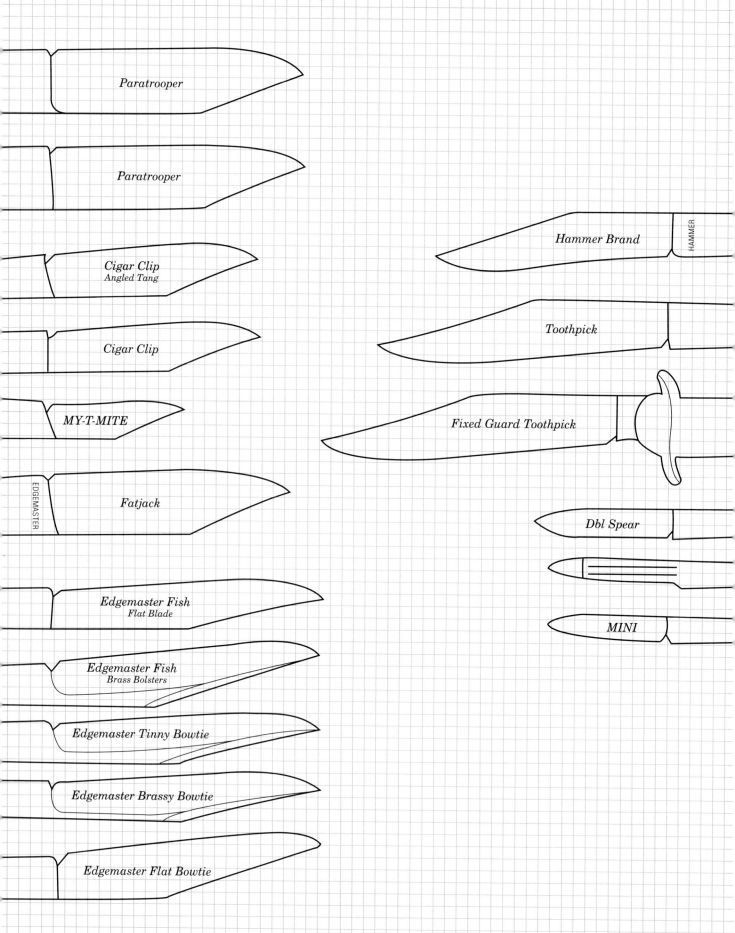

Paratrooper

Paratrooper

Cigar Clip
Angled Tang

Cigar Clip

MY-T-MITE

EDGEMASTER

Fatjack

Edgemaster Fish
Flat Blade

Edgemaster Fish
Brass Bolsters

Edgemaster Tinny Bowtie

Edgemaster Brassy Bowtie

Edgemaster Flat Bowtie

Hammer Brand

HAMMER

Toothpick

Fixed Guard Toothpick

Dbl Spear

MINI

Shursnap/Colonial

(Use Blade Grind As A Guide)

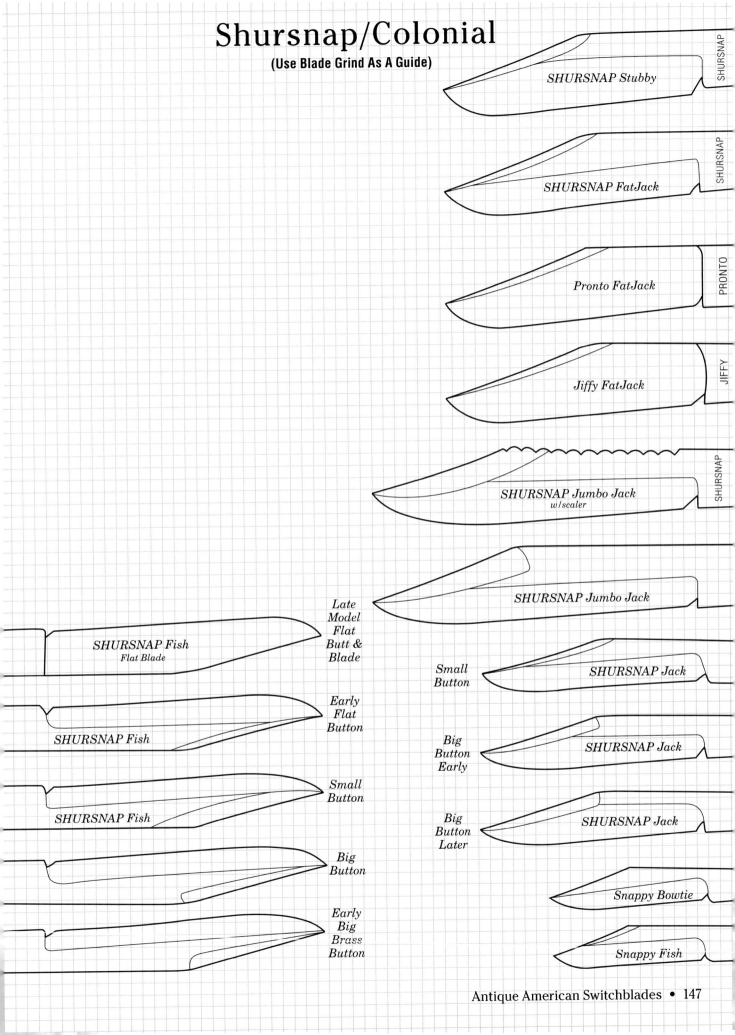

SHURSNAP Stubby

SHURSNAP

SHURSNAP FatJack

SHURSNAP

Pronto FatJack

PRONTO

Jiffy FatJack

JIFFY

SHURSNAP Jumbo Jack
w/scaler

SHURSNAP

SHURSNAP Jumbo Jack

Late Model Flat Butt & Blade

SHURSNAP Fish
Flat Blade

Small Button

SHURSNAP Jack

Early Flat Button

SHURSNAP Fish

Big Button Early

SHURSNAP Jack

Small Button

SHURSNAP Fish

Big Button Later

SHURSNAP Jack

Big Button

Snappy Bowtie

Early Big Brass Button

Snappy Fish

PRESTO

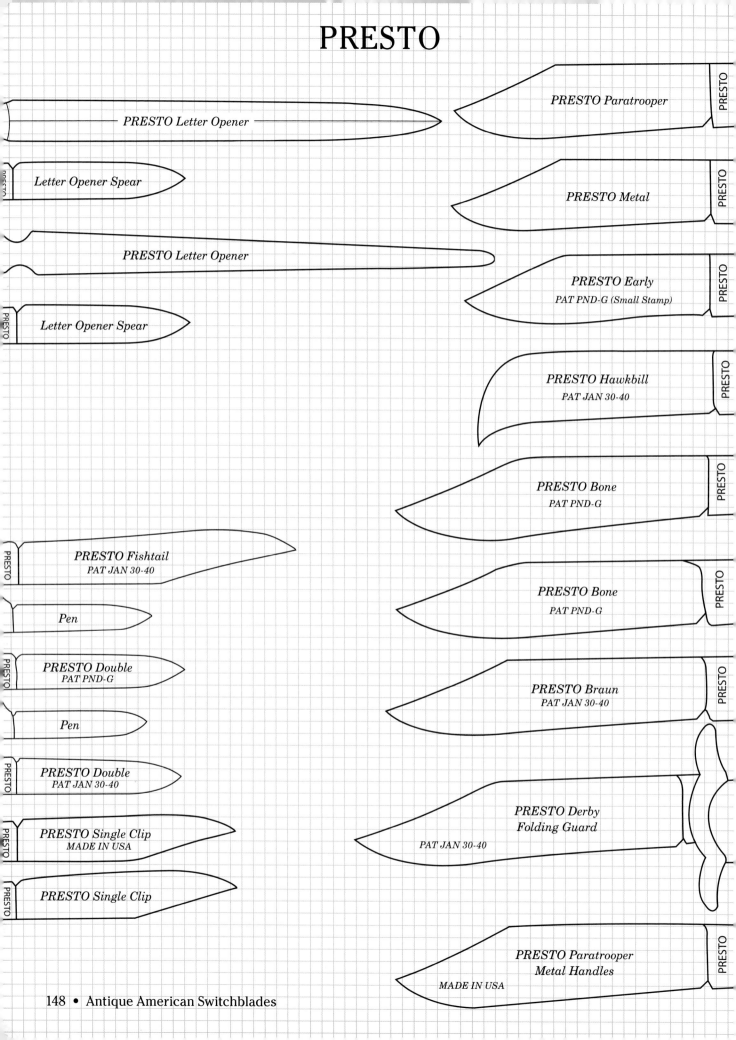

PRESTO Paratrooper

PRESTO Letter Opener

Letter Opener Spear

PRESTO Metal

PRESTO Letter Opener

PRESTO Early
PAT PND-G (Small Stamp)

Letter Opener Spear

PRESTO Hawkbill
PAT JAN 30-40

PRESTO Bone
PAT PND-G

PRESTO Fishtail
PAT JAN 30-40

Pen

PRESTO Bone
PAT PND-G

PRESTO Double
PAT PND-G

PRESTO Braun
PAT JAN 30-40

Pen

PRESTO Double
PAT JAN 30-40

PRESTO Single Clip
MADE IN USA

PRESTO Derby
Folding Guard

PAT JAN 30-40

PRESTO Single Clip

PRESTO Paratrooper
Metal Handles

MADE IN USA

Schrade Walden

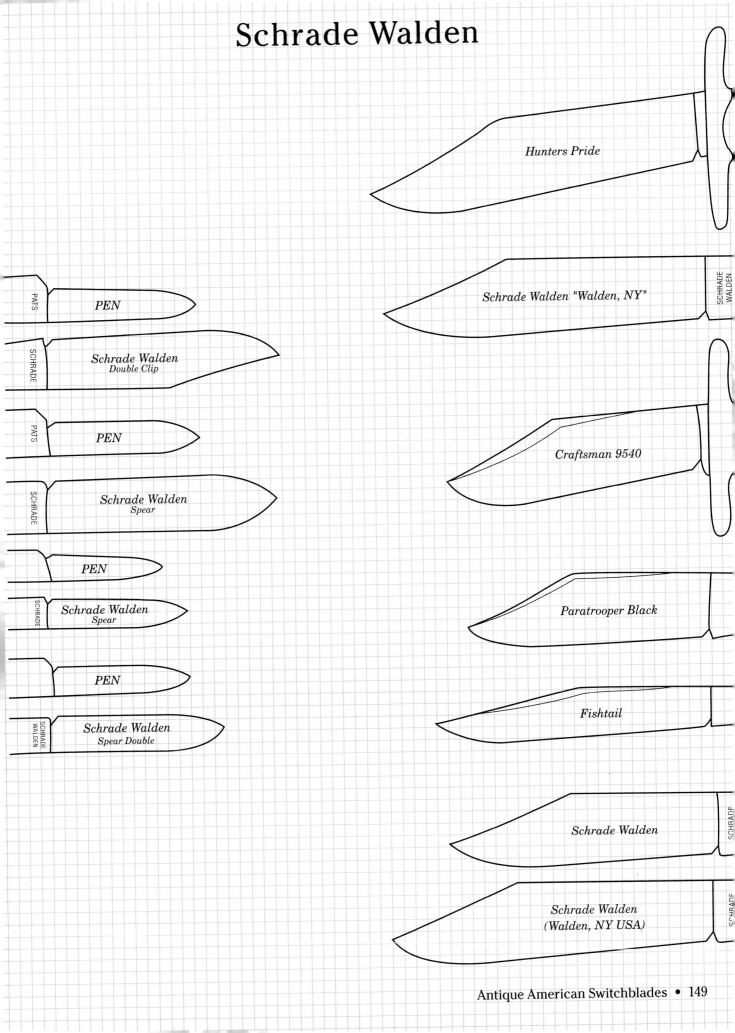

PATS

PEN

SCHRADE

Schrade Walden
Double Clip

PATS

PEN

SCHRADE

Schrade Walden
Spear

PEN

SCHRADE

Schrade Walden
Spear

PEN

SCHRADE
WALDEN

Schrade Walden
Spear Double

Hunters Pride

SCHRADE
WALDEN

Schrade Walden "Walden, NY"

Craftsman 9540

Paratrooper Black

Fishtail

SCHRADE

Schrade Walden

SCHRADE

Schrade Walden
(Walden, NY USA)

KA-BAR, Union Cut Co. & Keenwell

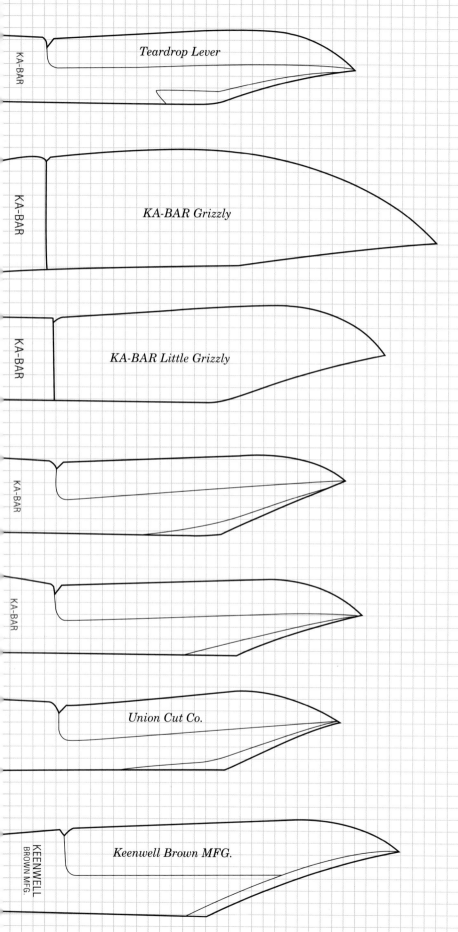

KA-BAR

Teardrop Lever

KA-BAR

KA-BAR Grizzly

KA-BAR

KA-BAR Little Grizzly

KA-BAR

KA-BAR

Union Cut Co.

KEENWELL
BROWN MFG.

Keenwell Brown MFG.

Schrade Cut Co.

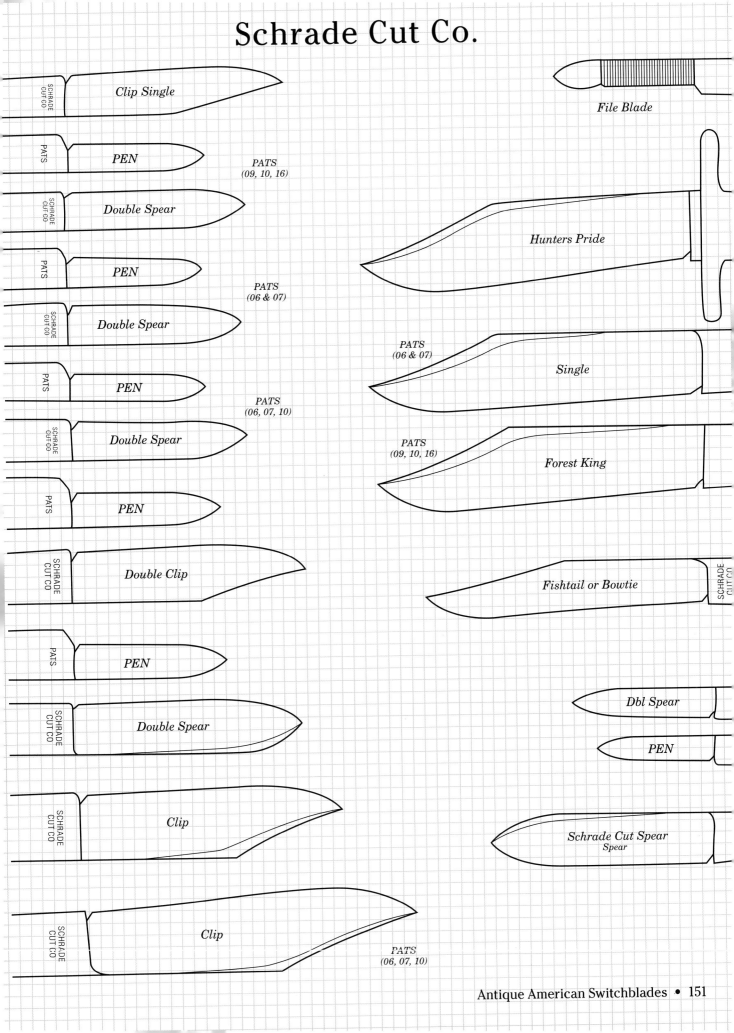

Clip Single

File Blade

SCHRADE CUT CO

PATS · PEN

PATS
(09, 10, 16)

SCHRADE CUT CO · Double Spear

Hunters Pride

PATS · PEN

PATS
(06 & 07)

SCHRADE CUT CO · Double Spear

PATS
(06 & 07)

Single

PATS · PEN

PATS
(06, 07, 10)

SCHRADE CUT CO · Double Spear

PATS
(09, 10, 16)

Forest King

PATS · PEN

SCHRADE CUT CO · Double Clip

Fishtail or Bowtie

SCHRADE CUT CO

PATS · PEN

Dbl Spear

SCHRADE CUT CO · Double Spear

PEN

SCHRADE CUT CO · Clip

Schrade Cut Spear
Spear

SCHRADE CUT CO · Clip

PATS
(06, 07, 10)

PRESS BUTTON KNIFE CO.
& CONTRACTS

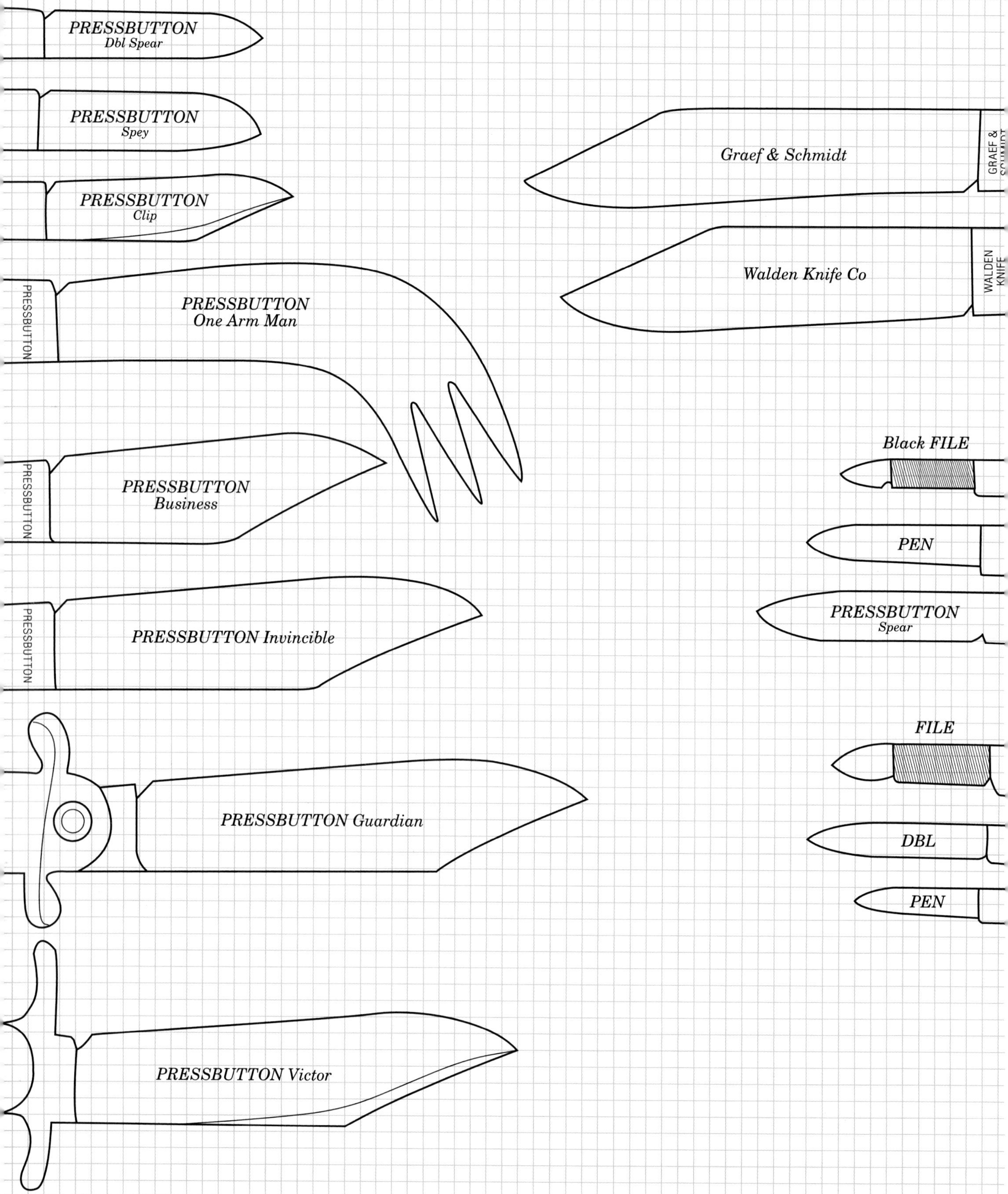

PRESSBUTTON
Dbl Spear

PRESSBUTTON
Spey

PRESSBUTTON
Clip

Graef & Schmidt

GRAEF & SCHMIDT

Walden Knife Co

WALDEN KNIFE

PRESSBUTTON

PRESSBUTTON
One Arm Man

Black FILE

PRESSBUTTON

PRESSBUTTON
Business

PEN

PRESSBUTTON
Spear

PRESSBUTTON

PRESSBUTTON Invincible

FILE

PRESSBUTTON Guardian

DBL

PEN

PRESSBUTTON Victor

Shapleigh & Norvell Shapleigh

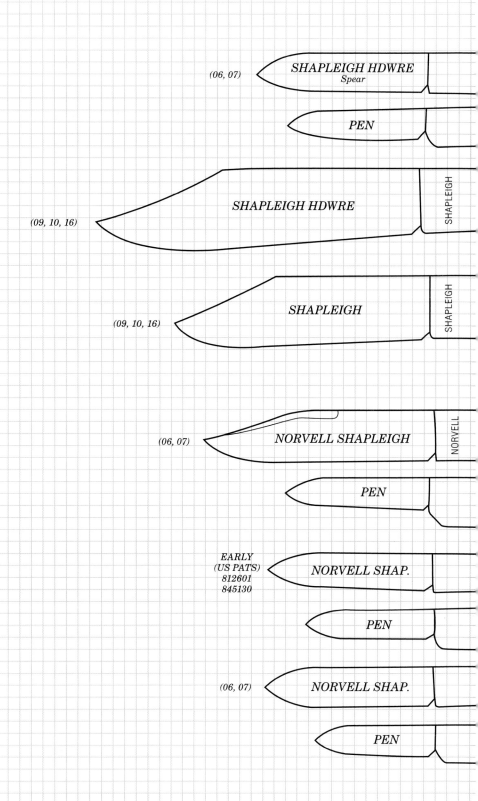

(06, 07)   **SHAPLEIGH HDWRE** *Spear*

PEN

(09, 10, 16)   **SHAPLEIGH HDWRE**   SHAPLEIGH

(09, 10, 16)   **SHAPLEIGH**   SHAPLEIGH

(06, 07)   **NORVELL SHAPLEIGH**   NORVELL

PEN

EARLY (US PATS) 812601 845130   **NORVELL SHAP.**

PEN

(06, 07)   **NORVELL SHAP.**

PEN

MISCELLANEOUS

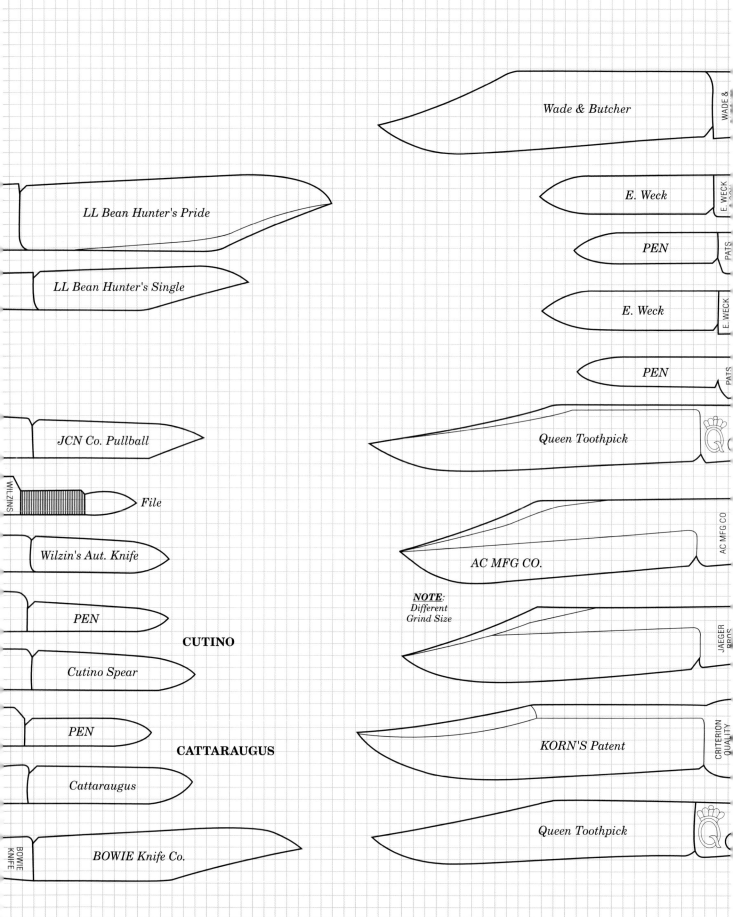

Wade & Butcher

WADE &

LL Bean Hunter's Pride

E. Weck

E. WECK

PEN

PATS

LL Bean Hunter's Single

E. Weck

E. WECK

PEN

PATS

JCN Co. Pullball

Queen Toothpick

Q

WILZINS

File

Wilzin's Aut. Knife

AC MFG CO.

AC MFG CO

PEN

CUTINO

Cutino Spear

NOTE:
Different
Grind Size

JAEGER BROS

PEN

CATTARAUGUS

Cattaraugus

KORN'S Patent

CRITERION QUALITY

BOWIE KNIFE

BOWIE Knife Co.

Queen Toothpick

Q

Celluloid

John Wesley Hyatt invented celluloid around 1870. It is a synthetic plastic made from cellulose nitrate treated with camphor and alcohol. The technical term is cellulose dinitrate or pyroxylin and is closely related to cellulose trinitrate, or nitrocellulose.

Celluloid is extremely flammable. It is also extremely easy to work with and giving knife makers a nearly perfect material for their handles! Knife makers now had a product that could be blended with pigments to achieve practically any color imaginable and when heated became very pliable and easy to form. They were more than willing to accept the risk for the reward. They did, however, take some precautions against damage from fire and explosion. One precaution was to build their celluloid storage building well away from their other buildings. Another interesting preventive measure was to build the storage building with a hinged roof so that if the celluloid ever exploded the force would go upward instead of outward.

The introduction of celluloid really opened up some possibilities that had not existed previously for knife makers. One of the most popular of these in the late 1800s was the picture knife. Pictures, art and advertising were fitted to a knife handle and covered with clear celluloid handles. Many of these knives were tailor-made for individual customers, meaning there are many "one-of-a-kind" picture knives out there. Aerial Cutlery Manufacturing Company of Marinette, Wis. was one company that jumped on the picture knife bandwagon. They were one of the leading producers in the world at one point. Aerial used this technique to handle a few of their K112 switchblade knives, which are extremely rare! Aerial also used other celluloid handle materials including Tortoise celluloid to handle the K112.

Celluloid knife handles started showing up on switchblade knives in the 1890s in Walden, N.Y. Press Button Knife Company used the material to handle some of their smaller double-bladed switchblades. When George Schrade and his brothers started up Schrade Cutlery Company in 1904 they too saw the advantages of using celluloid on their knives. They were even adventurous enough to put celluloid handles on their larger switchblade knives, but only in limited numbers. A large percentage of Schrade's switchblades made between 1904 and 1956 had celluloid handles. Other stampings that you will find with celluloid handles are: KaBar, CASE, Remington, Presto, Flylock, Challenge, Shapleigh Hardware and more.

Celluloid really is a beautiful and practical handle material, but there are drawbacks. Unfortunately it is not only flammable, it is also very unstable. A chemical reaction can cause the handles to completely deteriorate and in the process it releases a gas that will also corrode metal. If this process occurs when the knife is hidden away in a knife roll, the process can ruin other knives in the roll as well. If a knife starts to deteriorate I know of no way to stop the process. Extreme cold is believed to slow it down, but not stop it. Depriving the handles of oxygen will actually accelerate the process, so don't think you can save it by sealing it in a bag. It is not really known what starts this deterioration process. Some collectors think it will eventually happen to all celluloid handles, but I disagree. I think it takes something to activate the process. There are thousands of celluloid knives that have been lying in dresser drawers and trunks for nearly 100 years that still look as good as the day they were made, while others are no longer with us because of deterioration.

What I have learned about taking care of celluloid is the following:

1. Wipe the knives clean before storing
2. Store the knives in a dry place
3. Check on them regularly
4. DO NOT USE OIL on the handles!!!

I STRONGLY suspect that oil is the culprit that triggers this process. There may be other things that can do it also, but there are many collectors out there who are guilty of getting oil on these handles. I avoid putting anything on the handles. I just wipe them down with a clean, dry cloth. I would not even suggest using wax, simply because it may keep the celluloid from breathing. So far I've had good luck and as long as I keep them dry I'm not worried.

Patterns, Nicknames and Misc. Terminology

Aerial
>*Sportsman* Model K112- 4 5/8-inch, single-blade backspring release

Bowie Knife Company
>*Fishtail*- 4-inch, single-blade with tail at the bottom and checkered handles

Camillus
>*Model 80*- 3 1/8-inch, single-blade with backspring release near bottom or back of knife
>*MC1*- Orange handled paratrooper knife, Vietnam era

Case
>*Small lever*- 4 3/8-inch, lever released single-blade
>*Large lever*- 5 3/8-inch, lever released single-blade
>*Clasp Zipper*- 5 3/8-inch, zipper-release single-blade shaped like the big Ka-Bar Grizzly
>*Cokebottle Zipper*- 5 1/8-inch, zipper-release single-blade shaped like old coke bottle
>*Pullball*- 2 7/8-inch, single-blade
>*Jack*- 3 3/8-inch, single-blade
>*Double*- 3 3/8-inch, two blades with one at each end
>*Fishtail*- 4-inch, single-blade with tail
>*Bowtie*- 4-inch, single-blade with tail and finger guards
>*Small frame*- 4 1/8-inch, single-blade
>*Large frame*- 5-inch, single-blade
>*Folding guard*- 5-inch, single-blade with folding guards

Colonial
>*Mini Bowtie*- Term used to describe the smallest 2 ½-inch, Colonial "Snappy" with bolsters and guard
>*Mini Fishtail*- Term used to describe the 2 ½-inch, "Snappy" with no bolsters
>*Jumbo Jack*- Large 5-inch, closed Shur Snap with bolsters at both ends and finger guards
>*Stubby*- Shorter 4 1/8-inch, Shur Snap with bolsters at both ends and finger guards
>*Fatjack*- Shorter 4 1/8-inch, Shur Snap with NO bolsters, but has a lanyard ring. Stamped Shur Snap, Pronto and Jiffy
>*Jack*- 3 ½-inch, single-blade stamped Shur Snap. (Bolsters at both ends seems to be the most common)
>*Fishtail*- 4-inch, long with a tail at bottom, resembling a fish's tail
>*Bowtie*- Fishtail with bolsters at both ends and finger guards on top bolster

Edgemaster
>*My-t-Mite*- This is the smallest Edgemaster, measuring 2 ½ inches. Knife has a small bail and keychain
>*Jack*- This is a 3 7/16-inch, single-blade knife. No bolsters and one more pin in handle than Shur Snap jack
>*Fishtail*- 4-inch, with tail at bottom. Some had Copper Bolsters (Scarce)
>*Bowtie*- Fishtail with bolsters at both ends and finger guards. Marketing name was "Push-O-Matic"
>*Tinny*- bowtie with painted hollow tin handles that clip onto the liners
>*Brassy*- bowtie with brass handles that clip onto the liners
>*Fatjack*- 4 1/8-inch, with no bolsters, but has a lanyard ring. Blade shape is different than Colonial's models

Flylock & Challenge Cut Co.
>*Small double*- 2 7/8-inch, two blades with one at each end
>*Double*- 3 3/8-inch, with two blades with one at each end
>*Letter opener*- Large letter opener with 3 3/8-inch, single-blade switchblade attached to the end
>*Boy's Outdoor knife*- Term used to describe the 4 1/8-inch, single-blade knife
>*Outdoor knife* - Term used to describe the 5-inch, single-blade knife. Model with fish scaler called
>>*"Fisherman's knife"*
>*Folding guard*- This is the larger single-blade knife with folding guards

George Schrade Knife Co

Pullball- Term used to describe small flat knife with a clip blade and a small ball or die on end to activate blade (Also see Presto group for more knives made there.)

Imperial & Hammer Brand

Mini- Term usually used to describe the smallest Imperial "shell handle" switchblade measures 2 ¼ inches

Toothpick- 4 ¼-inch, long, wider at top, serpentine shaped & comes to rounded point at bottom

Serp or **Utility Jack** - Smaller version of toothpick with rounded ends. It's still serpentine shaped & measures 3 ½ inches

Press Button Knife Co

High school girl- This is an extremely rare 2 7/8-inch, single-blade knife

Small Double- This is a two bladed knife with a button on each end measuring 2 7/8 inches closed

Double- Two-blade knife with button on each end measuring 3 3/8 inches closed

Mechanic's Jack- Largest Press Button Knife Co. double with bone handles 3 11/16 inches. Several blade combinations

Business- Smaller of the large-frame Press Buttons measuring 4 inches closed. Clip or spear blade with etching

Invincible- Largest of the large-frame Press Buttons measuring 4 7/8 inches closed. Clip or spear blade with etching

Victor- This is the large frame knife measuring 4 7/8 inches with bone handles and Folding Guard. Clip blade with etching

Guardian- This is the large frame knife with bone handles and fixed-guard bolsters. Blade Etched

One Armer- This knife has aluminum handles that are curved. The blade has a built in fork for eating

Presto

Double- 3 3/8-inch, two blades with one at each end

Jack- 3 3/8-inch, single-blade

Fishtail- 4-inch, with tail at bottom

Bowtie- 4-inch, fishtail with finger guards on top bolster

Sportsman- 4 1/8-inch, single-blade

Hunter- 5-inch, single-blade

Derby- 4 1/8-inch, and 5-inch, models with fixed guard bolsters that resemble a derby hat

Schrade Cutlery Co. & Schrade Walden

Small double- 2 7/8-inch, two blades with one at each end

Jack- 3 3/8-inch, & 3 ¾-inch, single-blade knives

Double- 3 3/8-inch, two blades with one at each end

Large double- 3 ¾-inch, two blades with one at each end

Fishtail- 4-inch, with tail at bottom

Bowtie- 4-inch, fishtail with finger guards on top bolster

Small frame- 4 1/8-inch, single-blade

Large frame- 4 7/8-inch, single-blade

Hunter's Pride- These were the large frame knives with folding guards. Blades etched "Hunter's Pride"

Hunting Knife- This was a large frame knife with a saber-ground blade. Blade etched "Schrade Hunting Knife"

Forest King- Large frame single-blade knife with celluloid handles. Blades were etched "Forest King"

PLEASE NOTE: This list is not intended to be a representation of every model and is NOT a complete list. It is intended to provide information about the various knife names and nicknames listed by manufacturer as well as to give a general idea of what models were made by which manufacturers.

Miscellaneous Swithchblade
Tang Stamps

Tang Stamp	Dates Mfg	Manufacturer
AC Mfg Co, Marinette, Wis	1920-1940	Aerial Cut Co/Union Cut Co
American Auto Knife & Novelty	1892-1902	No information
Aut Knife Co	1891-1895	Automatic Knife Company
Buffalo Cutlery Co	1939-1944	Schrade Cutlery Co
Camco	1938-1950	Camillus
Case, WR & Sons	1920-1955	Geo. Schrade Knife Co & WR Case & Sons
Cattaragus	1920-1928	Flylock/Challenge
Crandall Cutlery Co	1905-1912	Crandall
Cutino Cutlery Co	1922-1935	Wucos, Germany
E. Weck & Son	1910-1925	Schrade Cutlery Co
Graef & Schmidt	1895-1900	Press Button Knife Co
Edgemaster	1954-1958	Edgemaster Co
Elliot Langley	1892-1923	Press Button Knife Co.
Hammer Brand	1949-1958	Imperial Knife Assoc Co Inc
Jaeger Bros, Marinette, Wis	1970's	Olsen Knife Co
JCN Co	1938-1948	George Schrade Knife Co
Jiffy	1953-1958	Colonial Knife Co
Keen Kutter	1892-1923	Press Button Knife Co/div. of Walden Knife Co
Keen Kutter	1924-1958	Schrade Cut Co/Schrade Walden
Keenwell Brown Mfg Co	1926-1936	A division of Union Cut Co
Norvell Shapleigh	1904-1917	Schrade Cut Co
LL Bean	1939-1958	Schrade Cut Co/Schrade Walden
Presto	1929-1956	George Schrade Knife Co
Pronto	1953-1958	Colonial Knife Co
Quick Point	1945-1950	George Schrade Knife Co
RC Kruschke	1891-1930	Robert Klass Company, Germany
Remington	1935-1941	George Schrade Knife Co
Schrado	1930-1941	George Schrade Knife Co
Shapleigh Hardware	1918-1958	Schrade Cut Co/Schrade Walden
Shur Snap	1949-1958	Colonial Knife Co
Simmons Hardware Co	1905-1912	Crandall Cutlery Co
Snappy	1950-1958	Colonial Knife Co
Torrey	1892-1923	Press Button Knife Co.
Utica Knife Co	1912-?	Utica Knife Co possible manufacture
Wade & Butcher	1912-1920	Schrade Cut Co
Walden Knife Co	1892-1923	Walden Knife Co predates Press Button Knife Co
Wilzin's Patent	1891-1895	Automatic Knife Co

Trademarks, Etches & Marketing Names

Name:	Used by:	Where seen
Business	Press Button Knife Co	Usually etched on the front of the blade on 4 ⅛-inch knife.
Camco	Camillus	Used on much of their cutlery including the #80 flylock switchblade.
Diamond Edge	Shapleigh Hardware Co	Etched on blades and on tang stamps
Edgemaster	Edgemaster Co?	stamped on the tangs.
FLY-LOCK	Challenge Cut Corp	Stamped on the back tang of most of their switchblade knives.
Forest King	Schrade Cut Co.	Etched on the front of the blade of the 4 ⅞-inch knives with smooth celluloid handles.
Guardian	Press Button Knife Co	Usually etched on the front of the blade on 4 ⅞-inch fixed-guard knife with no guards.
Hammer Brand	Imperial Knife Co.	Stamped on the tang of many of their early switchblade knives
Hunter's Pride	Schrade Cut Co.	Etched on the front of the blade on the 4-⅞ inch knives with folding guards.
Invincible	Press Button Knife Co	Usually etched on the front of the blade on 4 ⅞-inch-knife with no guards.
Jack-O-Matic	Imperial Knife Assoc Co Inc	On display cards for 4 ¼-inch toothpick knives stamped Hammer Brand.
Jaeger Bros.	Aerial Cutlery & Olsen Knife Co.	Stamped on the tang of much of their cutlery including the reproductionsof the K112.
Jiffy	Colonial Knife Co.	Stamped on the tang of some of the 4-⅛-inch fatjack knives.
Keen Kutter	Shapleigh Hardware Co	Name acquired from Simmons Hardware used for cutlery and other products.
My-T-Mite	Imperial Knife Assoc Co Inc	Used on display cards for 2 ½-inch switchblades stamped Edgemaster.
Presto	George Schrade Knife Co	Stamped on the tangs.
Pronto	Colonial Knife Co.	Stamped on the tang of some of the 4 ⅛-inch fatjack knives.
Push-O-Matic	Imperial Knife Assoc Co Inc	Used on display cards for 4-inch Bowtie switchblades stamped Edgemaster.
Remington Master Knife	Schrade Cut Co.	Etched on the front of the blade on the 4 ⅞-inch knives with folding guards.
Schrade Hunting Knife	Schrade Cut Co.	Etched on the front of the blade on the 4 ⅞-inch knives with folding guards.
Shur Snap	Colonial Knife Co.	Stamped on the tang of most of their switchblade knives.
Snappy	Colonial Knife Co.	Stamped on the tang of their 2 ½-inch keychain switchblade fishtails and bowties.
The Victor	Press Button Knife Co	Usually etched on the front of the blade on 4 ⅞-inch folding-guard knife.

Switchblade Manufacturers

Company Name	Location	Approx. Dates
1. Aerial Cutlery Co.*	Marinette, Wis.	1909-Present
2. Automatic Knife Co.	Middletown, Conn.	1891-1893
3. Bowie Knife Co.	Newark, N.J.	1945-1950
4. Camillus Cutlery Co.	Camillus, N.Y.	1902-Present
5. Case (WR Case & Sons)	Bradford, Penn.	1902-Present
6. Challenge Cutlery Co.	Bridgeport, Conn.	1905-1929
7. Colonial Knife Co.	Providence, RI	1926-2002
8. Crandall Cutlery Co.	Bradford, PA	1905-1912
9. Flylock Knife Co.	Bridgeport, Conn.	1925-1929
10. George Schrade Knife Co.	Bridgeport, Conn.	1929-1956
11. Hatch Cutlery Co.*	So, Milwaukee, Wis.	1890-1895
12. Imperial Knife Co.	Providence, R.I.	1916-Present
13. KA-BAR / Union Cut Co.	Olean, N.Y.	1923-1952
14. Keenwell Brown Mfg Co.	Olean, N.Y.	1926-1936
15. Korn's Patent*	Germany or N.Y.	1885-1895
16. Logan/Smyth	Venice, FL	1990 Approx.
17. Press Button Knife Co.	Walden, N.Y.	1892-1923
18. Queen Cutlery Co.	Titusville, Penn.	1922-Present
19. Russell Automatic Knife Co.	Chicago, Ill.	1891-1895
20. Schrade Cutlery Co.	Walden, N.Y.	1904-1946
21. Schrade Walden Cutlery Co.	Ellenville, N.Y.	1946-Present
22. Utica Cutlery Co.*	Utica, N.Y.	1910-Present
23. Walden Knife Co.	Walden, N.Y.	1874-1923

* May or may not have actually manufactured switchblades.

Bibliography

Goin's Encyclopedia of Cutlery Markings	John E. Goins	Copyright 1998
Levine's Guide to Knives and their Values	Bernard Levine	2nd & 3rd editions
Sargent's Premium Guide to Pocket Knives	Jim Sargent	Copyright 1986
New England Cutlery	Phillip Pankiewicz	Copyright 1986
101 Patented Knife Designs	Will Hanna	Copyright 1992
IBCA Price Guide to Antique Knives	J. Bruce Voyles	Copyright 1995
Schrade Cutlery Catalog 1926 reprint	A.G. Russell	1971
Pocket Price Guide Vol. 2	Sargent & Schleyer	Copyright 1982
Shapleigh's Hardware Catalog reprint	Barry L Keith	
Automatic Knife Reference Guide & Newsletter		